Workplace Trauma

Post-traumatic stress is a topical subject of increasing importance. Yet much of the writing on this subject so far has concerned stress suffered by people exposed to serious turmoil such as war and ethnic conflict. *Workplace Trauma* is an extremely welcome presentation of the subject of stress in the workplace.

The book explores the ways that traumatic events impact the psychological well-being of organisations and their employees. The effects of disasters, accidents, crime, injury and death are examined alongside examples of organisational trauma care programmes and reviews of the current thinking regarding post-trauma interventions. The insights generated are illustrated with case studies from the author's extensive experience of counselling victims of trauma at work.

The theory, research and practical advice contained in this volume will prove a valuable resource for organisations and practitioners seeking guidance on reducing the impact of psychological trauma.

Noreen Tehrani is a chartered occupational, counselling and health psychologist. She is the author of *Building a Culture of Respect*.

Workplace Trauma

Concepts, assessment and interventions

Noreen Tehrani

Brunner-Routledge
Taylor & Francis Group

HOVE AND NEW YORK

First published 2004
by Brunner-Routledge
27 Church Road, Hove, East Sussex BN3 2FA

Simultaneously published in the USA and Canada
by Brunner-Routledge
270 Madison Avenue, New York NY 10016

Brunner-Routledge is an imprint of the Taylor & Francis Group

Copyright © 2004 Noreen Tehrani

Typeset in Times by RefineCatch Limited, Bungay, Suffolk
Printed and bound in Great Britain by
TJ International Ltd, Padstow, Cornwall
Paperback cover design by Hybert Design

This publication has been produced with paper manufactured to
strict environmental standards and with pulp derived from
sustainable forests.

British Library Cataloguing in Publication Data
A catalogue record for this book is available from the British Library

Library of Congress Cataloging-in-Publication Data
Tehrani, Noreen.
    Workplace trauma : concepts, assessment, and interventions /
Noreen Tehrani.
        p. cm.
    Includes bibliographical references and index.
    ISBN 1-58391-875-2 (hbk) – ISBN 1-58391-876-0 (pbk)
    1. Post-traumatic stress disorder.   2. Industrial psychiatry.
3. Psychic trauma.   I. Title.
    RC552.P67T447 2004
    616.85′21–dc22   2004001602

ISBN 1-58391-875-2 (hbk)
ISBN 1-58391-876-0 (pbk)

Contents

Tables

Figures

Acknowledgements

This book is based on a PhD thesis undertaken at the University of Nottingham. My thanks go to Professor Tom Cox, my tutor, and the other members of the academic staff for their help and support.

I would like to record my appreciation for the courage shown by the many victims of trauma as we worked together to gain an understanding of their experience and to find a way out of their 'black hole' of despair.

I also wish to thank all the organisations and individuals that have provided me with this special opportunity to work with them in developing my ideas and approaches for responding to personal and organisational disasters.

Finally, I would like to thank my husband, Farhad, for his constant help and support during the eight years that it has taken me to undertake this research.

Preface

This book is concerned with traumatic stress in the workplace. My interest in this subject developed out of clinical and professional experience as a chartered occupational, health and counselling psychologist. My initial counselling experiences were gained in counselling individual victims of physical and sexual abuse. More recently, my work has taken place in organisational settings and has involved trauma debriefing and counselling distressed employees who were the victims of armed raids, disasters, violent physical attacks, verbal threats and abuse.

In the course of this work within organisations, I have received frequent requests for information and advice on:

- the nature and symptoms of post-traumatic stress;
- how an organisation can reduce the incidence of traumatic stress;
- which post-trauma interventions are most effective in the workplace;
- how employers can recognise when an employee is suffering from post-traumatic stress;
- the best way to monitor and evaluate trauma care programmes.

This book attempts to answer these questions.

Workplace trauma has been shown to have serious implications for employees and organisations alike, yet there has been little systematic research into the nature and extent of the problems created. It is known that there is a high level of under-reporting of traumatic incidents and there is a need to establish effective organisational policies, procedures and interventions if the problems are to be addressed.

This book describes the development of the concept of post-traumatic stress and then goes on to look at the causes and consequences of trauma in the workplace, offering practical solutions for organisations and the caring professions.

The book is in five interrelated parts. Part I sets the scene by looking at the development of the concept of post-traumatic stress and then reviewing the incidence and impact of trauma in the workplace. Case material illustrates the way that traumatised employees respond during and after the traumatic experience. Finally, Part I closes with an examination of the way that the law has influenced the development of post-traumatic stress.

Part II examines the need to develop and integrate trauma management and trauma care policies and the practical problems that face organisations supporting their workforce during and after a traumatic event. A range of psychological interventions is discussed, including crisis management, diffusing, debriefing and trauma counselling. An example of how a trauma care programme was developed within an organisation is presented to illustrate the issues that need to be taken into consideration by organisations wishing to create a similar programme. Because not all organisations have the internal resources to provide full trauma support, some guidance is also offered to those wishing to use an external provider of post-trauma care.

Part III describes the ways that psychological trauma can be measured and assessed, highlighting the problems of using some of the measurement tools in an organisation. The development of a new traumatic stress measurement tool designed for use in an organisational setting is described together with the process used to test its validity and reliability. This part of the book closes with a discussion on what is a successful outcome in an organisation and what kinds of criteria should be used to decide whether an intervention has been successful.

Part IV presents four case studies. The first pair examine the impact of acute and chronic traumatisation on employees. In the first the employees have been exposed to armed robberies and in the second to prolonged bullying. In the second pair, acute and chronic interventions are described and their effectiveness measured. In the acute intervention the employees had been exposed to victims of a train crash and were provided with debriefing and support. In the chronic intervention, employees whose workplace was destroyed by a bomb were found to be experiencing post-trauma symptoms two and a half years after the explosion. These employees had developed chronic post-traumatic stress and were provided with trauma counselling. The book closes with Part V, which is a review of the main issues that arise from the work described and suggests ways forward in the future.

Part I

Post-traumatic stress – history and development

The idea that stressful events can produce enduring, negative psychological states would appear logical. However, despite the efforts of notable pioneers in the field, it is only in the past two decades that mental health professionals have come to acknowledge post-traumatic stress as a valid psychological condition (Briere 1997). Unlike other psychiatric disorders, a diagnosis of post-traumatic stress requires an evaluation of precipitating factors as well as symptoms. The development of the post-traumatic construct is an active process with the definitions having been refined several times since their introduction by the American Psychiatric Association (1980). Chapter 1 describes the historical development of the construct of traumatic stress, looking at the portrayal of the traumatic experience in literature and in science. Chapter 2 shows how the traumatic experience is underpinned by the psychobiology of stress and traumatic stress. The chapter provides illustrations of the similarities and differences between stress and traumatic stress. In Chapter 3 there is an exploration into the ways in which trauma in the workplace can affect the employees and their organisation. Chapter 4 uses casework to illustrate common employee reactions and responses to exposure to traumatic incidents. The development of the case law and legislation is discussed in Chapter 5 together with the negative impact that the legal process can have on the recovery of trauma victims.

Chapter I

Post-traumatic stress: the history of a concept

Introduction

This chapter describes how, throughout history, writers and historians have recognised that following exposure to extreme stress and trauma, people may develop long-term emotional and psychological responses. However, this view took a long time to become established in psychiatry and as late as the nineteenth century there were few psychiatrists who accepted the notion that fear and horror were sufficient to cause a psychological disorder. The experience of dealing with dead and injured soldiers in the First World War provided the background and impetus to the development of new ideas on the origins of psychological trauma. This increase in knowledge has led to the development of a classification of post-traumatic stress disorder (PTSD) that is accepted throughout the world.

Trauma in literature

The idea that people can develop physical and psychological disorders following an exposure to a traumatic event that caused them fear or horror rather than a physical injury is not new. Literature has provided us with a rich source of powerful accounts of the human responses to war, murder, rape and other personal disasters. Authors such as Homer in the *Iliad* and Shakespeare in *Henry IV* and *Macbeth* create central characters whose dramatic symptoms and behaviours would today be diagnosed as indicative of post-traumatic stress (Trimble 1981).

Graphic descriptions of human responses to disasters, accidents and wars can be found in many historical documents (Trimble 1985). Samuel Peyps' *Diary* provides a good example of psychological trauma induced by a disaster. In Peyps' case, the disaster was the Great Fire of London, which occurred in September 1666. Pepys described his feelings as the fire spread towards his home and gave a vivid description of the terror experienced by the citizens of the city, unable to protect their homes and property from destruction. Six months later Peyps writes of his difficulty in sleeping due to nightmares caused by his experience of the fire and his panic at the news of a chimney fire some distance away (Daly 1983). The author Charles Dickens was a passenger on a train that crashed at Staplehurst in Kent in July 1868. In a letter to a friend, Dickens described his distress at being trapped for several hours surrounded by dead and dying passengers. Following the incident Dickens developed a phobia about travel by rail and described himself as 'not quite right within' and as 'curiously weak – weak as if I were recovering from a long illness' (Forster 1969).

Wars over the centuries have affected millions of people. In an account of life in the trenches in the First World War a soldier (Fred White of the 10th Battalion King's Royal Rifle Corps) said:

> It took years to get over it. Years! Long after, when you were working, married, had kids, you'd be lying in bed and you'd see it all before you. Couldn't sleep. Couldn't lie still. Many and many's the time I've got up and tramped the streets till it came daylight. Walking, walking – anything to get away from your thoughts . . . That went on for years, that did.
>
> (MacDonald 1988)

The nineteenth-century view of trauma

In contrast to wide recognition in literary works, medicine and psychiatry were resistant to the view that traumatic emotional experiences can profoundly and permanently alter a person's psychology and physiology (Van der Kolk *et al.* 1996). If a physician of the nineteenth century were to be asked what caused traumatic shock, the most likely response would be that it was due to organic damage to the nervous system. Most physicians of the time rejected any suggestion that an individual's perception or beliefs about a traumatic event were capable of bringing about the magnitude of change in the functioning of the brain that could result in a psychiatric disorder. The common belief of the time was that concussions to the head, injuries to the spinal cord or small cerebral haemorrhages alter psychic functioning, thereby causing the psychological symptoms (Trimble 1985). An example of the views of the time comes from Herman Oppenheim who said, 'functional problems are produced by molecular changes in the central nervous system, any suggestion that these difficulties could have an origin in an individual's perceptions of a traumatic event is incorrect' (Oppenheim 1889). This belief regarding the physical origins of psychological symptoms resulted in a proliferation of terms being used to describe a psychological disorder relating to specific experiences of the victim. Examples of some of the most common diagnoses of the time included 'spinal concussion', 'railway spine', 'irritable heart', 'soldier's heart' and 'shell shock' (Parry Jones and Parry Jones 1994). The giving of different names to what appeared to be the same condition was slowly challenged and by the end of the nineteenth century attempts were made to utilise the single diagnosis of 'traumatic neurosis' (Seguin 1890).

During the same period, the French neurologists Charcot and Janet were developing a second challenge to the traditional physicist view (Van der Kolk *et al.* 1996). Janet had painstakingly observed his traumatised patients and discovered that they tended to react to reminders of their trauma with responses that were more relevant to the original traumatic threat than to their current situation. Janet also found that these patients had difficulty in integrating the traumatic experience with their earlier life experiences, and consequently sometimes entered dissociative states as a way of dealing with these distressing memories. The work of Janet had a profound effect on Breuer and Freud. In *Studies on Hysteria* they said, 'hysterics suffer mainly from reminiscences, the traumatic experience is constantly forcing itself upon the patient and this is proof of the strength of that experience: the patient is, as one might say, fixated on his trauma' (Breuer and Freud 1955). Freud's views on the impact of actual traumatic events were overtaken by his beliefs about the importance of repressed infantile sexuality. Consequently, he never pursued any investigations of the real traumatic events that had occurred to his patients, preferring to concentrate on the Oedipal crisis that he believed occurred in early childhood.

The First World War

The First World War exposed large numbers of soldiers to trauma, and provided doctors and physicians with extensive experience in dealing with traumatic stress. This exposure brought about an increased awareness of the psychological aspects of the traumatic experience and caused many physicians to question whether physical injuries had any impact on psychiatric disorders. While some psychiatrists continued to cling to the notion that physical injuries were the *cause* of psychological disorder (e.g. Mott 1919), others rejected this approach. This dramatic change of view is illustrated by Charles Myres who had introduced the diagnosis of shell shock (Myres 1915) but went on to find that many soldiers exhibited the symptoms of shell shock without coming under fire. Myres wrote, 'my term shell shock is misleading . . . the true cause of the soldier's problems is the shock and horror of war' (1940).

Some of the resistance to the idea that soldiers could suffer a psychiatric disorder without any physical injury can be found in the Public Records Office in Kew, London. In the First World War, a number of soldiers were shot for cowardice. The documents relating to these men strongly suggest that many were suffering from post-traumatic stress, and yet it is clear that those making the decision as to which soldiers should be shot for cowardice and which needed treatment preferred an approach that used objective evidence such as a 'lesion of the brain' or 'damage to the heart', rather than the subjective judgements of psychiatrists on the soldiers' psychological symptoms (Moran 1945).

After the First World War, several war psychiatrists, experienced in dealing with the psychological impact of war trauma, left the forces and returned to civilian life. These psychiatrists recognised that civilian patients, who had been the victims of accidents or disasters, had symptoms similar to those they had seen on the battlefield (Merskey 1991). Unfortunately, there was little support for the view of these war psychiatrists that there was a 'common trauma syndrome'. One notable exception to this was Abram Kardiner. Kardiner began his career treating US war veterans. After leaving the army, he studied psychoanalysis with Freud. In the light of the knowledge and insights gained with Freud, Kardiner re-analysed his extensive clinical data on war veterans. The results of the re-analysis were published in *The Traumatic Neurosis of War* (Kardiner 1941), which provided a detailed analysis of a psychological trauma syndrome which he named 'psychoneurosis'.

The essential features of psychoneurosis were:

• persistence of startle response and irritability;

- proclivity to explosive outbursts of aggression;
- fixation on the trauma;
- constriction of general level of personality functioning;
- atypical dream life.

Kardiner claimed that war created a single syndrome, psycho-neurosis, and that this syndrome was essentially the same as traumatic neurosis, the syndrome of civilian life. (Kardiner 1941). His views provided a challenge to the American Psychiatric Association to address the confusion caused by the multitude of terms used to describe the same psychological conditions.

Recognition of traumatic stress

The American Psychiatric Association commissioned the development of a manual to provide a codification and classification of mental disorders. The first edition (American Psychiatric Association 1952) provided internationally acceptable statistical and diagnostic data which supported a classification of mental disorders. One of the psychiatric categories in this first edition of the manual (*DSM I*) was 'gross stress reaction', an acute reaction to extreme stress. The characteristics of gross stress reaction were similar to those for psychoneurosis apart from an additional situational precondition: 'the impact of the event to be so serious that it would have evoked overwhelming fear in any so-called normal person'. Strangely, the second edition of the manual (*DSM II*) removed gross stress reaction (American Psychiatric Association 1968). In the third issue of the *Manual* in 1980 (*DSM III*) the syndrome re-emerged, this time under a new name: 'post-traumatic stress disorder' (PTSD) (American Psychiatric Association 1980). In the most recent issue of the *Manual*, *DSM IV* (American Psychiatric Association 1994) there are six criteria relating to PTSD. The first describes the traumatic situation, the next three the trauma symptoms and the last two the duration and effect of the symptoms on the person's personal life and work (see Table 1.1)

One might expect that the status of post-traumatic stress would be well established among the medical and psychological researchers and practitioners of the twenty-first century. While this is generally true, there are still groups of psychiatrists who do not accept the existence of post-traumatic stress. An example is the assertion that 'traumatic life experiences do not cause a psychological disorder any

Table 1.1 DSM IV diagnostic criteria for post-traumatic stress

Criterion A: the person has been exposed to a traumatic event in which both of the following were present:
1 The person experienced, witnessed, or was confronted by an event(s) that involved actual or threatened death or serious injury, or threat to the physical integrity of self or others.
2 The person's response involved intense fear, helplessness or horror.

Criterion B: the traumatic event is re-experienced in one or more of the following ways:
1 Recurrent and intrusive distressing recollections of the event, including images, thoughts or perceptions.
2 Recurrent distressing dreams of the event.
3 Acting or feeling as if the traumatic event were recurring (includes a sense of reliving the experience, illusions, hallucinations and dissociative flashback episodes, including those that occur on awakening or when intoxicated).
4 Intense psychological distress at exposure to internal and external cues that symbolise or resemble an aspect of the traumatic event.
5 Physiological reactivity on exposure to internal or external cues that symbolise or resemble an aspect of the traumatic event.

Criterion C: persistent avoidance of stimuli associated with the trauma and numbing of general responsiveness (not present before the trauma), as indicated by three or more of the following:
1 Efforts to avoid thoughts, feelings.
2 Efforts to avoid activities, places, or people that arouse recollections of the trauma.
3 Inability to recall an important aspect of the trauma.
4 Marked diminished interest or participation in significant activities.
5 Feeling of detachment or estrangement from others.
6 Restricted range of affect (e.g. unable to have loving feelings).
7 Sense of foreshortened future (e.g. does not expect to have a career, marriage or normal life).

Criterion D: persistent symptoms of increased arousal (not present before the trauma), as indicated by two or more of the following:
1 Difficulty in falling or staying asleep.
2 Irritability or outbursts of anger.
3 Difficulty concentrating.
4 Hypervigilance.
5 Exaggerated startle response.

Criterion E: duration of disturbance is more than one month.

Criterion F: the disturbance causes clinically significant distress or impairment in social, occupational or other important areas of functioning.

more than life events cause depression' (Wessley 2000). There is a rather more serious debate on whether the restrictions in Criterion A (see Table 1.1) are too limiting. The situation created by *DSM IV* is that if an individual cannot demonstrate actual exposure to a situation which meets Criterion A, post-traumatic stress cannot be diagnosed. A number of researchers have expressed concerns over the use of Criterion A as a precondition for PTSD (Duckworth 1987; Ravin and Boal 1989). There is mounting clinical evidence (Scott and Stradling 1992b; Leymann and Gustafsson 1996) that chronic exposure to stressful conditions including organisational bullying and extreme pressure at work can lead to symptoms which are indistinguishable from those caused by a single traumatic event. If the key diagnostic feature of traumatic stress is symptoms, then *prolonged duress stress disorder* (PDSD) (Ravin and Boal 1989; Scott and Stradling 1992b) and *disorders of extreme stress not otherwise specified* (DESNOS) (Herman 1993) should be regarded as traumatic stress disorders. If, on the other hand, the diagnosis of traumatic stress retains the precondition of the Criterion A situational characteristics, then PDSD and DESNOS cannot be regarded as PTSDs.

International classification of diseases

While *DSM IV* has been influential in providing a recognised classification system, there is another system which is also in common use. The World Health Organisation included the category of PTSD in its most recent edition of the *International Classification of Diseases, ICD 10* (World Health Organisation 1993). Within this category, *ICD 10* describes three diagnoses: *acute stress reaction, adjustment disorder* and *PTSD*.

Acute stress reaction describes a transient disorder that develops without any other mental disorder. Symptoms of the acute stress reaction appear within minutes of the traumatic exposure, waning within hours. Adjustment disorder refers to states of subjective and emotional disturbance that arise in the period of adaptation to a significant life change or stressful event. Symptoms usually begin within one month of the occurrence of the stressful event and rarely exceed six months.

The diagnostic criteria of PTSD outlined in *ICD 10* are similar to those in *DSM IV* and involve the identification of a stressor which has the magnitude to cause the onset of the disorder. However, the process of making a diagnosis is different. The *ICD* approach recognises that other factors such as a pre-existing disorder or a vulnerable personality may play a role in the development of PTSD, but that these factors are neither necessary nor sufficient to explain its occurrence. The major difference between *ICD 10* and *DSM IV* is that *ICD 10* states that although emotional numbing is a common feature of the disorder it is not necessary for a diagnosis. (Joseph *et al.* 1997). The *ICD 10* diagnostic criteria for post-traumatic stress are as follows:

> This disorder should not generally be diagnosed unless there is evidence that it arose within six months of a traumatic event of exceptional severity. A 'probable' diagnosis might still be possible if the delay between the event and the onset was longer than six months, provided that the clinical manifestations are typical and no alternative identification of the disorder (e.g. such as anxiety or obsessive-compulsive disorder or depressive episode) is plausible. In addition to evidence of trauma, there must be a repetitive, intrusive recollection or re-enactment of the event in memories, daytime imagery or dreams. Conspicuous emotional detachment, numbing of feelings and avoidance of stimuli that might arouse recollection of the trauma are often present but are not essential for the diagnosis. The autonomic disturbance, mood disorder, and behavioural abnormalities all contribute to the diagnosis but are not of prime importance.
>
> (World Health Organisation 1993)

Discussion

It is important for workers in the field of post-traumatic stress to have some understanding of the history and development of the concept. The fact that the diagnostic criteria have taken over 100 years to evolve and the likelihood of further revisions in the next *Diagnostic and Statistical Manual* is evidence of the interest and active research in the area. The history of the development of the concept of post-traumatic stress clearly illustrates the value of clinical experience and the detailed observation of individual cases, which frequently contradicts and challenges existing knowledge and provides an important impetus for change. The *Diagnostic and Statistical Manual* has recognised these changes and developments by integrating the latest theoretical and clinical knowledge within a defensible codification. Whether Criterion A will be amended in future editions of the manual or new classifications created to include people whose PTSD-like symptoms result from chronic or prolonged duress rather than an acute trauma is a matter for further research and debate (Scott and Stradling 1992b).

Chapter 2

The psychobiology of traumatic stress

Introduction

The introduction of the classification of PTSD as a psychiatric disorder in 1980 has been followed by a dramatic increase in research into the biological underpinning of the disorder. This chapter begins with a brief review of the incidence of PTSD in the general population. The epidemiological findings challenge the early assumption that PTSD was a normal response to exposure to a traumatic event and suggest that PTSD is caused by a number of factors which include the pre-existing mental health and background of the individual, as well as the nature of the traumatic experience. The chapter then looks at recent research into the biological responses to trauma. While it is likely that the initial response to a traumatic event will be similar to that experienced in 'normal stress', there is mounting evidence that the hypothalamic-pituitary-adrenal (HPA) pathway behaves very differently in people with PTSD. This finding supports the idea that some people may have developed a predisposition for developing PTSD due to an earlier exposure to a traumatic event or other risk factor. Finally, the chapter looks at the brain and the structures most closely related to the trauma experience. Once again, traumatic stress is shown to be different to normal stress in the way it impacts on the functioning of the brain. The formation of an integration barrier blocks any processing of highly distressing trauma sensations and shuts down the language areas in the cortex. This prevents the trauma victim understanding or giving meaning to their experience as being particularly significant.

The epidemiology of traumatic stress

One of the most important findings of the large-scale epidemiological studies undertaken in the past ten years has been that of all the people exposed to traumatic experiences only a small proportion go on to suffer PTSD (Shalev and Yehuda 1998). This finding challenges the original conceptualisation of post-traumatic stress as a normal response to a traumatic experience. The finding has also led researchers to consider the other risk factors that may be important in the development of the disorder in addition to identifying which types of traumatic experience are most likely to result in the victim developing PTSD.

Many of the early epidemiological studies focused on groups of victims attending clinics, hospitals or treatment centres. The difficulty in the interpretation of these studies is that they examined the symptoms and responses of people who had sought clinical treatment or support. Consequently, the studies tend to under-record people who, following exposure to trauma, manage to get on with their lives without the need for any clinical treatment or support. Recently, a number of large-scale studies have been undertaken in the general population with subjects randomly selected from a particular geographical area. One such study was undertaken by Breslau in 1996 and involved a group of over 2000 adults between the ages of 18 and 45 from Detroit in the USA (Breslau *et al.* 1997). Breslau found that over 85 per cent of people had been exposed to at least one traumatic experience with the levels being slightly higher for males than for females. Despite the high incidence of trauma exposure, the prevalence of PTSD was relatively low with only 10.2 per cent of males and 18.3 per cent of females meeting the criteria for PTSD at any stage during their lifetime.

Breslau found that the risk of developing PTSD varied according to the type of trauma. Where the trauma involved a rape or sexual assault, the levels were 49 per cent and 24 per cent respectively, with much lower levels of PTSD being reported following a road traffic crash (2.3 per cent). Epidemiological studies have identified a number of other personal risk factors, the most significant being related to neuroticism, pre-existing anxiety or depression, a history of childhood abuse and earlier traumatic experiences (Bromet *et al.* 1998).

Unfortunately, there have been few epidemiological studies in the workplace. Two studies that have looked at PTSD in working groups show that following a disastrous bush fire in Australia, 16 per cent of volunteer firefighters suffered PTSD (McFarlane and de Girolamo 1996), and following the Kuwait/Iraq war, 9 per cent of American soldiers were found to be suffering from PTSD (Southwick *et al.* 1993). Current epidemiological studies have brought into question the most fundamental assumption of PTSD: that the disorder can occur to anyone exposed to a traumatic event. The important questions that need to be answered are whether some people have:

- a specific predisposition to PTSD;
- a predisposition to mental illness that can be triggered by adversity.

'Normal stress'

Stress research has shown that when physical or psychological demands are placed on an individual, a typical sequence of physiological responses is produced. The purpose of these responses is to maintain the stress reactions within 'safe' homeostatic boundaries. This homeosatic balance is achieved by reducing the impact of external demands on the individual's vital functions at the expense of secondary functions. An example of this protective balance is the withdrawal of blood from the skin to allow for an increase in the supply of blood to the vital organs. Selye (1956) described the stress responses as involving three phases: an *acute response*, *resistance* and either *recovery* or *exhaustion*. The mechanisms that the body uses to achieve homeostasis involve the operation of three biological pathways.

Biological pathways

The stress response is initiated, modulated and extinguished by the neural, the neuro-endocrine and endocrine pathways. The activation of these is a normal part of human physiological functioning. If these pathways become over-stimulated or are required to maintain their activity over a prolonged period of time (as can occur during and following a traumatic exposure), their functioning can be altered (Mitchell and Everly 1993). Briefly, the roles of the pathways are as follows:

The *neural pathway* consists of the nerves of the sympathetic and parasympathetic nervous systems which together make up the autonomic nervous system. The autonomic nervous system governs the activities of the cardiac and smooth muscle, the digestive and sweat glands and other endocrine glands such as the pancreatic gland and adrenal medulla. Although these functions are not under conscious control, there is a centralised regulation of these systems by the hypothalamus. Most of the organs of the body are connected to both the sympathetic and parasympathetic systems and the effects of these two systems are generally antagonistic.

The *neuro-endocrine pathway* consists of the sympathetic neural chain and the adrenal medulla. Stimulation of the neuro-endocrine pathway results in the release of the hormone adrenaline and noradrenaline. The neuro-endocrine pathway is responsible for the flight or fight response described by Cannon (1927). During the flight/fight response, the sympathetic activity causes rapid changes in the cardiovascular function that allow immediate exertion. The adrenaline and noradrenaline support the increased exertion by raising the metabolic rate and reducing gastrointestinal activity.

The *endocrine pathways* consist of two major pathways that have a role in the way that the body deals with stress. The first involves the anterior pituitary gland. When the anterior pituitary gland is stimulated it releases thyroid stimulating hormone (TSH). TSH stimulates the thyroid gland to produce thyroxin which increases the body's metabolic rate, raising the blood sugar levels, increasing respiration, heart rate, blood pressure and intestinal motility (Goodman and Gilman 1975). The second pathway is the HPA pathway. The stimulation of the hypothalamus causes the release of corticotrophin-releasing factor (CRF), which in turn initiates the release of adreno-cortico-trophin hormone (ACTH) from the pituitary. ACTH then stimulates the release of cortisol from the adrenal glands. Cortisol increases arterial blood pressure, mobilises fats and glucose from the fatty tissues, reduces allergic and inflammatory reactions and decreases white blood cells (Dryden and Yankura 1995).

Pathway interactions

The three pathways work together and their action is modified by the action of multiple feedback loops involving receptors on the pituitary, hypothalamus and other areas of the brain (Cullinan *et al.* 1995). This coordination of response is facilitated by the fact that receptors for adrenaline and cortisol are generally co-located in the brain (Yehuda 1998). Since the three pathways are stimulated during stress, it is unsurprising to find that adrenaline and cortisol are typically both elevated during the stress response. It is important to recognise however that adrenaline and cortisol have very different roles in the stress response (Yehuda *et al.* 1990). While it is the role of adrenaline to facilitate the availability of energy to the body's vital organs, the role for cortisol is to shut down these activities following the withdrawal of the stressful situation. A major function of cortisol is to restrain biological stress responses by initiating a termination of the activities of the sympathetic nervous system. As the neural pathway and neuro-endocrine pathways begin to shut down, the cortisol then begins to suppress the HPA pathway through the operation of the negative feedback loop, involving glucocorticoid receptors on the pituitary, hypothalamus and other brain receptors. This process restores the body to normal levels of blood cortisol. Munck and Guytre (1986) described cortisol as being more of an 'anti-stress' than a stress hormone and state that 'if the body's stress responses were not restrained by cortisol, the reactions that provide short term benefit in the acute aftermath of stress would ultimately produce long term damage'.

Traumatic stress v. normal stress

During a traumatic event, victims experience similar stress reactions as would occur as a response to normal stress; however, the intensity of the experience causes these physiological stress responses to breach the body's homeostatic barriers, causing organic damage which does not occur in non-traumatic stress (Shalev 1996). In research into post-trauma biological functioning, significant differences have been observed between the responses found in people suffering from PTSD and those suffering from chronic stress or depression (Yehuda 1998). Most significant is that in patients with PTSD, decreased levels of cortisol were found, but this was accompanied by an increased receptor sensitivity to the presence of cortisol and stronger inhibition negative feedback. The result of these changes is that the whole HPA system becomes much more sensitive and reactive to subsequent stress triggers. These changes are not found in patients with chronic stress or depression, whose symptoms followed the patterns which are much more consistent with the traditional concept of stress formulated by Selye in 1956. The chronically stressed and depressed patients had increased levels of cortisol but the decreased responsiveness of their receptors and the erosion of negative feedback resulted in the patients becoming less sensitive to further exposures to stress triggers. A summary of the differences between individuals suffering from chronic stress and PTSD is given in Table 2.1.

It has not yet been established whether the changes in the HPA pathway occur at the time of the original traumatic exposure or only develop later as an adaptation to the chronic symptoms of PTSD. When considered with the epidemiological studies it is difficult to say with any certainty that the alterations in the neuro-endocrine and endocrine pathways are solely due to exposure to traumatic events. It is increasingly obvious that despite comparable exposure to trauma, individuals without PTSD do not show the biological alterations found in those with PTSD and that other factors need to be considered.

Post-traumatic stress and the brain

The brain has an important role in the identification, accommodation and assimilation of the individual's internal and external experiences and needs (MacLean 1985). The evolution of the brain has created three major brain structures: the *brain stem and hypothalamus*, the *limbic system* and the *cortex*. Communication between these structures allows the traumatic incident to be recognised, processed and acted upon.

In the past, there have been major ethical and practical difficulties in studying the impact of a traumatic experience on the functioning of the brain. Because of these problems, much of the early trauma research involved animals (Maier and Seligman 1976; Hubel and Weisel 1977) or people who had already experienced a traumatic

Table 2.1 Differences between the actions of the HPA pathway in PTSD and chronic stress (Yehuda 1998)

PTSD	Chronic stress/depression
• Decreased levels of cortisol	• Increased levels of cortisol
• Increased cortisol receptor sensitivity	• Decreased cortisol receptor responsiveness
• Stronger negative feedback inhibition	• Erosion of negative feedback
• HPA system becomes more sensitised	• HPA system becomes more desensitised

event (Kolb 1987; Kosten *et al.* 1987). Recent advances in neuro-imaging methods allow brain structures and functions to be examined in detail. This is undertaken without discomfort or harm to the subjects and has revolutionised the way trauma is studied in the brain (Toga and Mazziotta 1996).

Brain structures involved in the PTSD response

A number of brain structures have been found closely associated with the trauma response. The most widely studied are the locus ceruleus, amygdala, hippocampus and cortex. When a person becomes involved in a traumatic experience, the sensory information is transported through the central nervous system or directly into the brain. Most of the sensory information is passed to the thalamus where some initial processing takes place. From the thalamus, the sensory information goes via the amygdala and the hippocampus to the pre-frontal cortex, and at each stage additonal processing takes place. When the information reaches the cortex and has been assigned meaning, it is fed back to the locus ceruleus and the amygdala. Connections to and from the locus ceruleus and amygdala to the hypothalamus, hippocampus and pre-frontal cortex are then able to affect the behavioural, autonomic and HPA response systems which in turn initiate and control the body's responses (LeDoux 1992).

Figure 2.1 illustrates the relationship between the thalamus, amygdala, hippocampus and pre-frontal cortex. Each brain structure is involved in the processing and interpretation of incoming sensory information. With a moderate activation of the amygdala, the cortex's potential for developing a verbal memory is enhanced. This process of creating a verbal memory is mediated by the hippocampus that has a role in creating short-term memories. Where there is extreme arousal the passage of information from the amygdala to the hippocampus is disrupted by the creation of an integration barrier. The barrier prevents information moving from the amygdala to the hippocampus with the result that traumatic sensations and impressions become trapped in the amygdala in an active form. The sensory information in the amygdala cannot be dispersed or changed without the intervention of the higher cognitive processes (Van der Kolk 1996).

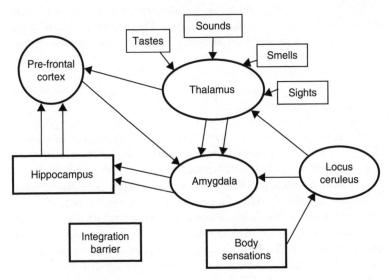

Figure 2.1 Schematic representation of emotional arousal pathways (after LeDoux 1992)

The effect of trauma on brain functioning

The locus ceruleus is involved in the access and retrieval of memories through its connections with the hippocampus and amygdala. When the locus ceruleus pathways of victims were stimulated, it was found that the victims experienced repetitive intrusive memories of their traumatic event (Van der Kolk *et al.* 1985). It has also been found that stimulating the locus ceruleus can cause feelings of intense fear, imminent death and an inability to sleep (Kaitin *et al.* 1986).

The amygdala is involved in the interpretation, the emotional strength and significance of incoming information (Falls and Davis 1995) and this is achieved by the creation of an internal sensory representation of the external world (Calvin 1990). Where the amygdala is stimulated in human subjects (Gloor 1992) a variety of emotions are elicited. These include fear, anxiety, pleasure and anger, with fear being reported most frequently. When subjects were asked to describe the cause of their fear, most described a distressing past or present life experience. In a study of PTSD patients using magnetic imaging, Van der Kolk (1996) found that visual re-experiences of a traumatic event (flashbacks) were accompanied by an increased activity in the amygdala.

The hippocampus plays a role in categorising and storing incoming stimuli in the short-term memory. The ability to learn from experience is dependent on the functioning of the hippocampus. The hippocampus processes new stimuli to decide whether the experience is rewarding or punishing (Gray 1987). Disruption to the hippocampus results in people becoming extremely responsive to environmental stimuli (Altman *et al.* 1973).

The use of neuro-imaging methods has enabled researchers to observe changes in brain activity as they occur. A number of studies that have exposed trauma victims to reminders of their traumatic experience have demonstrated a lateralisation of the victim's brain functioning (Rauch *et al.* 1998). In traumatised subjects, trauma reminders cause a right hemisphere lateralisation of cortical activity; the right hemisphere is involved in evaluating information for its emotional significance. At the same time, the left hemisphere (and most significantly the Broca's area, which is involved with the translation of personal experiences into language) showed little or no activity (Van der Kolk 1996). This finding is extremely significant as it means that during periods of extreme emotional and sensory demands the trauma victim is physiologically prevented from processing emotional information and is literally rendered speechless and out of touch with their feelings. The disruption of normal cognitive processing in traumatised people can also create sensory memories without any evaluation of the incoming information by the cortex (LeDoux 1992). This lack of processing of sensory information by trauma victims results in their becoming hyper-reactive to environmental stimuli (Van der Kolk and Ducey 1989).

Findings from studies into the brain suggest that where an individual has experienced an earlier traumatic event this could result in an increased sensitivity to subsequent traumatic experiences. This would be particularly true if there had been no opportunities for the sensory material already stored in the amygdala from previous traumatic exposures to be addressed.

Discussion

Early studies of traumatic stress disorders began by examining survivors of extreme events such as wars and major disasters. However, this approach failed to give adequate recognition to the fact that most people exposed to a traumatic event do not go on to suffer from PTSD. Epidemiological investigations indicate that the causes of

PTSD are multi-factorial and while the actual traumatic incident is an important factor, it is not the *only* factor in determining who will or will not suffer from the disorder. Investigations into the psycho-biology of trauma have established that PTSD brings about changes to the neuro-endocrine and endocrine pathways. By identifying the levels of adrenaline and cortisol in the bloodstream, it is possible to identify those people who are suffering from PTSD rather than from another form of mental disorder. The way that the brain deals with trauma-laden information by preventing it from being processed and given meaning has an enormous implication for the way trauma interventions are designed. If sensory memories are to be moved out of the amygdala for processing in the hippocampus and cortex it is essential that the original levels of fear and horror are not re-stimulated. If re-stimulation does occur it is likely that the integration barrier will be formed with the result that the sensory information remains stuck.

Chapter 3

An employee's response to trauma[1]

Introduction

This chapter looks at the responses of employees to traumatic incidents at work. Although organisational policies and procedures have a strong influence on employee behaviours at times of trauma, the psychological contract formed between the employee and the organisation is an equally powerful influence. The employee's responses to trauma are described in a three-phase model. This model separates the responses at the time of the trauma from the acute responses following the trauma and the chronic responses, some of which may last for many years. Typical employee responses at each trauma phase are illustrated with case material taken from workplace settings. Finally, the chapter returns to the importance of the psychological contract and describes how organisational care programmes can be enhanced or damaged by the way the organisation deals with the aftermath of the trauma and its traumatised employees.

The psychological contract

The multiple relationships within organisations are complex. Employer and employee expectations and responsibilities are established, some are formalised in legal contracts and some in health and safety legislation. Other expectations are created from the attitudes and beliefs of employees and come to form an unwritten psychological contract. The psychological contract is difficult to define; Schein (1980) described such contracts as 'Unwritten sets of expect-

1 Based on Tehrani, N. (1998) Dealing with trauma at work – the employee's story, *Counselling Psychology Quarterly*, 11(4): 379–92. www.tandf.co.uk

ations operating at all times between every member of an organisation and the various managers and others in that organisation'. Schein explained that although the psychological contract is unwritten, it is a powerful tool for determining behaviour within organisations.

When a traumatic event occurs in the workplace, employee and employer behaviour is partly determined by policies, procedures and legal standards. Failure to observe these laws and rules can result in the employee being disciplined or the organisation being punished by the law. The psychological contract also has an effect on the behaviour of employees, and organisational failures to meet obligations under the psychological contract can lead to a loss of morale, anger and delayed recovery.

Three phases of trauma

An employee's reactions to trauma fall into three main phases: a) immediate reactions at the time of the trauma; b) acute reactions in the month following the trauma; and c) chronic or long-term reactions. Each phase involve a number of characteristic responses (American Psychiatric Association 1994). Research has shown that the magnitude and duration of trauma responses is determined by a number of factors, the main ones being the intensity and nature of the traumatic event, the employee's perception of the trauma, the employee's level of training and their preparedness to meet the demands of the trauma, plus the availability of appropriate support (Feinstein and Dolman 1991).

Mitchell (1993), in an explanation of the differences in trauma responses, described two protective barriers that can reduce the development of post-trauma stress by a process of *trauma immunisation*. The first barrier protects the employee from the immediate psychological impact of trauma. This barrier is developed through pre-trauma training and mental preparation. The barrier enables the employee to reduce the likelihood of personal identification with the traumatic event and facilitates the development of effective personal defences against the traumatic experience. The second defence barrier protects employees who have breached the first barrier and are suffering from acute traumatic stress. The second barrier requires the provision of effective organisational and peer support, debriefing and counselling (see Figure 3.1).

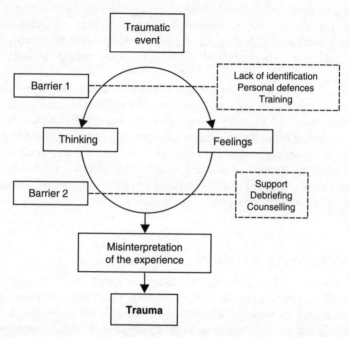

Figure 3.1 Barriers to the experience of trauma in organisations (after Mitchell 1993)

Responses to traumatic events in the workplace

DSM IV (American Psychiatric Association 1994) describes the immediate psychological reactions to trauma as intense fear, horror and helplessness. The three classical behavioural response patterns to trauma have been identified as escape (flight), aggression (fight) and freezing (Cannon 1927; Gray 1971). Many employees, particularly those from the emergency services, exhibit a fourth response, which is to 'deal' with the demands of the traumatic situation. Green *et al.* (1985) found that employees were able to deal with traumatic situations providing that their perception of the magnitude and nature of the trauma was balanced by their perceived ability to deal with it. Green found that the greater an employee's confidence in their ability to cope, the more likely the employee would be to deal effectively with the traumatic event. A comprehensive model of an individual's response to extreme stress is found in the transactional model (Cox and MacKay 1976; Cox 1990). This model views an individual's responses to stressful situations as a complex and dynamic system of transactions between the individual and their internal and external environments. Stress is the result of an imbalance between a perceived demand and a perceived capability to meet that demand. This imbalance is experienced in emotional, psychological and physiological responses, the consequences of which are fed back as new or additional demands.

Many employees, including those who work in the emergency services, banks and retailing, face traumatic situations as a normal part of their work. These traumatic situations include such events as dealing with death and disasters, armed raids, physical attacks, threats of violence and severe verbal abuse. The physical demands of handling a traumatic situation can be considerable (Holoday *et al.* 1995), however the psychological demands are no less daunting, particularly as the traumatic situation may challenge personal values or abilities to meet organisational expectations (Parkes 1975).

The illustrative case studies that follow present some common employee reactions to trauma at each of the three trauma phases. Where published accounts exist these were used to illustrate the responses; however, where there was no illustrative account, new case material has been used from the accounts of employees describing traumatic experiences, drawn from the author's personal case notes. These are the examples where no source has been given.

Immediate trauma responses

The demands which face an employee during a traumatic incident can be numerous and sometimes contradictory. This faces the employee with the dilemma of which demand to meet first. Although training can increase the likelihood of a particular behaviour or course of action, the employee's own values and beliefs determine which behaviours are selected. Lazarus and Folkman (1984) suggested that when an individual faces extreme stress three things are considered: a) Is there anything I can do to stop it?; b) Do I need to stop it?; and c) What is the best way to stop it?

In Case 1, the cashier had to decide whether to sound the alarm or to hand over the money to an armed robber. She assessed the situation and decided that if she handed over some of the money this may prevent the gunman from shooting. When the gunman left she felt it was safe to set off the alarm. In this incident, the cashier satisfied her need to protect her colleagues, her wish to protect the organisation's money and her duty to call the police.

Case I
Things happened very quickly, one minute it was a normal day, the next there was a gunman demanding the money. I had to think quickly but it seemed to me that the raider was very nervous and if I pressed the alarm, he may shoot someone. I did not want to give him the money but there was no alternative. I only gave him the money which was visible and as soon as he had gone I set off the alarm.

In the workplace, people often form strong social relationships. These relationships frequently involve feelings of responsibility, affection and friendship. In Case 2, a cleaner became involved in an armed raid and believed that it was her duty to look after a pregnant cashier who had been tied up by the raiders. When the cashier became distressed, the cleaner did her best to look after her despite the real danger to her own life and well-being.

Case 2
The cleaner saw that the cashier was having problems. She was five months pregnant and shaking violently. Despite being told to keep quiet the cleaner kept shouting at the raiders to untie the cashier's hands. Talking about the raid later the cleaner said that she had not considered the possible danger to her own life, all she was concerned about was the welfare of the cashier and her baby.

A job role can define the behaviours that are appropriate when dealing with traumatic situations. Bystanders may look to the emergency service workers to deal with traumatic situations calmly. Employees with a strong role image will try to meet those role requirements even when the traumatic incident has a direct impact on their own lives. In Case 3, a police officer tried to maintain her professional image despite being involved in the incident personally. When she became overwhelmed by her emotions, she expressed shame for her reactions.

Case 3
A female police officer had hit a pedestrian with her police car. When her supervisor and the ambulance arrived she was sitting on the pavement cradling the injured woman's head, and directing a recruit to take statements from bystanders. After she had reported what she had done to the supervisor she began crying uncontrollably. Later

she was more concerned about crying in front of her supervisor than about the accident.

(Joyce 1989)

Raphael (1986) found that in organisations with cultures which regard the expression of emotions or fear as unacceptable signs of inadequacy, employees were likely to hide all signs of emotion or distress. In many traumatic situations the natural physiological and behavioural responses may become difficult to prevent or hide. Where the traumatic impact on an employee is so severe that there is a loss of control of the bladder or bowel, or where the experience of terror is so extreme as to cause freezing, the employee may be exposed to the additional distress of peer ridicule and shaming. In Case 4, a bank clerk experienced feelings of intense shame and disgust after running away from the scene of an armed raid.

Case 4
A gunman threatened a bank clerk. The gunman swore, cursed, and threatened to kill the clerk unless the money was handed over. The ordeal lasted a few minutes but the bank clerk was terrified. When the gunman left, the clerk ran into the toilets where he stayed until he felt able to face his colleagues. Later the clerk said that he felt debased and dirty.

(Parkinson 1993)

Where employees lack the coping skills, knowledge or competence to deal with the demands of a traumatic event, they may become disorientated and disorganised. Weisaeth (1983) found that 25 per cent of workers involved in a fire in a paint factory displayed inappropriate freezing, aimless wondering or purposeless hyperactivity. Raphael (1986) found a greater occurrence of freezing when the victim's resources were overwhelmed by the demands of the trauma situation. In Case 5 a young man is faced with two competing courses of action.

Case 5
During a North Sea oil rig disaster a young man froze when he was faced with the choice of helping a trapped man he knew or saving his own life. This dilemma was only resolved when the dangers to his own life increased to such an extent that he had to fight for his own survival.

(Jaatun 1983)

There is a common belief of invulnerability in most people (Janoff-Bulman 1985), and this has led many victims of trauma to delay their recognition of danger (Scheppele and Bart 1983). In Case 6 a supervisor, involved in a raid on a mail train, found it difficult to believe that an armed robbery was taking place until he was struck on the head by the gunman.

Case 6

It had been a normal kind of day and when the train came in all I was thinking about was getting it unloaded. A man came up to me, he was in uniform, he shouted at me to lie on the floor. Although he had a gun in his hand, I thought it was some kind of joke. The gunman hit me on the head with the gun and I fell to the ground. It was only then that I realised that it was for real.

When the reality of the traumatic situation becomes difficult to handle, some employees may dissociate from the full reality of their experience (McFarlane 1995). *Peritraumatic dissociation* is common in victims of trauma. During the dissociative experience, the employee may encounter out of body experiences. Dissociation results in the individual having the sense that their body is distorted, that time is speeded up or slowed down, or other sensory information is distorted or changed (Marmer *et al.* 1997). In Case 7 a gas engineer was involved in a major explosion, and as he fought for his life, he experienced an out of body experience.

Case 7

I was just starting to use the welding machine when the explosion happened. From that time everything became unreal. It was as if I was floating above the trench watching what was happening to me. I saw myself as if I was a different person and yet I knew it was me. I remember getting out of the trench but I cannot remember much else after that.

Barriers to the experience of acute traumatic stress

Where employees have been trained and are mentally prepared to meet the demands of a traumatic situation, there is a reduced incidence of psychological trauma (Mitchell and Everly 1993). The support of peers and colleagues at the time of the trauma has been found to help employees deal with the traumatic situation without developing traumatic stress (Green *et al.* 1985). In the emergency services, peer support sometimes takes the form of black humour, which provides a means of diminishing or depersonalising the traumatic event (Joyce 1989). The use of black humour by police officers dealing with particularly distressful incidents is illustrated in Case 8.

Case 8

I have seen an officer waving the severed leg of a railway victim and telling his colleague he would hit him with the soggy end. It is hard to relate a piece of meat wearing a sock and shoe to the original wearer.

(Joyce 1989)

Despite extensive training and experience, personal identification with the trauma victims can occur. This is particularly true when personal relationships are involved. In Case 9, a policeman was called to a murder. A man he knew had just killed his wife's lover. The policeman became upset because he identified with the husband's distress and helplessness.

Case 9

I've seen hundreds of dead bodies over the years but I cannot take it any more. I was called to a murder; the husband stabbed his wife's lover . . . there was blood everywhere . . . I had been called out to domestics between him and his wife. He was actually a very nice guy, but his wife would try the patience of a saint. I just felt sorry for the husband. I cried at the scene, there was this ***** body in the bedroom and the husband downstairs like a lamb.

(Scott and Stradling 1992a)

A lack of personal identification acts as a barrier to the acquisition of acute traumatic stress, however sometimes the identification and trauma responses may only become established later (American Psychiatric Association 1994). In Case 10, a cashier suffered delayed onset of traumatic stress when she eventually recognised the significance of an armed raid.

Case 10

I was involved in this armed raid but no one got hurt and I was back to work after a couple of days. About six months later the same gang hit another office. This time they shot someone. It was only then that I realised that I could have been killed and started having the nightmares.

Reactions during the following month

After a traumatic event, a number of typical trauma responses can be observed. These can be separated into the *primary* and *secondary* responses. The primary responses relate directly to the trauma and include the symptoms of avoidance, re-experience and increased arousal. The secondary responses involve the employee's reactions to the primary responses. Common secondary responses include irrational beliefs such as 'There must be something wrong with me because I feel so bad', 'I should be able to cope with this' or 'I will never feel the same again?' (Shalev 1996). The immediate physiological and psychological responses to a traumatic event are frequently re-experienced in the following month. Smith *et al.* (1990) observed that the re-experience of responses placed significant demands on traumatised employees and prevented an early return to a normal life and work. In Case 11 a postman describes the effect of being held up in an armed raid.

Case 11

Sometimes when I am sitting in my home I get the same feelings that I had when the gunman was behind me. That was the worst vulnerability I have ever felt. I begin to shake and feel sick to the stomach. This can last for quite a long time. It is difficult to explain how it feels but I think that I must be losing my mind.

The presence of distressing intrusive memories and disordered arousal can lead trauma victims to avoid people, situations or places which remind them of the incident. This avoidance is particularly significant when the traumatic incident occurred in the workplace (Tehrani 1995). In Case 12 an engineer injured in an explosion found that he could not go back to his original job and asked to be given work in the office.

Case 12

The company has been good to me; I just could not face going back to my original job. I find it difficult to go anywhere near the place the explosion happened. If I smell gas I begin to panic. My life has totally changed since the explosion and I still feel guilty when I think about what happened to the others.

An employee who narrowly escapes death when others are killed can experience feelings of guilt (Hodgkinson and Stewart 1991). In Case 13 a survivor became obsessed with reading the list of dead victims as if to check for his own name.

Case 13

I must be going mad. I was looking at the alphabetical list of the dead in the newspaper, and thought over and over again that's where I could have easily have been between the G and the L. I could not put the paper down. This week I have just gone over and over the events of the day in my mind. I am stupid; I just cannot concentrate at work. I am shattered when I go to work because I am not sleeping.

(Scott and Stradling 1992a)

In Case 14 a lorry driver who survived the Zeebrugge ferry disaster and saved the lives of numerous passengers could not come to terms with the death of lorry drivers he failed to save. He committed suicide three years after the disaster.

Case 14

When the ferry went down the driver was on the ferry's vehicle deck. Frozen with fear he heard the vehicle groaning under the weight of the vehicles above and he thought he would die. He smashed his suitcase through the window and escaped into the water. As he swam towards the exit he heard the screams of trapped lorry drivers. He climbed out onto the side of the ship where he was one of the first to smash portholes, let down ropes into the ship and begin the rescue. He had saved the lives of many passengers, yet he did not remember these actions. All he remembered was the unanswered screams of the lorry drivers. 'They were drivers like me and I did nothing to help them.'

(Hodgkinson and Stewart 1991)

Military training is designed to help soldiers cope with the trauma and consequences of armed conflict (Murphy *et al.* 1995). Sometimes dilemmas may emerge which bring personal values in conflict with those of the army. Where the soldier's role is as a peacekeeper in a civil war the difficulties can become even more acute (Laufer *et al.* 1985). The soldier in Case 15 was involved in the Vietnam War, and years later he still felt guilt for having killed civilians.

Case 15

I felt good about knocking out the machine gun. I felt bad about killing the people. We killed five civilians and the machine gunner ... I'm trying to forget the entire incident. I wish I had not killed those people. I have dreams about it. It was surreal, you know I very clearly saw them die and I felt very responsible.

(Murphy *et al.* 1995)

In the immediate aftermath of a traumatic event, organisations have to manage additional demands. Managers and employees may be required to speak to the families of deceased colleagues, dead bodies may need to be identified, police interrogations and identity parades take place and where the trauma story is of public interest, employees may be exposed to the media. This can be particularly distressing to vulnerable employees who, in a state of shock, may reveal information which is personally damaging or distressing (Ochberg 1993). The security van driver in Case 16 became very angry about the way that the press and television reporters handled the hostage situation. He was upset that the story was on the news before he had an opportunity to contact close family members.

Case 16

I was told that my family was being held hostage and that they would be killed if I did not help the robbers. When the incident was finished, I returned home to find that reporters surrounded my house. The trauma of the blackmail and handing over the cash was much less upsetting than having reporters outside my home and my name and address given out on the news.

Barriers to the development of post-traumatic stress

Where employees are provided with adequate post-trauma support following a traumatic event, the level of distress can be reduced and the employees make a rapid recovery (Health and Safety Executive 1995). Inadequate organisational support for trauma victims and their families can damage workplace relationships and delay recovery. In Case 17 the security van driver had been held up in an

armed raid. He was very angry about his manager's failure to show
any concern for his well-being.

Case 17

I got back to the office after the raid. My manager was working on the
computer and did not even turn around. He asked me how I felt and if
I would be able to do the job the next day as he was short of staff. Is it
too much to expect your manager to show a little concern? How can
I believe that the organisation cares about me after that?

Distressed employees are often avoided by colleagues afraid of
doing the wrong thing and making matters worse. Flannery *et al.*
(1996) found that where organisations provided training for managers in providing support for traumatised employees there were significant reductions in the incidence of post-trauma stress. In Case 18 a
driver compares the different approaches of a trained and untrained
manager.

Case 18

The first time I was involved in an incident the manager did not know
what to do. He just expected me to go on with the job, although I had
been threatened with a gun. The last time was very different. My
manger seemed to want to help me and understood what I was going
through.

Trauma victims need to understand what has happened to them,
and telling their story is one way that victims regain control
over their lives (Raphael 1986). In criminal attacks, the employee
may have to make a number of statements to the police and to
the organisation. Although these interviews allow the employee
to recount what has happened, the purpose of the interview is to
prevent crime or catch criminals and not to help the employee.
A *debrief* is different. Here, employees are encouraged to explore
the facts, emotional content and meaning of what has
happened, with the aim of reducing the negative impact of the
trauma (Newman *et al.* 1997). The need to talk is illustrated in
Case 19.

Case 19

I felt I must tell someone what it was like. You couldn't know if you
weren't there. And people talk about physical things – but it is the

emotions that count. It's what's left in your mind afterwards that really leaves scars.

(Raphael 1986)

The rehabilitation of traumatised employees is an important part of the recovery process. During the acute stage, employees can develop phobic or avoidance behaviours. Returning to the workplace or site of the trauma helps the employee deal with the incident and begins to re-establish normal life (Tehrani 1995). In Case 20 a postman has been attacked on his round. His manager gradually rehabilitated him to returning to work by encouraging him to mix with his workmates and then to go out on a round with another postman.

Case 20
I came back to the office to talk to my manager and my workmates. My manager said I could go out with a colleague for the first week, but that was no good. I had to be able to do the job on my own. It was hard at first but after a day or two it got easier.

Chronic and long-term reactions

It is estimated that around 14 per cent of the working population in the USA suffer from post-traumatic stress (American Psychiatric Association 1994). Only a small minority of employees exposed to traumatic situations go on to develop PTSD and those who suffer traumatic stress symptoms frequently find their symptoms become resolved over time (McFarlane 1996). For some employees the impact of an early trauma lies hidden, only emerging when the employee is faced with strong reminders of the traumatic event (Gibson 1991). The driver in Case 21 suffered trauma reactions when he experienced road conditions similar to those that were present on the night he was attacked.

Case 21
I thought that I had handled the trauma well and had not had a symptom for over six months. Then this night I was driving the van out of the yard and I started to panic. It was as bad as anything I had suffered before was. It was the lights shining on the wet road that did it. It was just like the night I was hijacked.

Employees with mild or transient post-traumatic stress usually continue to work, although some may not be able to return to their original jobs. Where an employee suffers full-blown PTSD it is difficult to continue working (Keane *et al.* 1985). In Case 22, a soldier describes the post-trauma symptoms that he regularly experienced at night. The distress caused by the psychological reactions to trauma produces a similar sense of powerlessness as was experienced at the time of the original trauma.

Case 22
For no obvious reason I had suddenly been overwhelmed by a crescendo of blind unreasoning fear, defying all logic and insight . . . nothing that General Galtieri's men had generated compared with the terrors that my own mind invented that night. Having looked at death full in the eye on a windswept isthmus outside Goose Green and again, but two weeks later, on a barren hillside called Wireless Ridge, I think I can honestly say I no longer feared death or the things real and imagined that usually become the objects of phobias. I was afraid that night of the only thing that could still frighten me, myself. I was terrified of losing my control.

(Hughes 1990)

McFarlane (1996) describes PTSD as a failure of recovery rather than a response to a traumatic event. Employees who have experienced a traumatic event at an earlier stage of their lives are often unaware of the part the trauma still plays in their behaviours and attitudes. Many employees will discover ways to reduce traumatic arousal such as avoiding stimuli which remind them of the trauma, or numbing their responsiveness to all experiences. This numbing reduces the pain of the trauma but also affects the ability to take pleasure from normal life events and lowers potential at work (Shalev 1992). The engineer in Case 23 was managing to work reasonably well, however he suffered frequent bouts of depression and relationship difficulties.

Case 23
An engineer had suffered sexual abuse in childhood. In his work he was regarded as competent, but not dynamic. He had received average reports from his managers. He was transferred to a new manager who had a reputation for bullying. The engineer had difficulty in dealing with the manager and became withdrawn and depressed. The

engineer then began to re-experience the childhood sexual abuse in flashbacks and nightmares.

Exposure to traumatic events may also affect social relationships. McFarlane (1987) found that victims of Australian bush fires were inclined to be irritable, aggressive and avoid any shared activities. Following the Armenian earthquake in 1988, survivors showed an increase in marital discord and interpersonal violence (Goenjian *et al.* 1994). Case 24 describes how a marital relationship was badly affected by the impact of a traumatic experience. In this case the husband survived when a ferry sank and his wife, who was to have accompanied him on the ferry, also suffered trauma reactions but these were unacknowledged by her husband.

Case 24
A 55-year-old married man involved in a major shipping disaster had a particularly miraculous escape. He suffered physical injuries and severe PTSD. Being self-employed his business began to fall apart and he was virtually house bound. He and his wife began to drink heavily and he admitted to hitting his wife. He had no interest in sexual relations and eventually he filed for divorce.

(Joseph *et al.* 1997)

Substance abuse is a common response to chronic traumatic stress (Keane and Wolfe 1990). Alcohol, one of the oldest treatments for trauma, reduces psychological trauma symptoms but any cessation of drinking causes a rebound effect, in which victims experience sleep loss, nightmares and other traumatic intrusions (Abueg *et al.* 1995).

Case 25
An unmarried woman aged 22 suffered from accidental gas poisoning in an incident in which two friends were killed. She reported extreme anxiety in situations involving confinement (queues, trains, the tube and when driving). She felt apathetic, feeling that there was no point to life. Although she was still working she reported trying to avoid thoughts and feelings about the tragedy. She was drinking up to 15 pints of beer at the weekend.

(Joseph *et al.* 1997)

In their study, Dansky *et al.* (1997) found that 40 per cent of alcoholics met the criteria for PTSD. The young woman in Case 25 suffered a range of post-trauma symptoms including the abuse of alcohol.

Discussion

This review of case studies illustrates the different ways employees react to trauma and provides an indication of the impact of the organisation on those reactions. Organisations employing workers in roles where there is a risk of trauma are required to provide an appropriate level of support to meet the needs of traumatised employees (Health and Safety Executive 1995). The introduction of trauma care can be problematical when, despite the organisation's best intentions, their employees form negative views of their motives. In organisations that place a high value on cost saving, the introduction of a trauma care programme can be greeted with suspicion from employees. The programme may come to be regarded as the organisation's way of saving money by getting employees back to work quickly and by reducing the cost of litigation. Organisations can give conflicting messages to their workers by rewarding employees for 'having a go' while claiming that their employees are their most valuable asset. Organisations that find it difficult to accept the expression of strong emotions may find that employees will avoid showing their feelings in order to reduce the likelihood of being ridiculed by workmates. Where the expression of normal reactions to trauma is suppressed, secondary problems such as depression, alcoholism, relationship difficulties and suicidal tendencies may develop. The introduction of integrated trauma care programmes appears to address many of the difficulties of trauma care in the workplace, and when they are sensitively introduced (Tehrani 1995) they have brought about essential cultural changes and improved employee well-being.

Chapter 4

Traumatic stress in the workplace

Introduction

The full extent of the incidence of traumatic events within the workplace is difficult to assess due to a lack of reliable data. It is known that many workplace situations meet the criteria for traumatic exposure. It is likely therefore that a large number of employees will have been exposed to situations in the workplace with the potential for causing them post-traumatic stress or other trauma-related disorders. While it is generally recognised that employees working in the emergency services face traumatic and distressing situations as a normal part of their working life, and as a result may suffer psychological problems (Mitchell and Everly 1993; Violanti and Paton 1999; Alexander and Klein 2001), there is less recognition of the psychological needs of workers who experience other forms of traumatic event in their place of work. Employees working in industries not routinely exposed to major incidents or disasters are less likely to be provided with awareness training and post-traumatic support (Income Data Services 1994). This chapter describes some traumatic incidents that are commonly encountered in the workplace and then goes on to discuss the main groups of employees who are at risk of exposure to traumatising situations. Finally, the chapter emphasises the need for organisations to take a proactive approach in dealing with workplace trauma.

Major incidents in the workplace

There is no universally recognised definition of a major incident or disaster. The definition used by the police and fire services in the UK describes a major incident as any emergency that requires the implementation of special arrangements by one or more of the emergency services, the National Health Service or the local authority. A major incident is likely to involve:

- initial treatment, rescue and transport of large numbers of casualties;
- involvement either directly or indirectly with large numbers of people;
- handling a large number of enquiries likely to be generated both from the public and the news media;
- the need for the large-scale combined resources of two or more of the emergency services;
- mobilisation and organisation of the emergency services and supporting bodies (e.g. local authorities) to cater for the possibility of death, serious injury or homelessness affecting a large number of people (Home Office 1994).

This definition, although useful, does not include major incidents involving military conflict or disasters that occur at sea or in the air. Table 4.1 provides a list of major incidents that can happen in the workplace. While the list is not exhaustive, it gives an indication of the types of incident that can have a major impact on the operation of the organisation and the well-being of the workforce.

Major incidents and disasters cause death, physical injury and

Table 4.1 Major incidents causing traumatic stress

Technological disasters e.g.	Natural disasters e.g.
• Collapse of buildings	• Floods
• Fires	• Earthquakes
• Release of toxic substances	• Hurricanes
• Loss of ships/aircraft	• Fires
Criminal activity e.g.	**Terrorism e.g.**
• Murder	• Bombs
• Hostage-taking	• Mass shooting
• Shooting	• Release of poisonous gas
• Contamination of products	• Sabotage
Armed conflict e.g.	**Peacekeeping e.g.**
• Hand-to-hand fighting	• Body recovery
• Land mines	• Snipers
• Death/injury of colleagues	• Civil unrest
• Serious injuries	• Dealing with atrocities

suffering to a large number of employees each year (Health and Safety Executive 1990). A statistical review of accident statistics (Health and Safety Executive 1999a) provides the numbers of fatal and major injuries that were reported during 1998/9. However, these figures are estimated to be less than half the total number of major injuries that occurred. Table 4.2 provides a summary of fatal and major injuries and Table 4.3 shows the industries whose employees had the highest levels of fatal or major injuries in 1998/9.

Most fatal injuries and major injuries are caused by falling or by being hit by a vehicle, object or machinery. Although there was only one death reported as being due to an act of violence, almost 600 people suffered major injuries due to violent attacks. Workers in the construction industry are the most likely group to be killed or seriously injured at work. While the physical cost of these incidents is high it is important to remember that the nature of these events is likely to result in psychological injury to those directly involved as well as to their colleagues and other witnesses.

Table 4.2 Types of accident that resulted in death or major injuries to employees in 1998/9 (adapted from Health and Safety Executive 1999a)

Incident	Killed	Major injuries
Falls	49	8662
Struck by moving vehicle	38	899
Hit by falling or flying objects	36	4184
Contact with moving machinery	17	1674
Contact with electricity	16	205
Trapped	11	647
Acts of violence	1	591

Table 4.3 Fatalities and major injuries by industry for 1998/9 (adapted from Health and Safety Executive 1999a)

Industry	Killed	Major injury	Total incidents per 100k workers
Agriculture, hunting, forestry, fishing	46	665	353
Extractive utility supply	10	545	412
Manufacturing	71	8066	393
Construction	66	4299	1146
Service industry	65	14219	397

To prepare for these major incidents some organisations have developed business continuity plans. However, few of these continuity plans adequately deal with the psychological needs of the employees most closely affected (Tomkinson 1999).

Other traumatic events

For most employees, exposure to traumatic incidents is much less dramatic than a major incident. Events such as workplace violence (Lipsedge 2000), bullying (Leymann and Gustafsson 1996) and victimisation (Joseph *et al.* 1997) together with exposure to a wide range of other stressful incidents including accidental injuries can lead to traumatic stress. Unlike major incidents which affect a relatively small number of employees, interpersonal conflicts and other traumatic experiences have a profound effect on the physical and psychological well-being of a large number of employees (Wynne and Clarkin 1995). Unfortunately, many of these traumatic incidents go unreported and therefore the size of their impact on employee health is largely unrecognised. The under-reporting, although unfortunate, is less surprising when one considers the attitudes held by many workers exposed to high levels of violence, victimisation and abuse. These workers have come to regard personal attacks and violent abuse as 'part of the job'. This 'macho' culture has been found to be particularly prevalent in hospitals and doctors' practices (Brady and Dickson 1999), the police force (Paton and Smith 1999), in public houses (Beale 1999) and in the construction industry (Reid 2000).

Whilst individual incidences of violence, abuse or victimisation may not immediately result in psychological trauma to the exposed employee, the prolonged exposure and gradual build-up of traumatic experiences can lead to a cumulative form of traumatic stress (Scott & Stradling 1992a). There is a wide range of incidents that can lead to employees suffering from traumatic stress. Table 4.4 lists the types of organisational incident that may lead to employees experiencing traumatic stress.

Employees at risk

Almost everyone will experience a traumatic event at some point in his or her life. In a community study in the USA it was found that 81 per cent of men and 74 per cent of women had been exposed to at

Table 4.4 Four types of traumatic event found in organisations

Operational	Interpersonal
• Exposure to biological hazard (AIDS)	• Death of a colleague
• Exposure to a carcinogen (asbestos)	• Witnessing a colleague being injured
• Exposure to noxious fumes	• Exposed to a violent strike/ picketing
• Destruction of workplace	• Suicide of colleague at work
• Institutionalised victimisation	• Bullying
• Community opposition to project	• Victimisation and verbal abuse
Criminal	**Injuries caused by**
• Bomb threat	• Vehicle crash
• Mugging	• Equipment failure/misuse
• Blackmail	• Small-scale fires
• Violent attack/threats	• Lifting and handling

least one traumatic event in their lives (Stein *et al.* 1997). However, it is important to recognise that the employee need not be directly involved in the traumatic or distressing event to experience traumatic stress symptoms. Following a traumatic event, it has been found that three groups of employees are vulnerable to post-traumatic stress:

• the primary victims;
• rescuers and carers;
• colleagues and other witnesses.

While the psychological impact of a traumatic event on the employees in each of the three categories follows the same general pattern (Van der Kolk and McFarlane 1996), each group requires special care and consideration from their organisation to facilitate their recovery.

Victims

Some occupations carry a higher risk of exposing workers to traumatic situations than others. For example, workers in the construction, fishing and mining industries are more likely to be exposed to situations involving death and injury than are workers in the insurance or finance industries. A survey of 149 construction companies showed that the most frequent traumatic event reported involved an employee being seriously injured at work (63 per cent), with on-site fatalities occurring in 30 per cent of the organisations (Reid 2000).

However, in less dangerous occupations the unexpected horror of being held up by an armed raider, involved in a car or rail crash, or being trapped by a fire can affect almost anyone. In the USA a major source of traumatic stress is the incidence of workplace murder. Up to one in six of all the murders that are committed in the USA occur in the place of work (Toscano and Weber 1995). In a study that looked at a typical week in the USA it was found that 20 workers are murdered and 18,000 assaulted in the workplace, the highest levels of risk being experienced by taxi-cab drivers, bailiffs, police officers, petrol station attendants and security guards (Jenkins 1996). A random survey of 600 American workers found that 19 per cent had been harassed, 7 per cent had been threatened and 3 per cent had been physically attacked at work in the previous year (Warshaw and Messite 1996). Reviews into the incidence of violence at work have shown that some tasks carry a greater risk of the employee experiencing a traumatic event than others (Incomes Data Service 1994; Chappell and DiMartino 1997). Table 4.5 lists the roles that have been most frequently associated with workplace violence.

Reported violence in the workplace is growing, and has led many European governments to issue guidelines on handling the impact of violence. However, this has not significantly increased organisational awareness of the need to introduce appropriate organisational policies and practices (Wynne et al. 1995). Finland is one of the few countries to have undertaken a systematic study of the incidence of violence at work. Heiskanen et al. (1991) found that the reported cases of violence at work rose from 16 per cent of the total number of violent incidents in 1980 to 23 per cent of the total number reported in 1988. In the UK a survey of violence in the retail trade showed that each year 0.5 per cent of staff experienced physical violence, 3.5 per cent threats of violence and 8.1 per cent verbal abuse (Brooks and Cross 1996). Far from being a rare event, workplace trauma involving major incidents, interpersonal conflict,

Table 4.5 Job tasks associated with workplace violence

• Caring for people in distress	• Undertaking money transactions
• Controlling and inspecting	• Providing services
• Delivering and collecting	• Enforcing laws or regulations
• Providing/delivering education	• Working at night
• Carrying expensive equipment	• Working alone

untimely death and injury is a growing concern. A review of fatal accidents by the Health and Safety Executive (1990) shows that in the UK around 500 people die at work each year and several hundred thousand lose time from work through work-related illness or injury.

Rescuers and carers

The impact of dealing with the dead and injured victims of traumatic incidents has been well documented (Joyce 1989; Brown and Campbell 1991; Orner et al. 1997). A study in the UK that measured the levels of stress symptoms in a random sample of ambulance workers found that a significant number were suffering from undiagnosed post-traumatic stress (Thompson and Suzuki 1991). In Australia, a study of volunteer firefighters found that 16 per cent had symptoms of PTSD 41 months after dealing with a major bush fire (McFarlane 1988b). In the police force it was found that 85 per cent of the personnel involved in traumatic incidents experienced traumatic stress reactions (Rivers 1993). These findings show that despite extensive training and experience, emergency workers are still vulnerable to the effects of post-traumatic exposure. A study that asked firefighters to describe the incidents which cause the most distress found that dealing with dead or injured children, fires in high-rise buildings, multiple casualty accidents and the threat of personal mutilation or death were regarded as highly distressing (Dyregrov 1989).

An emergency worker's personal involvement with trauma victims is generally for relatively short periods of time and this reduces the likelihood of over-identification or the formation of attachments with the primary victim. Carers, such as first-aiders, medics, nurses and counsellors, who have a longer-term involvement with trauma victims, sometimes develop a psychological or emotional attachment that may cause them problems. In a study of carers, Figley (1993) described a secondary traumatic stress syndrome which he called 'compassion fatigue'. Figley suggested that compassion fatigue was 'the natural consequent behaviour and emotions resulting from knowing about a traumatising event experienced by a significant other – the stress resulting from helping or wanting to help a traumatised or suffering person'. Compassion fatigue involves many of the symptoms found in burnout (Maslach and Jackson 1981), however, in compassion fatigue the carer exhibits the same post-traumatic stress symptoms of re-experience, avoidance and hyperarousal as are experienced by the person for whom they are caring.

Colleagues and witnesses

There has been little research in the UK into the impact of trauma on the primary victim's colleagues and other witnesses. This may be due to the fact that English law specifically excludes payment of damages for nervous shock to witnesses unless there are close family links to the primary victim. (*McFarlane* v. *EE Caledonia Ltd* 1994; *Robertson* v. *Forth Road Bridge Joint Board* 1995). A particularly relevant case was that of *Frost and others* v. *Chief Constable of South Yorkshire Police and others* (1996). This case is better known as the Hillsborough disaster. The police, who were personally involved in rescuing the dead and injured football fans at Hillsborough, received compensation for their injuries, while police officers who were present but not involved in the rescue were not compensated. Although witnesses and absent colleagues are unlikely to succeed when making a claim for compensation, they frequently experience post-traumatic stress symptoms (Muss 1991; Mitchell and Everly 1993). The way that organisations communicate with and support absent colleagues and witnesses following a traumatic incident has a large impact on the speed of recovery of these employees and the morale of the working team (Reid 2000).

Organisational responsibility

Traumatic situations impact employees in different ways depending on whether they are involved as victims, rescuers or bystanders. When organisations are undertaking their risk assessment of organisational working conditions it is important they identify not only the range and severity of traumatic incidents that might occur but also how these incidents would impact all the potential victims. Some organisations have adopted a proactive approach to assessing the risk of traumatic stress which identifies the underlying levels of stress symptoms experienced by employees, audits the impact of incidents and assesses the effectiveness of systems used to manage its provision of trauma care (Tehrani 1995). The development of systems and procedures for managing disasters and other traumatic incidents is discussed in Part II.

Discussion

With around 1.5 per cent of workers reported as being involved in a fatal or other accident at work and the known under-reporting of these incidents (Health and Safety Executive 1999a), it is clear that a large number of workers are exposed to incidents that may cause physical and psychological trauma. While, many organisations concentrate on the victims of major incidents, traumatic stress is just as likely for employees who experience a fall, road crash or being hit by a flying object. Although employees injured in the traumatic incident can go on to suffer post-traumatic stress or other psychological disorders, other employees are equally susceptible to psychological injury. It is important for all organisations, particularly those with high levels of exposure to traumatic incidents, to be aware of the need to provide support for rescuers, counsellors and supporters as well as to fellow workers and other witnesses.

Chapter 5

Workplace trauma and the law[1]

Introduction

Many workers are exposed to traumatic experiences during the course of their work. This chapter looks at how the law affects the way that organisations handle workplace trauma and how the operation of the law can make trauma symptoms worse. The perspective taken in this chapter is predominantly English, with the recognition that there are differences in the legal approaches of common law, typified by the legislature in England, Scotland, the USA, Canada and Australia, and those of the civil (Roman) law that dominates Europe. An important feature of common law is the emphasis it places on the duties of the organisation in addition to the protection it provides for employee rights (Leighton 1999). This chapter describes the development of English case and statute law in the area of traumatic stress and examines how the law has been applied to employees following a traumatic experience in the workplace. The chapter then looks at the impact of the law on the psychological well-being of traumatised individuals. Finally, there is a brief discussion of the difficulties caused by the failure of trauma researchers to provide clear guidance to lawyers and organisations on the most effective and appropriate way to support employees following a traumatic incident.

The size of the problem

The number of employees who become involved in a traumatic incident at work is difficult to estimate, since traumatic events are known

1 Based on Tehrani, N. (2002) Workplace trauma and the law, *Journal of Traumatic Stress*, 15(6): 473–7, by permission of Kluwer Academic Publishers.

to be under-reported (Incomes Data Services 1994) and within Europe, only Finland has undertaken large-scale studies of the incidence of trauma at work (Heiskanen *et al.* 1991). A review of workplace trauma literature (Rick *et al.* 1998a) described eight major occupational groups affected by traumatic incidents. These groups are workers from the military, transportation, emergency services, finance, health care, off-shore oil and gas industries, the nuclear industry and 'other industries'. In many organisations the number of traumatising events that occur in a given period of time can be predicted, therefore these organisations have a common law and statutory duty to provide appropriate care, training and support for their employees.

Post-traumatic stress and the law

Perhaps more than any other psychological or medical disorder, PTSD has been influenced by the law (Napier and Wheat 1995; Pitman *et al.* 1996). While human beings have probably reacted with fright, horror and distress to traumatic events since the beginning of time, the concept of a traumatic event leading to a psychological disorder is a relatively new phenomenon. The law has a role in protecting employees from harm by developing and imposing laws on organisations in the form of rules, regulations and duties. One of the objectives of this legislation is to reduce the incidence of traumatic events. The legal tool used to achieve a reduction of trauma in the workplace is the assignment of a *duty of care* to organisations to protect their employees from foreseeable harm. If a traumatic event does occur, and an employee is harmed, the law decides whether the harm was due wholly or partly to organisational negligence in carrying out its duty of care. Where negligence is proved, the law will decide how the organisation should be punished and the settlement required as compensation for the employee for the pain, distress and damages that resulted from the traumatic experience.

Legal recognition of psychological assessments

The recognition of psychological damage as a valid compensatable disease has been slow to gain recognition. Before the early twentieth century the initial response to claims for psychological damages in courts of law was to deny liability (Cooke 1995). In more recent times lawyers have begun to recognise PTSD as a mental illness that is caused by the psychological impact of an external event. This recognition represents an important landmark for psychology and the law (Pitman *et al.* 1996). The legal recognition of a psychological diagnosis increases the importance of accurate assessment tools and processes to diagnose the psychiatric injury (Raifman 1983). However, even with the accurate measurement tools that are available, other factors may influence the results including a lack of trust between the victim and the assessor or the stress caused by the assessment process (Fowlie and Alexander 1992).

The tort of negligence

Liability for negligence has existed for centuries but until the nineteenth century it was not based on the concept of a duty of care. Liability where it did exist was confined to the very narrow context of individual relationships, such as those found in the contracts between sellers and buyers. Today, laws relating to negligence come from two sources: a) statute law – that is, the legislation that is passed by an Act of Parliament or a Directive from the European Community; and b) common law.

In brief, a *tort* is an injury resulting from a wrongful (intentional or negligent) act of omission or commission. In order to be successful in a tort action the claim must pass through a series of filters. First, the defendant must be found to have borne a duty of care to the plaintiff. Second, the defendant must have been the cause of the plaintiff's reasonably foreseeable injury. Finally, the plaintiff must have suffered some damage (Spaulding 1988).

Duty of care

The duty of care was first recognised by the House of Lords in the case of *Donoghue* v. *Stevenson* (1932). In this case the victim was a woman who found the decomposed remains of a snail in a bottle of ginger beer. Miss Donoghue successfully sued the manufacturers of the ginger beer for causing her to suffer illness as a result. In his judgement, Lord Aitkins said:

> The rule that you are to love your neighbour becomes in law, you must not injure your neighbour; and the lawyer's question, Who is my neighbour? receives a restricted reply. You must take reasonable care to avoid acts or omissions, which you can reasonably

foresee, would be likely to injure your neighbour. Who then, in law, is my neighbour? The answer seems to be – persons who are so closely and directly affected by my act that I ought reasonably to have them in contemplation as being so affected when I am directing my mind to the acts or omissions which are called in question.

(*Donoghue* v. *Stevenson* 1932)

Employer's duty of care

The duty of care an employer owes to employees is defined in national and European legislation and in common law. The Health and Safety at Work Act 1974 places broad general duties on employers to protect the health, safety and welfare at work of their staff. Section 2(1) of the legislation states that 'it shall be the duty of every employer to ensure, so far as is reasonably practicable, the health, safety and welfare at work of all his [*sic*] employees'. Section 2(2) sets out more specific duties covering plant and systems of work; articles and substances, information, instruction, training and supervision; place of work and working environment.

The document Management of Health and Safety at Work Regulations (Health and Safety Executive 1999b) requires employers to assess the risks to the health and safety of their staff. This assessment process enables employers to identify preventative and protective health and safety measures. The regulations also require employers to remedy health and safety hazards identified in risk assessment. An employer's common law duty of care towards employees is based on the general principle that an employer will be regarded as negligent if steps are not taken to eliminate a risk which is known or ought to be known about. The definition of a risk in law is that it is a *real* risk and not merely a possibility that would never influence the mind of a reasonable person. An employer's duty to take reasonable care of the health, safety and welfare of employees is illustrated in the case of *Wilsons and Clyde Coal Co. Ltd* v. *English* (1937) where it was held that 'The obligation is threefold, the provision of a competent staff of men, adequate material, and a proper system and effective supervision'.

In recent years, an employer's duty to employees has been summarised as the need to take reasonable care to:

• provide a safe place of work;

- provide safe plant and equipment;
- provide competent and safe staff;
- lay down a safe system of work in all circumstances (Walden 1994).

An employer's vulnerability to claims of negligence depends on the efforts they have taken to remove or reduce all reasonably foreseeable risks. It is a requirement of law that employers maintain that degree of knowledge of potential risks and hazards that might be expected of any reasonably prudent employer. A 'reasonable degree of knowledge' in law is determined by a number of factors:

- the state of relevant technical, scientific or statistical knowledge at the time of the incident;
- the body of advisory material which is available within an industry;
- the general statutory, regulatory and advisory material produced by the Health and Safety Executive (Walden 1994).

Case law

The following five cases have been selected for their role in shaping the responsibilities of organisations towards their employees. In reading the case law it is important to recognise that the law of tort is not based on whether or not an employee is suffering from post-traumatic stress but rather on whether the organisation fulfilled its duty of care towards the employee.

Piper Alpha disaster (McFarlane v. EE Caledonia Ltd 1994)

Mr McFarlane was employed on the oil rig Piper Alpha. The disastrous fire on the rig in July 1988 resulted in the deaths of 167 people, including two men from the *Sandhaven* fast rescue craft and another man who died in the Aberdeen Royal Infirmary. At the time of the disaster, Mr McFarlane was on the support vessel *Tharos*. The *Tharos* approached the burning oil rig to carry out firefighting and rescue functions, however, Mr McFarlane was not involved in these activities but watched the events prior to being evacuated by helicopter. Mr McFarlane was not successful in his claim for compensation as the court did not regard him as a primary victim of the disaster, nor was he able to demonstrate any close ties of love and affection for any of the primary victims.

The Court of Appeal dealing with Mr McFarlane's case identified two categories of people to whom a duty of care may be owed: participants and witnesses. The primary victims or participants included those who were closely involved with the event and as a result of their proximity suffered psychiatric injury. These participants were judged to be owed a duty of care by their employer because their presence in the proximity of the traumatic event was reasonably foreseeable. The Court of Appeal considered that there are three situations in which a participant in a trauma can be viewed as a primary victim:

- if they were in the actual area of the danger but through luck escaped physical injury, but feared for their life;
- if they were in no actual danger, but because of the sudden nature of the event thought that they were in danger;
- if they were not originally in the area of danger but entered it later as a rescuer.

The second category of people, onlookers, witnesses and bystanders, were judged to consist of those who are the passive and unwilling witnesses of injury caused to others. In the second category, duty of care is only extended to people who have close ties of love and affection for the actual victims.

Hillsborough disaster (Frost and others v. Chief Constable of South Yorkshire Police and others 1996)

The Hillsborough disaster involved the death and injury to spectators shortly before the start of a football match. The deaths resulted from too many people being allowed into crowd control pens. The crowd control problem had resulted from a decision by a senior police officer to open an outer gate which allowed additional spectators into an area in the football ground which was already overcrowded. Lord Justice Taylor (Taylor 1989) said that although there were other causes for the disaster, the main reason was a failure of the police to have a clear strategy to control the fans. The liability for the deaths and injuries was accepted by the chief constable, Sheffield Wednesday Football Club and the club's engineers. Fourteen police officers on duty in the fatal pens were awarded £1.2 million in an out of court settlement. A second group of police officers, not in the pens, also claimed compensation. The Court of Appeal found that the claimants should be compensated because of the employer's duty of care to employees. Lord Henry regarded the four officers as participants because they were directly involved in the consequences flowing from their employers' negligent actions in crowd control. They were on duty at the ground close to the horror scene, dealing with the dead and injured. They had no choice but to be there and were involved in dealing with the disaster. It was that involvement that led to their frustrations at being ineffective and helpless, in addition to the guilt and shame relating to negligent police decisions that caused or contributed to the accident (Walden 1994). This ruling was later overturned in the House of Lords by a majority ruling from the five Law Lords. Lord Steyn said:

> In an ideal world all those who suffered as a result of the negligence ought to be compensated. But we live in a practical world where the tort system imposed limits to the classes of claim that ranked for consideration as well as to the heads of recoverable damages. That resulted of course in imperfect justice, but it was by and large the best the common law could do.
>
> (*Frost and others* v. *South Yorkshire Police and others* 1996)

Forth Road Bridge (Robertson v. Forth Road Bridge Joint Board 1995)

In this case Mr Robertson and Mr Rough, who were employed by the Forth Road Bridge Joint Board, witnessed an accident in which a colleague was blown off the bridge and killed. Mr Robertson and Mr Rough were not compensated for their nervous shock because the court decided that they had not been in any personal danger at the time, nor were there any particularly close ties of love and affection with the deceased. In addition neither of the two men attempted a rescue. Lord Hope said that even taking account of the special relationship between employer and employee, the Forth Road Bridge Joint Board had not failed in its duty of care to Mr Robertson and Mr Rough:

> The existence of the relationship between the employer and the employee may be said to remove the risk of having to compensate the world at large, because it does to some extent restrict the

numbers of persons who are likely to be involved in the incident. Nevertheless the numbers may still be very considerable if the enterprise is a substantial one and has numerous employees.

(*Robertson* v. *Forth Road Bridge Joint Board* 1995)

The King's Cross fire (Hale v. London Underground Ltd 1993)

Mr Hale was a fireman involved in the King's Cross station fire. As one of the first firefighters to arrive, Mr Hale braved the fire half a dozen times to retrieve six bodies. During the blaze he crawled out for more oxygen and returned again to rescue people despite learning of the death of Colin Townsley, his station officer. London Underground, who had admitted liability for the fire, were found to be negligent in preventing the fire occurring and Mr Hale was awarded £147,683 damages in the High Court for post-traumatic stress as he had been shown to be a participant and rescuer in the disaster.

Falklands War (Findlay v. MoD 1994)

In this case, Mr Findlay went to the High Court with the claim that the army had failed to diagnose and treat his PTSD sustained in the Falklands War. He joined the army in 1980 and in 1982 sailed to the Falklands. In an assault on Mount Tumbledown his battalion suffered nine fatalities and over 40 of the remaining men in the battalion were injured. Mr Findlay witnessed the horror of a chaotic night-time battle in which one of his friends was shot in the jaw and shoulder. He tried to save his friend by undertaking field surgery and was later found to be suffering from severe post-traumatic stress and major change in personality. His lawyers were able to show that despite the army's knowledge of the impact of traumatic events on soldiers they made no attempt to diagnose or treat Mr Findlay's post-traumatic stress (Beggs 1994). This case is particularly important to organisations as it underlines the legal responsibility they carry to diagnose and treat employees involved in work that places them in situations of intense danger or trauma.

Armed Forces group action (Multiple claimants v. MoD 2003)

The claimants were former members of the Armed Forces who claimed that they had sustained psychiatric injuries because of exposure to the stress and trauma of combat. The judge ruled that any members of the Armed Forces that saw action before May 1987 were not eligible for compensation because at that time the Ministry of Defence was protected by crown immunity. Post-1987 the judge said that the Ministry of Defence was protected from liability due to combat immunity and as a result there was no duty to maintain the normal safe systems of work as would be the normal employer's duty of care.

Effects of litigation on traumatised employees

The capacity of the incentive of compensation to reinforce psychiatric symptoms is embodied in the concept of *compensation* or *accident neurosis* and *secondary gain* (Miller 1961). While it is recognised that some people may be exaggerating their symptoms in order to receive increased levels of compensation, recent studies have generally refuted such findings. These studies (e.g. Kelly 1981; Tarsh and Royston 1985; Koch *et al.* 2000) have shown that in most cases trauma symptoms continue well after compensation has been paid.

There is an increasing body of research that suggests that the litigation process itself has an adverse influence on the primary trauma symptoms through a process of re-traumatisation (Pitman *et al.* 1996). Constant interrogations and interviews by lawyers, police and consultants has the effect of undermining the trauma victim's adaptive efforts to avoid unnecessary reliving of unpleasant memories, bringing about high levels of arousal and distress. The impact of serial interviews and assessment is particularly undesirable when conducted in the adversarial setting of the law (Fowlie and Alexander 1992). Many victims of a traumatic experience will accept a less than adequate financial settlement rather than face the psychological distress of telling and retelling their traumatic story to a string of expert witnesses or the possibility of being aggressively cross-examined in court (Scott 2000).

Delays and the inadequacy of the legal system have also been shown to further traumatise victims (Napier 1991). Most trauma victims have difficulty in understanding the complexities of the legal system and do not have access to appropriate and timely information on the legal process. This lack of knowledge and involvement can result in disillusionment with the law and an increased level of symptoms (Tehrani 1999b).

Managing trauma in the workplace

Within organisations, case law and legal statutes place specific requirements on the employer to provide and maintain a safe working environment and to keep abreast of current knowledge and research in the area of traumatic stress. In order to meet their legal responsibilities, organisations need to discharge their duties to develop a systematic approach to managing the risk of traumatic stress (Tehrani 1995). Unfortunately, the guidance and information provided to help organisations deal with trauma in the workplace is less than helpful. The two reports produced by the Institute of Employment Studies on behalf of the UK Health and Safety Executive (Rick *et al.* 1998a, 1998b) are not particularly useful to organisations in developing systems and processes. These reports do little more than review the existing literature and raise concerns over the effectiveness of existing approaches to the management and treatment of traumatised employees, without offering organisations alternative ways forward. While it has been shown that the legal process can have a negative impact on the psychological well-being of victims of trauma, it is also true that the current unresolved debate on the benefits or otherwise of debriefing and trauma counselling is also unhelpful. Given the growing body of negative literature relating to trauma debriefing and counselling, organisations are uncertain whether providing debriefing as part of a post-trauma care programme will increase rather than decrease their vulnerability to litigation (Freckelton 1998).

The future

The effect of the litigation process on an individual suffering from post-traumatic stress can be devastating. Not only is the length of time between the incident and final settlement often excessive but the actual process itself can cause additional psychological injury. The new rules and procedures developed by Lord Woolf (Woolf 1996) and set out in *Civil Procedures Rules* (1998, 1999) should help to reduce the distress caused to traumatised individuals by the operation of the legal system. The *Rules* increase the level of pre-action contact, ensure an earlier and better exchange of information and encourage an early settlement of cases without the need to resort to litigation. The *Rules* also promote the use of a single joint expert witness who will provide evidence to the court on behalf of defendants and claimants. The use of such experts should reduce the number of times a traumatised individual is psychologically assessed. The adoption of the new *Rules* by the English courts will result in more cases being settled out of court through consultation and compromise rather than through the legal adversarial route. This change in civil procedures brings the operation of English law closer to the inquisitorial system prevalent in Europe.

For the organisation, the major problem faced is the lack of clear directions on which procedures and interventions are effective and appropriate in supporting vulnerable employees. The responsibility to assess and manage the risk of traumatic incidents occurring is essential, as is the need to provide appropriate training and support for employees undertaking work with risk of traumatic exposure. What is more difficult is how to support traumatised employees following a traumatic event. This uncertainty is likely to continue until workers in the field of trauma provide more evidence on the effectiveness or otherwise of post-trauma care, including debriefing and counselling. In the meantime it is important for organisations to protect their employees and themselves by monitoring and evaluating their trauma care programmes to ensure that their employees are recovering rather than being made ill by post-trauma interventions (Tehrani 2000c).

Summary: Part I

Post-traumatic stress is not a new phenomenon, and has been written about in literature for at least a thousand years. However, it has only recently been recognised as a psychiatric disorder. The major influences on the development of the construct of post-traumatic stress have been major disasters, including war, where the work of Abram Kardiner was particularly influential. There has been a constant review and revision of the criteria that define post-traumatic stress and even the current formulation has been challenged for its failure to include chronic traumatic exposures such as are found in domestic violence and bullying. The current diagnostic criteria that put the major emphasis on the situational or objective features of the traumatic event rather than on how the event was perceived may not be a valid approach.

One of the major findings of trauma research has been the fact that most people are able to deal with their traumatic experiences well, and it is *uncommon* for people to develop PTSD even after a major traumatic experience. These findings have caused some workers to suggest that post-traumatic stress is a result of a failure in recovery rather than related to the nature of the traumatic exposure. There are a number of classic post-traumatic stress symptoms. Re-experience is unique to post-traumatic stress and involves having nightmares, flashbacks and physiological reactivation. Two further symptoms are avoidance of anything related to the traumatic event and hyperarousal.

An understanding of the underlying biological processes is helpful in understanding the psychological symptoms of traumatic stress and recent work by Yehuda and LeDoux provides the answers as to why certain symptoms are associated with traumatic exposure. It is possible that a better understanding of the biological basis of the psychological response will be helpful in the development of more effective treatment regimes. It has also been suggested that the biological indicators of post-traumatic stress may become a more reliable assessment tool than clinical psychometric assessment.

Where trauma occurs in an organisation, there is a need for the employer to protect the health and well-being of the workforce. In order to meet its duty of care the organisation needs to be fully aware of those employees that are particularly vulnerable and the situations that are most likely to cause post-traumatic stress. The longer-term effects of trauma can be extremely distressing and may involve anxiety, depression, dissociation and social problems such as alcoholism and the inability to maintain relationships.

The law attempts to protect employees by placing a duty of care on the employer. In order to meet this duty the organisation has to put in place a number of policies and procedures including ensuring that there are adequate risk assessments, safe practices and post-trauma support for employees that become involved in traumatic events. Unfortunately, the law itself can cause further harm to victims of traumatic exposure. The main difficulties involve the length of time it can take to bring a case to court and the use of multiple assessments. However, many employees have been successful in claiming damages from their employer for failure to provide a safe place of work, safe practices and procedures and support.

Post-traumatic stress is a controversial area of study with active debate about when a diagnosis is appropriate. The symptoms of this disorder are distressing and therefore anything that can be done to help the victims should be welcomed. Where the traumatic events occur in the workplace there are special requirements on the organisation to protect employees or face the consequence of expensive litigation.

Part II

Dealing with disasters at work

When a crisis or disaster occurs within an organisation it is important that the organisation has already undertaken some planning to ensure that it has the resources and systems in place to manage the situation effectively. Chapter 6 briefly describes the steps that organisations need to put in place to protect their employees from harm. One of the most important aspects of this planning involves the duty to undertake regular risk assessments to identify anything that might be hazardous to the physical or psychological health of employees. The focus of Chapter 7 is on the changing requirements for support required by employees and their families affected by traumatic events. The needs at the time and immediately following a traumatic exposure are very different to those during the following weeks and months. This chapter introduces the aims and process of diffusing, debriefing and trauma counselling. It is not always easy for organisations to introduce a comprehensive trauma care programme, however in the UK the Post Office introduced such a programme for some of its employees in 1993 (Chapter 8). The programme, which began by providing support for its most vulnerable employees, has evolved over the years to include most of the Post Office businesses. However, not all organisations are big enough or have the internal resources to develop their own trauma care programme and may as a result wish to have these services provided by an external provider. The choice of provider of services is not easy and there is little information available for organisations to help them decide which provider to select. In Chapter 9, information and guidelines are given to help organisations decide which supplier meets their needs most appropriately.

Chapter 6

The management of crises and disasters, and their relationship to business continuity

Introduction

Organisations are now more aware of the need to undertake risk assessments and business continuity planning in order to prepare themselves for a range of crises and disasters that may impact their organisation (Heath 2001). Until recently, much of this planning has involved examining the risks to business systems, resources and operations. However, one of the areas that is often left out of this planning process is the management of disasters that may have an impact on the health and well-being of people – including employees, customers and the public. In this chapter, some of the principles of risk assessment, crisis management and business continuity are described. The chapter begins with a brief definition of what constitutes a 'disaster' from a range of different perspectives. Some of the basic principles of risk assessment crisis management and business continuity are described, together with examples of what organisations should be doing to provide practical and emotional support for their employees and families. Finally, suggestions are made on the way that appropriate communication can reduce the impact of the disaster on those affected.

Crises and disasters

Despite many attempts to define what makes a particular incident or situation a disaster, no single definition has gained universal acceptance. The problem is that the same incident can be viewed from a number of different perspectives, with the result that what is disastrous from one perspective is not necessarily disastrous from another. The sense of being affected by a disaster is a subjective experience that may relate to personal, social, civil, organisational and humanitarian events. For an individual, the death of a friend or colleague in an accident at work could be regarded as a disaster, whereas for the organisation disasters are events that can put the business at risk. An example of an organisational disaster is the contamination of mineral water with benzene. The way Perrier handled this disaster almost resulted in the collapse of the company, (Peregrine 1993). Many disasters affect organisations *and* employees, such as the Manchester bomb in which the emergency services, hospitals and businesses in the vicinity of the bomb were affected (Tehrani 1999a). A wider definition of disasters that encompasses most types of disastrous event was developed by Beverley Raphael (1986). The following definition is an adaptation of Raphael's: disasters involve overwhelming events and circumstances that test the adaptational responses of a community, organisation or individual beyond their capability, and lead, at least temporarily, to a massive disruption in the functioning of the community, organisation or individual.

While much of the research into disasters has concentrated on major civil, technological or humanitarian events (e.g. Arata *et al.* 2000; Norris *et al.* 2001; Porter and Haslam 2001), it is important to remember that the personal disasters associated with smaller-scale incidents can prove to be highly damaging to organisations and employees. In this chapter, the emphasis is on helping organisations deal with workplace disasters that have an impact on employees, the aim being to help organisations prevent or reduce the likelihood of traumatic incidents occurring and where an event has occurred to prevent a crisis turning into a disaster.

Managing the crisis

In the past ten years there has been an increasing awareness of the need to develop crisis management and recovery plans to protect the organisation from the worst effects of disasters (Freestone and Raab 1998). Much of the emphasis in businesses' crisis management has, until recently, concentrated on incidents and events that have a disruptive effect on business operations. There has been little emphasis on events that may have a detrimental impact on the health and well-being of employees, customers and the public. This attitude is illustrated in a business continuity definition of a crisis as 'any event or activity with the potential to negatively affect the reputation or credibility of a business' (Caponigro 1998). Given this emphasis on operational issues it is not surprising that the business literature dealing with crisis management focuses on the need for organisations to identify and assess the risks to the business operation (Hiles and Barnes 2001). As a result of this focus, business risk assessments are commonly confined to a relatively small number of business areas such as the loss of vital equipment, resources, public image and customer satisfaction (Vancoppenolle 2001). Frequently neglected by organisational crisis managers is the need to assess the risks to employees should a disaster or other traumatic incident occur in the workplace.

Preparing for the crisis

One of the difficulties an organisation faces when dealing with a disaster or crisis is that each situation is likely to be different and therefore it is hard to anticipate and prepare for all the possible eventualities. Despite these difficulties in preparation, it is important that organisations endeavour to manage crises effectively. Crisis management requires the organisation to anticipate the kinds of disastrous event which might happen and then to identify ways to eliminate or reduce the potential impact of these events. Due to the unpredictability and speed of crisis development, it is important to recognise that crises need to be handled differently to the other more predictable events that occur in organisations. In most cases, it has been found to be impossible to manage crises using the same organisational structures as are used to deal with everyday emergencies (Quarantelli 1988), and in a crisis a much more flexible and teamworking approach is needed (Flin 1996). Where organisations have failed to put a crisis plan in place, chain reactions may occur which if left uncontrolled can create more damage to the organisation and employees than the initial incident (Reid 2000). The effective management of a crisis requires preparation and planning which should be part of the normal process of risk assessment, crisis management and business continuity. It has been shown that many organisations find themselves learning how to deal with a crisis while in the midst of the catastrophic event. The pressure and stress of the events can lead to an overloading of those involved, with the result that poor decisions can be made and appropriate actions not taken at the right time (Hiles 2001). The purpose of crisis management planning is to eliminate, modify or reduce exposure to crises and to develop business recovery plans (Heath 2001).

The first part of this process is to look at the risks. It has been found that when examining the psychological risks to employees, some events are more likely to cause traumatic stress reactions than others. The European Foundation (2000) found that events which involved the sudden death or serious injury of an employee, colleagues or members of the public were particularly damaging. However, physical assaults, particularly those causing actual injury, or verbal threats of violence during which the employee believes that they might be injured or killed can also cause psychological injury. The Health and Safety Executive (1998) developed a risk assessment process to help organisations identify and prevent avoidable risks. Figure 6.1 is based on the Health and Safety Executive's model and illustrates the steps that should be taken to reduce the risks to people from traumatic events in the workplace.

Identifying the risks

The best starting point when looking at the risks and hazards in the workplace is to identify the current situation. This information can be found in security reports, accident books and sickness absence data. Although it is important to know what has happened it is equally important to identify near misses – that is, incidents that could have happened but were avoided. The circumstances that caused the near miss should be established, together with the possible outcomes had the incident not been prevented. Having identified a range of risks it is helpful to go through a 'what if' analysis (Reid 2000). A 'what if' analysis requires the risk management team to think creatively and to identify what could result from the range of crises that may occur in their workplace. To be successful the analysis needs to be at a time when there is no crisis, so that the whole situation can be anticipated without the panic of the actual event. Table 6.1, shows a simple 'what if' analysis related to the possibility of a violent attack at work. However, each item identified in the analysis can lead to other problems and ways in which the crisis can be prolonged or intensified. The second stage of the analysis involves identifying what should be put in place to reduce the risk and where a risk cannot be avoided. The initial trauma risk assessment, the 'what if' analysis and the processes identified for responding to the outcomes of the crisis form the starting point for the crisis management plan.

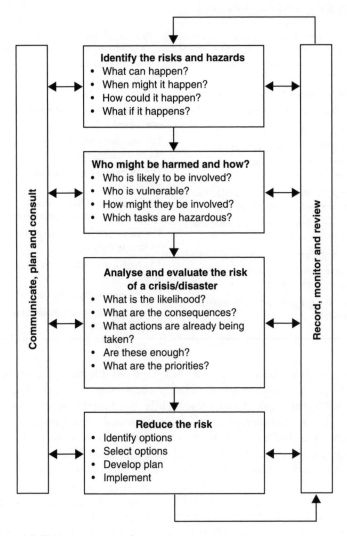

Figure 6.1 Risk assessment and management process

Who might be harmed?

Many people can become traumatised by exposure to crises at work. Organisations should try to identify the potential victims of every situation in their crisis plan and then make sure that an appropriate level of support is provided to each group of victims. Although it is

Table 6.1 A simple 'what if' analysis

An employee has been injured in a violent attack by a client: what if . . .

The employee cannot get to a telephone?	The employee is a Muslim?
Urgent medical attention is required?	The employee cannot work for six months?
There are no ambulances available?	The attacker begins to stalk the employee?
The employee is HIV+	
The employee is a single parent?	The attacker's friends threaten the life of the employee?
There is no one to look after the children?	The employee begins to have nightmares?
The children are waiting outside the school gate for their mum?	The employee is diagnosed as suffering from post-traumatic stress?
The employee is estranged from her violent husband?	The employee sues the organisation for lack of duty of care?
The employee's parents live in Africa?	The employee dies following the attack?
The children have nowhere to go and turn up at the office?	The media take up the case?
The manager goes off work with stress?	A major customer is lost because of the bad publicity?

not always possible to say who will be most affected by a specific incident, it is important to identify those who were closely connected to the incident and consequently may find it more difficult to cope. Crises and disasters can have a profound impact on everyone involved including those directly involved, absent colleagues, the helping professionals, families and the community. While it may not be necessary to provide the same level of support to all groups, an awareness of the potential needs of each group is essential (Rothberg and Wright 1999). Table 6.2 shows a traumatic event that involved an armed raid on a post office. In this incident, an armed raider broke into a post office in the morning. After threatening the sub-postmaster and staff, he escaped with £2000 in cash. The getaway car then hit a pedestrian. Ten different groups of people were involved, all of whom required some support as a result of the raider's actions.

Table 6.2 People vulnerable to traumatic stress following a post office raid

Victim	Reason for involvement	Vulnerability
Sub-postmaster	Lived on the premises. Behind the counter when the gunman came into the shop. Initially refused to hand over the money.	Feels responsible for the shop and guilty about his inability to protect staff and family.
Two counter staff	Threatened by the gunman who told the sub-postmaster that he would shoot the staff if the money was not passed over.	Feared for their lives. Unable to control what was happening to them. Angry.
Customer and child	Told to get onto the ground. The child started to scream and the gunman told the customer to shut him up or he would be shot.	Terrified that the gunman might shoot the child.
Sub-postmaster's wife	Heard a noise and looked down the stairs. Hid on the landing when she saw the gunman.	Ashamed that she did nothing to help her husband.
Customer's husband	Saw the gunman run out of the shop and gave chase but was shot at and wounded.	Thought that he was going to die.
Pedestrian	Hit by the getaway car and seriously ill in hospital.	Having flashbacks of the car coming out of nowhere and hitting him.
Area manager	Came to the post office to help but felt inadequate.	Feels ashamed at not being able to help.
Sub-postmaster's children	Heard the shots from upstairs and are now having nightmares about the gunman.	Having flashbacks about the gunshots. Feel unable to talk to parents.
Counsellor	Has been doing too much trauma counselling and is beginning to find it difficult to cope.	Suffering from compassion fatigue. Needs a break.
A postmaster from another office	Had a raid earlier in the year and, although he was fine, now realises that he could have been shot in his own raid.	Own trauma reactivated by the new incident.

Reducing the risk of traumatic stress

The most appropriate way for organisations to support employees is to reduce the incidence of violence and accidents at work. This process involves the organisation examining the situational and individual factors that may have a bearing on the prevention of violence and accidents. Table 6.3 illustrates these factors and the steps that can be taken to reduce the likelihood of employees becoming exposed to, or damaged by, traumatic incidents.

Table 6.3 Reducing the incidence of traumatic stress at work

Situational factors	Area for consideration
Security systems	Are they appropriate and effective? Are they sited appropriately? Are they regularly maintained? Are the employees trained to use them?
Procedures	Have they been designed to reduce the incidence of trauma? Are they easy to understand and practical? Are they reviewed regularly? Are the ideas of the employees taken into consideration when looking for improvements?
Emergency support	Is there a way for employees to summon help? Are emergency tests run? Does everyone know how to use the emergency support systems?
Organisational culture	Does the culture encourage cooperation? Are employees able to talk about how they feel? How do senior management demonstrate caring? Do employees believe that they will be supported?
Clothing	Do employees have suitable clothing for their work? Does their clothing protect them from injury/harm?
Equipment	Do employees have the right equipment to do their job? Is the equipment regularly maintained?
Working environment	Is the working environment safe? What is being done to improve the working environment? Is there adequate lighting?
Personal factors	Area for consideration
Skills and attributes	Have the essential skills and attributes required for the role been identified? Are the selection criteria clearly defined? Is the selection process adequate?

Training	Is there appropriate induction training? Is there training in dealing with difficult situations or customers? Have the employees been adequately trained in using safety equipment? Is there regular update training? Have the employees been trained in healthy living techniques?
Attitude	Do employees have an understanding of the need for safety and security? Can employees handle difficult and demanding situations?
Support	Is the organisational culture supportive of individuals? Do employees have access to an occupational health service? If there are fatalities, does the organisation provide practical support to the family?
Counselling	Do the employees have access to specialist counsellors and debriefers? Is the counselling service regularly audited and assessed?
Ability to relax	Do employees know how to use a range of relaxation techniques? Are relaxation seminars available for all employees?
Support from family and friends	Do employees have the support of family and friends? Can employees talk about their problems to others?

After identifying all the preventative options, it may not be possible to implement them all within the organisation. In such cases, it may be necessary to decide on the priority of the options to be undertaken. This decision should be determined by an assessment of the likelihood of each of the hazards occurring together with the potential harm that the hazard can inflict on the employees and organisation (Haslegrave and Corlett 1999).

Making the plan work

Having identified the main hazards and introduced the preventative options, the formal crisis management plan then needs to be written. The crisis management plan should contain the findings from the risk assessment together with any preventative strategies that are to be engaged to reduce the likelihood of incidents occurring. The plan should also provide the means by which records can be kept to monitor progress against the plan's objectives. Where a particularly serious hazard exists, care should be taken to ensure that the strategies identified in the plan to address the hazard are regularly reviewed in order to identify potential improvements. The crisis management plan needs be communicated to employees and consultations should take place with the representatives of the employees to ensure that any employee concerns are fully addressed within the plan.

Dealing with the aftermath

Despite the best endeavours of crisis planners, disasters happen. Within the oil industry, a support charity (Sim 2001) has worked with the industry to identify some of the actions that organisations should have in place to support employees and their families involved in a disaster. These include the need to:

- designate responsibilities for handling the care of those employees and others affected by the incident or disaster during the immediate crisis and the subsequent aftermath and recovery periods;
- describe the main features of the crisis management, aftermath and recovery management plans;
- provide guidelines to help those involved in managing the crisis to identify when the crisis management ends and aftermath/ recovery management begins;
- provide resources for the training of those with responsibility for dealing with traumatised employees and their families.

Currently there is no legislation in the UK on the level and standard of post-incident support. This is not the case in the USA where a document produced by the US National Transportation Safety Board (2000) describes the level of care and support required under US law to support victims of aviation disasters. While this legislation does not cover victims of other transportation or workplace disasters, the principles described are relevant to other crisis and disastrous events. Table 6.4 provides a list of areas covered by this legislation. The aviation industry has, as a result of this legislation, introduced a wide range of support services to their own staff, those

Table 6.4 US Federal Family Assistance Plan for aviation disasters

Responsibilities

1	Make initial notifications to family members of victims involved in the aviation crash based on the manifest documents and other available information.
2	Monitor search and recovery operations conducted by the local jurisdiction and offer assistance where needed.
3	Determine the status and location of the victims.
4	Obtain approval of the local medical examiner to provide federal assistance.
5	Assist the local medical adviser in the identification of fatalities and the notification of their families.
6	Provide psychological and logistical support and services to victims and their family members.
7	Provide daily briefings to families on the progress of recovery efforts, identification of victims, the investigation, and other areas of concern.
8	Arrange for a memorial service for the fatalities and their family members.
9	Provide for the return of personal effects.
10	Maintain contact with victims and their families to provide updates on the progress of the investigation and other related matters.

injured in air crashes and to the families of bereaved passengers and employees.

Handling communications

Effective communication both within the organisation and to the world at large is vital following a disaster. Communications with the press, while difficult, are important. It is often useful to engage a professional media consultant to assist in the development of the crisis management plan and to advise at the time of crisis. Equally important is the way the organisation communicates its care and concern to employees, as this can have a long-term effect on morale and relationships within the organisation. It has been found that if the organisation is open, honest and committed to frequently updating employees on the crisis, then employees will act as loyal ambassadors who support their company's actions (Reid 2000). However, if the organisation withholds information and fails to answer reasonable questions, the employees are likely to become highly critical and may even give negative information to the media. The messages that should be given out during a disaster should include:

- facts about the current status;
- concern and compassion for those injured/killed and their families;
- an assurance that the health and well-being of all employees is of top priority and that everything is being done to find the cause of the disaster;
- that all contact with the press should be through a named company spokesperson;
- notification of when the next update will take place.

These communications need to be conveyed rapidly to all the organisation's work sites and may involve a special meeting, email or formal announcements.

Discussion

Organisations need to spend time developing risk assessments and crisis management plans that bring together the needs of the organisation and employees within a single crisis management/business continuity plan. These plans should not only deal with major organisational disasters but also those events that could have a devastating impact on individual members in the workforce. In industries where there is a high level of risk, the major effort should be to reduce the likelihood of an incident occurring. However, even with the best preventative programme it is possible that traumatic events will occur. Organisations have a responsibility to provide a reasonable level of support care for their employees and this will involve providing immediate practical support which should be part of a more comprehensive trauma support programme. The nature and content of the psychological element of the crisis management plan is described in Chapter 7.

Post-trauma interventions: crisis management, diffusing, debriefing and trauma counselling

Introduction

There is an increasing recognition that a significant number of people exposed to a traumatic experience will go on to develop severe and sometimes prolonged psychological reactions (Breslau *et al.* 1997). Much of the research has been into survivors of disasters (Green *et al.* 1990; Kenardy and Carr 2000; Lundin 2000) and the emergency service personnel involved in rescue (Alexander 1993; Violanti and Paton 1999; Robinson 2000; Mitchell and Everly 2001). However, there is an increasing interest in the impact of traumatic events on a wide range of workers exposed to traumatic experiences at work, including victims of violent attacks (Flannery 2000), accidents (Mayou 1997) and other traumatic events (Tehrani *et al.* 2001). It is not surprising that given the negative psychological impact of traumatic exposure, many organisations have introduced interventions designed to reduce the incidence of post-traumatic stress reactions and to speed up the process of recovery. With increasing interest in the field, the effectiveness of early interventions (Raphael and Wilson 2000; Orner and Schnyder 2003) and later treatments (Foa *et al.* 2000a; Wilson *et al.* 2001) has been reviewed.

In this chapter, four post-trauma interventions are described: *crisis management, diffusing, debriefing* and *trauma counselling*. Each is appropriate for use at a particular time following a traumatic incident. The role of each intervention in helping the organisation and employee survive a personal disaster are discussed and the need to introduce appropriate auditing and monitoring is highlighted.

The timing of trauma interventions

Following a traumatic experience, those involved require a range of practical, physical and psychological support, the balance of which changes over time. In the early stages, the emphasis is likely to be on immediate medical treatment for injuries and practical support for victims and their families. Over time other needs may emerge such as the need to re-establish feelings of personal safety and security, the need to deal with psychological symptoms that may have emerged and the need to understand how the traumatic incident fits into the rest of a person's life.

Figure 7.1 illustrates the four interventions and their relationship each to the other. However, it is important for organisations to recognise that there may be a continuing need for aspects of an earlier intervention. For example, there may be a long-term need for social support and organisational caring over several weeks or months following a traumatic incident.

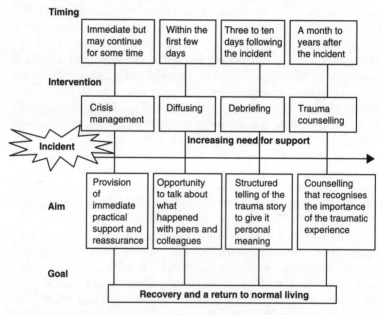

Figure 7.1 The timing and goals of post-trauma interventions

Managing a crisis

Dealing with a crisis and its immediate aftermath requires sensitive management if it is to be successful. The way that employees are handled during and immediately after a crisis has a strong influence on their recovery and rehabilitation (Gibson 1991). The responsible manager has the role of ensuring that those involved in the crisis situation are provided with the consideration, help and support they require. This can be difficult when the manager is also a victim of the incident. The focus of the early stages of the crisis recovery period is to ensure the immediate safety and well-being of employees and members of the public, and where appropriate to call the emergency services. The help that is provided should be sensitive to the employees' feelings of emotional and practical chaos and should seek to aid them in a way that does not add to their feelings of being totally out of control and overwhelmed. At a time of crisis or during the immediate aftermath it is unhelpful to attempt to interpret or explain what is being said or expressed by shocked employees (Kennedy 1991).

Social support

Following any traumatic incident there is a need for social and practical support. Social support has repeatedly been found to be a critical component of recovery or lack of recovery. It has been shown (Andersson *et al.* 1997) that high rates of psychosocial complications after road traffic injuries coupled with poor social support produces a risk of post-traumatic stress. In victims of urban violence (Landsman *et al.* 1990) it was found that three years after the traumatic experience the levels of psychological distress were predicted less by injury severity than by subsequent financial, employment, family and other social difficulties. Following a traumatic experience, employees have certain expectations of their employers and if the organisation fails to live up to these it is likely that employees will become even more traumatised (Silver 1986). Table 7.1 highlights some of the social issues that need to be considered following a traumatic incident.

Psychological support

In the first hours after an incident, the organisation should ensure that the immediate practical, physical and emotional needs of all

Table 7.1 Examples of issues to be considered as part of the crisis management plan

Crisis management	Aftermath and recovery management
• Access to emergency services • First aid or medical treatment • Initial contacting of families or partner • Setting up reception centres for victims and families • Availability of supporters • Availability of blankets, warm clothing and food • Transporting employees home • Setting up a telephone help desk • Transport for families to location of incident or to hospitals • Accommodation for families close to the location of incident • Child and elder care facilities • Immediate financial support to victims and families • Immediate personal support for employee(s) from organisation • Line manager contact/responsibilities • Handle the media • Availability of crisis leaflets and written information	• Funeral arrangements • Setting up a disaster fund • Book of condolences • Organising a memorial service • Communications within the organisation • Arranging regular visits to traumatised employees • Continuing contact with families • Sensitive handling of the investigatory and legal implications of incident • Provision of relevant human resources information (e.g. pay, insurance and pensions) • Availability of counselling and other psychological support for employee(s) and family members • Encouraging contact with colleagues • Legal representation • Support in court hearings • Rehabilitation programmes • Arranging medical severance or ill-health retirement

those involved are met. The organisation should provide information on the availability of debriefing and the normal symptoms of trauma. The traumatised employees should be made aware of the support that is available at an early stage, however it is not appropriate to begin the debriefing process during this period as the employees are in shock. In incidents involving one or two employees the supervisor or manager may be in the best position to provide this immediate support, but where the supervisor or manager is also a victim a designated person should take over responsibility for managing the crisis. The organisation is responsible for ensuring that the first line managers and others are aware of their responsibilities during and following a traumatic incident. Examples of material produced to support an organisation in dealing with a traumatic incident (Tehrani *et al.* 2001) are provided at the end of this chapter. The first provides guidance for the organisation on the processes involved in helping employees and families deal with the emotional impact of a traumatic event. The second is a simple handout that can be given to employees and their families to explain some common responses to a traumatic event and how to get help should these symptoms of traumatic stress not diminish. The third lists the kinds of skills and competencies that are essential for those chosen to handle a crisis and its aftermath.

Diffusing or defusing?

The term *primary defusing* was introduced by Mitchell in 1983 (Mitchell and Everly 2001). More recently, it has been known simply as *defusing*. Mitchell said that he chose the word because it suggested that a dangerous or difficult situation was being rendered harmless. *Diff*using, on the other hand, is a term suggested by Tehrani *et al.* (2001). The aim of diffusing is to assist in the gradual diffusion or melting away of the strong emotions and responses associated with a traumatic event. This is achieved through the creation of an environment in which the traumatised person can be heard and supported.

Defusing

Defusing is a small-group process that usually occurs on the same day, preferably within a few hours of the incident. It is a shortened version of critical incident stress debriefing (CISD) and offers an opportunity for the people involved in the traumatic event to talk briefly about their experiences before they have time to rethink the incident and reinterpret its meaning. Defusing is much less structured than a CISD and consequently is easier to organise and manage. It usually takes around 20 minutes to an hour to complete, and the process has eight goals:

1   The rapid reduction of intense reactions to the traumatic event.
2   The normalising of the experience, enabling employees to return to normal life as quickly as possible.

3 The re-establishment of the social network of the working group so that employees do not isolate themselves from each other.
4 The sharing of information about the incident between all participants.
5 The restoration of cognitive processes disrupted by the incident.
6 The provision of practical information for dealing with stress.
7 An affirmation of the value of every member of personnel to one another and to the organisation.
8 The development of an expectancy of recovery.

The defusing process

The defusing process is made up of three main parts. The introduction, exploration and information. The introduction is similar to that of CISD but is undertaken in a shorter period. The exploration is more open than that found in CISD. Anyone who wishes to speak is encouraged to do so. There is no order in the process and anyone can remain silent if they wish. The defusing team will ask a number of questions of the group that help to explore what has occurred, the nature of the incident, their part in it, the roles played by others and the nature of the interactions. The defusing team may also ask the group about their symptoms of distress.

Each defusing will be different. Sometimes the employees will have a lot to say, sometimes very little, but as the group relaxes they tend to give more details of their experiences. When the discussion on the incident appears to be coming to a close or where the discussion begins to look at side issues, the defusing team should close this part and move onto the information phase.

The information phase involves passing a considerable amount of information to the group. It should cover:

• an acceptance and summary of the information provided by the group during the exploration phase;
• questions raised by the group;
• a normalisation of the experiences and reactions of the group;
• training in practical stress survival skills;
• details of a CISD session if required;
• availability of ongoing support from the defusing team;
• a final summing up and closure of the session.

Diffusing

In contrast to defusing, diffusing is a much less formal approach and is more concerned in enabling employees opportunity to talk to each other and the 'diffuser' as and when they feel comfortable to do so. This is not a *process* but rather an *approach* designed to create a safe and supportive environment in which employees are given the opportunity to talk or not to talk about what has occurred. Diffusing would normally take place the day after the incident and would involve those affected coming together in an informal setting. The focus of the diffusing is an acknowledgement of what has occurred and then a description of what the organisation is able to do to help. The employees are encouraged to ask questions about the next steps. During the diffusing, employees are provided with detailed information on the practical and emotional support available from the organisation, together with details of the debriefing session that is being arranged. During the process, the main skills are those of listening and clarifying what has been said. This is achieved using summary and paraphrase. During the diffusing there is no exploration of the incident by the diffuser, but rather an opportunity for the employee to describe the incident at their own pace and in their own way. The rationale behind diffusing rests in the belief that the employees are best able to handle the event when given the opportunity to work at their own pace.

Debriefing

Psychological debriefing has become a widespread and popular post-trauma intervention over the past 15 years. Friedman (2000a) describes *psychological debriefing* as an intervention conducted by trained professionals shortly after an incident that allows victims to talk about their experiences and receive information on 'normal' types of reaction to such an event. Although several methods of psychological debriefing have been described, most researchers regard it as a single-session, semi-structured crisis intervention designed to reduce or prevent adverse psychological reactions and responses to the traumatic event (Bisson *et al.* 2000). Originally, psychological debriefing was used as an intervention with a group of emergency service personnel, victims of the same traumatic event. The aims of debriefing are to review in detail the facts, thoughts, impressions and reactions following a traumatic incident as well as providing information on typical reactions to critical events (Dyregrov 1997). Bisson *et al.* (2000) describe the purpose of psychological debriefing as providing survivors of a traumatic experience with an opportunity to review their impressions and reactions to the trauma in an atmosphere where psychiatric 'labelling' is avoided. During the debriefing, the debriefer will also provide assurances that the participants are normal people who have experienced an abnormal event.

The increase in frequency of civilian disasters in the 1980s, coupled with expanding knowledge on the effect of traumatic exposure, led a number of mental health professionals to develop psychological debriefing as a group intervention. Debriefing was primarily designed for emergency workers involved in handling traumatic situations (Mitchell 1983; Dyregrov 1989; Armstrong *et al.* 1991), however, Raphael focused her group debriefing model on the primary victims of disasters (Raphael 1986).

In this section, four current and popular models of group debriefing are described. These are Mitchell's (1993) critical incident stress debriefing (CISD), the psychological debriefing models of Dyregrov (1989) and Raphael (1986) and Armstrong *et al.*'s (1991) multiple stressor debriefing models (MSDs). Although there are differences between these models, the generic term 'psychological debriefing' will be used to describe all of them. The common feature is that they all have a structured format and clear introduction to formal group meetings, and are held shortly after the traumatic event. A summary of the four models is given in Table 7.2.

Mitchell's model

The CISD protocol that Mitchell (1993) describes is a group process of seven distinct phases. Prior to this, Mitchell had used a six-stage model (Mitchell 1983). During the introductory phase, confidentiality is emphasised and the outline of the CISD explained. A good *introduction* increases the motivation of the participants to become involved in the process. Mitchell then moves rapidly into the *actual incident itself* with standard questions such as 'What was your job?' and 'Who arrived first?'. At this stage emotions are only acknowledged and the participants are assured that their feelings are normal. Mitchell then moves to the *thought phase* with the question 'What was your first thought when you came off automatic pilot?' Participants are urged to talk, although it is emphasised that they

Table 7.2 Comparison of stages in four models of debriefing

Mitchell	Dyregrov	Raphael	Armstrong
Introduction/ rules	Introduction/ rules	Introduction/rules	Introduction/rules
Facts	Expectations and facts	Initiation into disaster	Identification of events that are most troubling
Thoughts	Thoughts and decisions	Experience of disaster	
Reactions	Sensory impressions	Negative/positive aspects and feelings	Feelings and reactions to difficult events
Symptoms	Emotional reactions	Relationships with others	Coping strategies, past and present coping strategies
Teaching	Normalisation	Feelings of victims	
Re-entry	Future planning/ coping	Disengagement	Termination
	Disengagement	Review and close	Focus on leaving the disaster and returning home

will not be forced to say more than is comfortable for them. The fourth phase is a *discussion of the reactions*. In this phase questions such as 'What was the worst thing about this event for you?' and 'What aspects of the event caused you most pain?' are asked. These questions typically elicit the most powerful emotional reactions in the debriefing. Participants are encouraged to speak as openly and freely about their emotions as possible, focusing on extreme fear or on the feelings that were unexpected or hard to accept, where these occurred. The fifth phase of the debriefing model is concerned with *symptoms of distress* and questions such as 'How have you been since the incident?' will be asked and the symptoms that occurred at the scene reviewed. The sixth phase is concerned with *teaching*. General information is given regarding the identified stress reactions and the 'normal' nature of these. Specific advice regarding issues such as diet, increased risk of accident, alcohol consumption, effects on relationships and lack of libido are discussed. The debriefing is closed with a *summary* of what has happened during the session and any remaining questions answered.

Dyregrov's model

The Dyregrov model of psychological debriefing (1989) builds on Mitchell's work, however there are some significant differences. Unlike Mitchell, who begins the debriefing at the scene of the trauma, Dyregrov starts his debriefing process *before the incident* with questions such as 'How did you come to learn about this incident?' Dyregrov also looks at the decision-making process of the participants during the *thinking stage* of the debriefing, with questions such as 'What did you do?' followed by cognitive questions such as 'Why did you decide to do that?' Dyregrov uses this form of questioning to help participants reduce their tendency to self-blame. He then goes on to discuss *sensory information* gained at the incident (e.g. 'What do you see, hear, touch, smell or taste?'). This level of sensory detail is missing from Mitchell's model. Dyregrov then concentrates his attention on the *normalisation of reactions* both at the time of the incident and currently. The planning and coping stage in this model is similar to Mitchell's re-entry stage. Although the models of Dyregrov and Mitchell are similar, Dyregrov places a greater emphasis on normalisation of reactions and responses, which he suggests may be safer for the participants.

Raphael's model

Raphael's (1986) model is not as prescriptive as Mitchell and Dyregrov. Like Dyregrov, Raphael begins the debriefing *before the incident* and asks participants about the level of preparation or training that they had received prior to the experience. In the *experience of the disaster stage*, Raphael asks questions such as 'Was your life threatened?', 'Did you lose anyone close to you?' and 'What kinds of things happened to you personally?' Although this kind of information may emerge from the Mitchell and Dyregrov models, Raphael is much more direct in her questioning. In the *positive and negative aspects of feelings stage*, Raphael looks at areas explored by Mitchell and Dyregrov in their reactions stages but adds questions on the positive aspects such as 'Did you feel good about anything that you did?' or 'Did you have a sense of fulfilment?' In the *relationships with others stage*, Raphael explores the participants' feelings about their colleagues and others during and after the incident. This is similar to Dyregrov's future planning and coping stage and is not found in Mitchell's model. Raphael also has a stage of *looking at feelings for other victims*, which is not found in either of the other two models. In the *disengagement stage*, Raphael focuses on what has been learnt from the experience and how this can help the participants or others in the future.

Armstrong's model

Armstrong *et al.* (1991) designed the multiple stressor debriefing (MSD) model for use with emergency personnel. The model is a modification of the Mitchell defusing model but with similarities to Raphael's approach. The purpose of this model is to address the problem of the disaster workers involved having multiple contacts with victims, long hours and a poor working environment. The MSD model has four main stages. In the first stage, *disclosure of events*, the purpose of the debriefing and the rules are outlined. The participants are then asked to describe in detail which aspects of the disaster are most troubling to them. The second stage, *feelings and reactions*, involves asking the participants about their feelings and reactions to the incidents they have experienced. This process is facilitated by the debriefer and uses visual aids. In the third stage the emphasis moves to *coping strategies* and the participants are given information on the normal and abnormal responses to stress – again, this stage is supported by the use of visual aids. The participants are then asked how they coped with stress in the past and how they are currently coping. Wherever possible the debriefer will try to use practical coping strategies identified by the group participants themselves rather than introducing new coping patterns. In the final stage, the participants are asked how they feel about *leaving the disaster site*. Then the emphasis changes to saying goodbye to co-workers and preparing for returning home or to other responsibilities. Before leaving the debriefing room there is a discussion of what has been accomplished and emphasis is placed on the need to continue to talk to partners and significant others. At the end of the debriefing, any remaining questions are answered and referrals made where necessary. The main difference between this model and the others is the emphasis on past reactions to stressors and coping styles.

Individual debriefing models

While the creators of most group debriefing models maintain that their models should only be used with groups, there have been attempts to use adaptations of these models with individual victims of traumatic stress (Armstrong 2000). Indeed, many of the studies undertaken to evaluate debriefing have been done using individual trauma victims (e.g. Hobbs *et al.* 1996; Lee *et al.* 1996; Bisson *et al.* 1997). Unfortunately, the protocols for individual debriefing interventions are rarely provided and have been criticised as being inadequate and potentially harmful (Dyregrov 1998). An individual debriefing model was developed in the British Post Office (Tehrani and Westlake 1994) to support lone employees affected by physical violence, threats of physical violence, hijacking and being taken hostage. This model involves five stages: *introduction, facts, thoughts, feelings* and *close*, with the introduction setting the rules of the debriefing, the facts stage identifying in detail the sensory memories relating to the traumatic experience, the thoughts phase taking the sensory and factual experiences and establishing the positive and negative thinking related to those experiences, and the emotions stage relating to thoughts and sensory information. The closing phase allows time for summarising the incident and for undertaking education on the normal symptoms of trauma. In addition, there is an opportunity to discuss the use of existing and new coping skills.

Trauma therapy and counselling

Where an employee's post-trauma responses do not subside within a few weeks, it may be necessary to consider the introduction of trauma therapy or counselling. Many therapeutic approaches have been advocated for treating post-traumatic stress, including cognitive behavioural therapy (Foa *et al.* 2000a; Scott and Palmer 2000), psychodynamic therapy (Marmer *et al.* 1995; Bailly 2003) and eye movement desensitisation and reprocessing (EMDR) (Shapiro 1989; Mansfield 1998). Counsellors and therapists working with victims of trauma generally agree that the therapeutic process can be divided into three stages:

- establishing trust;
- trauma focused therapy;
- disconnecting from the trauma and reconnecting with family, friends and society (Friedman 2000a).

The outcome of exposure to a trauma is not always negative. Surviving a trauma may also lead to an enhanced appreciation of one's vulnerability, sensitivity and emotional experience (Tedeschi and Calhoun 1995). The goal of the therapy is to gain some mastery of the traumatic experience and to use the knowledge gained to positive effect.

Cognitive behavioural therapy

It is common for victims of traumatic exposure to feel destabilised in the immediate aftermath, but within a few weeks most will have regained their balance. Cognitive behavioural therapy is based on the principles of learning and conditioning which suggest that re-experience and arousal symptoms are due to classical conditioning being elicited by environmental stimuli. Avoidant behaviours on the other hand are under operant control (Rothbaum *et al.* 2000) and have been subject to a number of different therapeutic techniques. Earlier therapies have focused on the two-factor theory of conditioned fear (Mower 1960), while more recently, emotional processing theories (Foa and Kozak 1986) and social cognitive theories (Resick and Schnicke 1992) have gained acceptance.

The most frequently used cognitive behavioural techniques include the following.

- *Exposure therapy.* This technique involves prolonged exposure to anxiety, provoking stimuli without relaxation or other anxiety-reducing methods. Typically, the employee will be asked to create a tape-recorded narrative of the traumatic event and then listen to the tape with their eyes closed. Initially the employee will experience extreme distress but after multiple exposures the level of anxiety falls.
- *Systematic desensitisation.* In this therapy the employee is taught relaxation techniques prior to being exposed to a reminder of the trauma. The employee is then helped to substitute a relaxation response for the anxiety response previously caused by traumatising stimuli.
- *Stress inoculation training.* This technique was originally developed as an anxiety management technique. It includes education, muscle relaxation training, breathing training, role-play and thought stopping.
- *Cognitive therapy.* This therapy works on the premise that it is the interpretation of the event, rather than the event itself, that determines mood states. The employee will be taught to identify

irrational or dysfunctional thoughts, challenge them and replace them with more logical and beneficial thoughts.

• *Assertiveness training.* This is not normally used as a stand-alone therapy but as a component of other approaches. The training focuses on developing an assertive response in place of the anxiety response typically elicited by a trauma reminder.

Psychodynamic therapy

Psychodynamic therapy has been used to treat victims of trauma for over 100 years. Psychodynamic approaches emphasise the impact of the traumatic event on the person's self-concepts and view of others. The approach seeks to understand the context of the traumatic memories and the defensive processes through which the unconscious transforms repressed memories into maladaptive symptoms. Psychodynamic treatments last from between 12 sessions to several years. Brief psychodynamic therapy has been developed specifically for use with victims of trauma (Brom *et al.* 1989). This therapy involves retelling the story to a calm empathetic and non-judgemental clinician during which the employee develops more adaptive defences and coping strategies. Employees also learn to identify how current life situations can set off trauma memories and symptoms.

Lindy (1996) describes the relationship between the therapist and the client as one in which the therapist:

• maintains an empathetic relationship with the client in the here and now;
• uses words to describe feelings in the here and now which can also be applied to the 'then and there' of the trauma;
• encourages the client to reconstruct the trauma memory;
• uses the client to find the right words to describe their uniquely traumatic experience.

The most common symptom identified in psychotherapy is the alternation between over-controlled states and poorly-controlled states, resulting in an approach avoidance struggle involving a difficulty in staying with the feelings without taking defensive flight or being overwhelmed. The therapy process encourages the victim to review their memories of the trauma and to express feelings and identify distorted meanings. The therapy is successful when the trauma victim is able to talk about the traumatic event without being overwhelmed.

Eye movement desensitisation and reprocessing (EMDR)

This form of treatment is controversial and was developed by Shapiro (1989) on the basis of a chance observation that took place when her eyes followed the waving of leaves during a walk in the park. She found that this brought about the cognitive processing of information that had been troubling her. Shapiro suggests that the process of EMDR facilitates the connection of appropriate information into a positive emotional and cognitive schema. In EMDR, eye movements or other alternating right/left stimuli are used to trigger a physiological mechanism which activates the information processing system and enables the negative experience to be processed in such a way that it no longer triggers negative psychological responses. In the EMDR protocol, a client is asked to identify and focus on a traumatic image or memory. The therapist then elicits negative belief statements about the memory. The client is asked to rate the statements on an 11-point distress scale. The therapist then asks the client to generate positive feelings about the memory, which are rated on a 7-point scale of how much the client believes the positive statement. The client is then asked to do four things simultaneously:

- visualise the memory;
- rehearse the negative thoughts;
- concentrate on the physical sensations of the anxiety;
- visually track the therapist's index finger, which is rapidly passed back and forth 30–35 cm from the client's face.

At the end, the client is asked to blank out the memory and take a deep breath. The client then brings back the memory and thoughts. The eye movements continue until the level of distress equals 0 or 1 at which stage the client is asked to describe how he or she feels about the positive cognition and gives it a rating.

Discussion

In order to reduce the impact of traumatic events in the workplace, organisations need to be aware of the range and purpose of a large number of psychological interventions. Some are very clearly in the domain of the organisation. It is the organisation itself that is in the best position to undertake a comprehensive risk assessment and to decide on what support it is willing to provide to assist employees and their families to overcome the impact of a traumatic event. Defusing, debriefing and trauma counselling are psychological techniques that few organisations would be expected to fully understand and therefore it is important that they are aware of the effectiveness of each of these interventions in protecting the health and well-being of their workforce.

Incident support material

Guidance on handling employees following a traumatic event

Try not to rush into the situation where your help is required. Try to keep to a calm and even pace. Being over-reactive is confusing and increases distress in people who are already upset.

Gain as accurate a picture as possible of what is involved and who might be affected. Where helpers rush into a situation and begin doing things without any planning or preparation they can become over-involved and part of the problem rather than part of the solution.

Where a decision needs to be made, be decisive. Constant changes in arrangements increases the distress.

Personal disaster creates distress in those touched by the event. Distress is necessary and a normal part of the process of adjustment. Normal responses to a personal crisis may include:

• Incomprehension	• Withdrawal	• Numbness
• Confusion	• Denial	• Mood swings
• Worry	• Insomnia	• Fearfulness
• Vigilance	• Sweating	• Anger
• Anxiety	• Dizziness	• Rage
• Apprehension	• Tension	• Guilt
• Flashbacks	• Loss of interest	• Agitation
• Nightmares	• Avoidance	• Crying
• Depression	• Slowing down	

The greater the shock the more severe the distress. The severity of the person's response to the distress may peak at any time; it may increase for a time after the event and then decline. It may be helpful to let everyone know that they will not always be as distressed as they are now and that they *will* recover.

What you can do

Listen. It will be helpful to the person to tell you what happened – they may become calmer simply by being able to share the experience. It is important for helpers to reduce the stress to manageable proportions. The first step for a victim is to be able to understand exactly what has occurred. At this stage, it is the victim's meaning that is important. Sometimes people will express negative thoughts and feelings about themselves at this stage. It is important not to try to correct or challenge, as this will tend to make the person more negative.

Assess the situation. Often the most important way of assisting recovery is to do the *practical* thing. Make sure that people have all the practical things that they need. If someone is cold, hungry, worried about family or unwell, these are the first things that need to be sorted out. It is only then that they will be able to think about what has happened.

Assess the people. Some people will be able to cope, but others will find it difficult. Are any of the people particularly vulnerable, have they other problems, are special relationships involved? As far as possible let everyone make their own decisions about the help they want or need, but make sure that they know that help is always available.

Later support. Keep a check on everyone and work out with each person how much help they might need over the next few days/weeks. Continue to take the time to listen, be clear about the facts but be ready to:

• accept the person's distress, anger or pain;
• let them talk – be prepared to listen: *you do not have to offer any solutions*;
• acknowledge the normality of their responses to the disaster.

The process of working through involves talking about what happened, and is rarely smooth. The changes from feeling bad to feeling OK may involve occasional setbacks. This is normal and setbacks are usually followed by further improvements.

Talking will help. Take your cue from the person; let them focus on whatever they want to talk about. It has been found that generally people find it easier to talk about what *happened*, more difficult to talk about *what they think* and more difficult still to talk about *what they feel*. Talking in all these three areas will help, but only when the person is able and ready.

Self-care. Those involved in supporting can be left with the feeling that they did not do enough. In order to deal with difficult situations, supporters may find themselves making an effort to shut out their own feelings. It is important that supporters have someone they can talk to about *their* experiences as a supporter.

Traumatic stress: advice for distressed employees and their families

Dealing with sudden death, accidents and other traumatic experiences can leave you feeling confused, angry, isolated and shocked.

We would like to offer you some help to overcome your difficulties by:

- being there to listen;
- arranging further help or counselling.

Talking over what happened with someone who cares can help.

There are a number of common reactions to severe shock

You may feel:

- Angry
- Jumpy
- Alone
- Anxious
- Numb

- Tense
- Emotional
- Guilty
- Down
- Worthless

- Irritable
- Restless
- Tearful
- Tired
- Depressed

You may also have bad dreams or nightmares There may be problems with concentration, eating, sleeping or sex. All these reactions are normal and should begin to fade in the next day or so. However, sometimes feelings do not go away or they start at a later date. If this happens you may need to consider asking for professional help.

Helpful hints

Do
- Talk about your feelings
- Ask for help
- Speak to your GP
- Try relaxation to unwind
- Go back to work
- Take exercise

Do not
- Drink alcohol
- Take un-prescribed medication
- Cut yourself off from colleagues
- Get over-tired
- Skip meals
- Bottle things up

If you would like more help please talk to:

Or phone:

Skills for helpers

Observation skills	Listening skills
• Gathering information about the situation • Assessing how others feel • Establishing the causes and nature of the behaviours of others • Self-observation and awareness • Recognition of changes in emotions and attitudes • Distinguishing between statements and behaviours	• Reflecting thoughts and feelings • Matching the mood of others in the situation • Demonstrating attention by providing verbal and non-verbal feedback • Clarity of expression of emotion and attitudes • Appropriate body language and eye contact
Responding skills	**Networking skills**
• Skills in the use of paraphrase and summary • Fluency of speech and non-verbal aspects of speech • Clarity in the disclosure of factual information • Appropriate disclosure of feelings • Ability to use questions to elicit important information without distress	• Ability to work with others in a team • Being able to discuss differences of approach/ opinion calmly • Ability to develop and build on the ideas of others • Ability to time actions in a way that recognises the needs of others • Ability to communicate concerns openly and non-aggressively
Training and education	**Communicating concern**
• Provide skills, feedback, advice and coaching • Offer simple information and advice suitable for the occasion • Recognise and offer additional information and support to those who need it • Explain to colleagues and other helpers what you are doing	• Skills in greeting, making requests, talking to strangers • Offering praise, encouragement and congratulations • Showing sympathy • Providing explanations • Offering apologies for things that could have been done better • Being assertive without being aggressive

Chapter 8

Introducing trauma care into an organisation[1]

Introduction

In the early 1990s, one of the UK's largest employers, the Post Office, identified the need to introduce an appropriate organisational response designed to reduce the incidence of psychological trauma caused to employees when traumatic incidents occurred at work. The strategy that evolved was to develop a trauma care programme that could be adapted to meet the specific needs of each of four Post Office businesses. When introducing the programme the businesses were prepared to accommodate its needs. This accommodation included the modification of existing policies relating to: a) the selection and training of employees; b) operational security; c) risk assessment; and d) police liaison, and a commitment to introduce methods for monitoring and evaluating post-trauma care.

This chapter describes how the programme was introduced together with the issues that were faced. In addition, the chapter outlines some of the problems that had to be overcome before the programme was acceptable to the businesses and the workforce. Some early evidence of the effectiveness of trauma care on reducing sickness absence is also presented.

Post Office Trauma Care Programme

In 1992, the Post Office was organised as a number of separate businesses, each with its own managing director and board of directors (see Figure 8.1). The Post Office Corporation provided a number of

1 Based on Tehrani, N. (1995) An integrated response to trauma in three Post Office Businesses, *Work & Stress*, 9: 380–93. www.tandf.co.uk

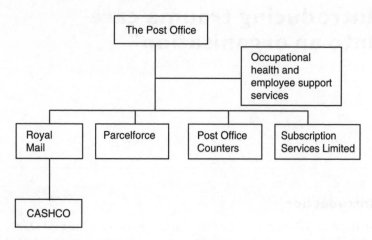

Figure 8.1 The Post Office organisation 1992–7

central services including the occupational health and employee support service. In the autumn of that year a number of senior managers working within the Post Office became concerned about the increasing levels of attacks on employees and decided that there was a need to provide post-trauma care for employees exposed to traumatic events. Over the next three years the four Post Office businesses, CASHCO, Subscription Services Limited, Royal Mail and Post Office Counters introduced trauma care programmes. The different organisational needs of each of the Post Office businesses required individual trauma care programmes to be designed, however it was found that flexibility could be achieved while retaining a core trauma programme common to each of the trauma care programmes.

CASHCO

Royal Mail CASHCO was a strategic business unit of Royal Mail and one of the UK's leading cash in transit companies. It was the first of the Post Office businesses to indicate a wish to introduce trauma care for its workforce. Due to the nature of its business, CASHCO was particularly susceptible to violent attacks from criminals. During a meeting of the CASHCO board of directors a decision was taken to undertake a benchmarking exercise and risk assessment of the traumatic events that were occurring in the business in order to identify the size and nature of the problem. These exercises showed that although CASHCO employees were at no greater risk than other employees within other cash in transit businesses, there were times when employees were exposed to frightening incidents and experiences. However, CASHCO had no comprehensive plans for dealing with major incidents such as hostage-taking or even for the more common incidents such as violent attacks on crew members. While the support of occupational health nurses and employee support advisors was available to distressed CASHCO employees, there was no comprehensive trauma care programme as had been adopted in some other organisations involved in similar work. In 1992, there was little information available on the human factors involved in the management of organisational trauma programmes. McCloy (1992) had discussed the need for effective management of trauma in organisations and developed a three-stage model involving immediate action, short-term management and long-term management of the outcomes of a traumatic exposure. It was not until the next year that the Health and Safety Executive provided guidelines on the prevention of violence to staff in banks and building societies (Health and Safety Executive 1993). As these guidelines emerged, the principles were adapted to create a framework for the Post Office's Trauma Care Programme.

The programme to be developed for CASHCO needed to take account of the nature of the cash carrying business. Crew members were employed to transport high-value items including cash from the cash centres to Post Office Counters. Consequently, a significant number of employees became victim to armed raids, hijackings and physical attacks. The first objective of the Trauma Care Programme therefore was to reduce the number of attacks on CASHCO crews by training all employees to develop a culture where the security of personnel, systems and the goods carried was given the highest priority. CASHCO management came to expect all their crew members to conform to, and carry out, all the CASHCO security systems and procedures. In order to achieve this conformity of behaviour, a significant investment in training and monitoring was undertaken by CASHCO. This focus on security was regarded as essential as not only did it protect the crew members from attack but it also reduced the incidence of robbery.

Within each CASHCO van was a driver and another crew member. The two employees working together as a team was an important aspect of the CASHCO culture where 'looking out' for your partner became an important means by which crew members could avoid becoming victims of crime. It was important that CASHCO's trauma care programme took account of the fact that there would normally be two crew members involved in every traumatic incident. There was therefore a requirement to debrief two people at the same time.

The CASHCO debriefing model

In 1992, there was little guidance for counsellors and psychologists on how to deal with traumatised employees. A number of books had been written on dealing with disasters (e.g. Figley 1985; Raphael 1986; Hodgkinson and Stewart 1991), however, these focused on the experiences of members of the emergency services or members of the public who had become victims of disastrous floods, fires or earthquakes. Although there were some helpful insights to be gained from these books there were different problems to be faced with the CASHCO crew members who typically had been taken hostage, hijacked, involved in armed raids or violent attacks. Whatever the model of debriefing chosen it would have to take account of the following facts:

- the crews were dispersed all over the UK;
- crews were made up of two people;
- crew members were expected to comply with all CASHCO procedures;
- breaches of security would always be reported;
- teamworking was essential.

As there were few psychologists experienced in dealing with traumatised employees, the main source of information on how to provide support was two papers describing crisis management and debriefing (Mitchell 1983; and Dyregrov 1989) (see Chapter 7). The Mitchell and Dyregrov debriefing models were examined and although they provided a helpful starting point they were not detailed enough or in a form that could be easily adapted for use in CASHCO. Tehrani (2000b) developed a model of debriefing that was adopted by CASHCO. The debriefing model was designed for the use of CASHCO depot managers, as it was believed that they were in the best position to provide the immediate and ongoing support that was important to the recovery of traumatised crew members. The First Line Debriefing Model (see Table 8.3, p. 110) was made up of four stages: introduction, story, information and close. In CASHCO the introduction was particularly important as it emphasised the fact that although personal information would be kept confidential, any breaches in security could not be treated in the same way. The introduction also asked the two crew members to allow each other to take a full part in the debriefing by taking turns in telling the story of what had happened. The First Line Model of debriefing was later adapted for use in the other Post Office businesses.

Subscription Services Limited

Subscriptions Services Limited, having heard of the CASHCO trauma care programme, wanted a similar programme for its television enquiry officers. Subscription Services was involved in administering the collection and recording of television licence fees on behalf of the BBC. The enquiry officer's role was to visit the houses of those people for whom no record of a licence existed on the database. Where there was no satisfactory explanation for the absence of a licence, the enquiry officer would arrange for the householder to be prosecuted. Regardless of whether the householder had a television licence or not, the enquiry officer was never a welcome figure on the doorstep. Because of this negative perception, enquiry officers suffered a relatively high level of verbal and physical abuse. Enquiry officers normally worked alone and were home based. There was a need therefore for them to be self-sufficient and resilient in their ability to deal with the pressures of their role.

The Subscription Services debriefing and diffusing models

The trauma care programme developed for Subscription Services had to take account of the fact that the traumatised enquiry officers would generally be on their own, away from any immediate colleague support and frequently in the middle of a hostile working environment, such as a run-down housing estate. The need to provide immediate support resulted in the introduction of open telephone lines to the enquiry officers' managers. An enquiry officer's manager would take responsibility to handle the immediate needs of the officer over the telephone and would then arrange a debriefing session within the next two days. However, there were also other differences between the needs of the CASHCO and the enquiry officers in that much of the violence experienced by enquiry officers was constant but of a relatively low level, involving verbal abuse, threats, physical pushing and jostling. The prolonged duress suffered by these employees eventually resulted in *prolonged duress stress* (Scott and Stradling 1992a). To cater for the slow build-up of prolonged duress stress a special diffusing session was introduced at the end of each monthly team meeting. These sessions were designed to help enquiry officers share their experiences and consult with their peers to identify new ways of dealing with the stresses and traumas of the job.

Royal Mail

Before Royal Mail introduced its trauma care programme, an audit of the existing programmes was commissioned. This audit looked at the programmes that were being delivered to CASHCO and Subscription Services together with the services that Royal Mail was currently receiving. Because of the audit (Cox *et al.* 1993) the trauma care programmes, training and systems provided to CASHCO and Subscription Services were adopted by Royal Mail. However, the audit was also supportive of improving the programme with additonal services provided by the Post Office's Employee Support Service. The audit marked the final stage of creating the Post Office's core Trauma Care Programme (see Table 8.2, p. 107). The final programme not only involved the use of the First Line Debriefing Model, but also introduced a new model of psychological debriefing (Tehrani and Westlake 1994), referrals for trauma counselling and psychiatric care, and processes for evaluating and monitoring the benefits of the programme. The trauma care approach was accepted by Royal Mail for introduction for all its postal workers in 1994/5.

Post Office Counters

At that time, Post Office Counters was the largest retailing organisation in the UK with over 18,000 outlets, some of which were run by employees of the Post Office and others by agents or sub-postmasters. In 1996, Post Office Counters decided to introduce trauma care for all the workers in the crown and sub-post offices. The Post Office core Trauma Care Programme was adapted for Post Office Counters with additional training to help the network managers deal with the immediate aftermath of a raid on a post office. As many of the incidents in post offices involved more than one employee, in addition to the First Line Debriefing Model for debriefing individuals, a group debriefing model was developed to deal with raids involving several employees. Trained occupational health nurses and employee support advisers undertook the group debriefing.

In a period of three years, the Post Office had introduced trauma care to most of its workforce. However, each business had been able to make adaptations to the programme to allow for the organisational and operational needs of their business.

Features of the Post Office Trauma Care Programme

One of the main concerns of the business managers at the time of introducing the core programme was that the policies and procedures used to deliver a trauma care programme were consistent with the recommendations of the Health and Safety Executive (1993). Before any work began on developing the trauma care programmes a number of risk assessments were undertaken (Tehrani 1995). The assessment process involved gathering information from managers and employees and examining incident reports and sickness absence data. This assessment enabled risk profiles to be developed for each business. Overall, the risk data indicated that there were three main categories of incident in the Post Office; these included attacks on employees that were:

- related to robbery or attempted robbery;
- expressions of anger or frustration directed at an authority figure;
- random attacks sometimes with a sexual connotation in which the attacker had no particular motive other than personal gratification.

The result of the risk assessment for each of the four businesses is shown in Table 8.1.

The different profiles of the four businesses can be seen with CASHCO's attacks generally involving robberies, with a high incidence of hijacking and threats of violence where firearms and noxious substances were the common weapons. Subscription Services employees on the other hand had been much more likely to be the victims of an anti-authority or random attack. These attacks frequently involved being bitten by dogs, threats of violence and verbal abuse. Royal Mail suffered rather lower levels of attack than the other three businesses. The attacks on Royal Mail employees often involved Royal Mail vehicles being hijacked and taken to a place where the items within the vans were stolen. Postal workers were also likely to be attacked by dogs, threatened with knives, bats or fists. Post Office Counters' employees experienced the widest range of

Table 8.1 Degree of risk from traumatic occurrences for Post Office employees

	Post Office business			
	Royal Mail	*Counters*	*CASHCO*	*Subscription Services*
Category of attack				
Robbery	**	***	***	—
Anti-authority	*	**	—	***
Sexual	*	—	—	*
Random	**	—	—	***
Nature of attack				
Family or colleague taken hostage	—	*	*	—
Hijacking of vehicle	***	—	***	*
Kidnap (held against will)	**	***	**	*
Physical attack	**	**	**	**
Dog attack	***	—	—	***
Witness to traumatic event	*	***	***	—
Road traffic crash	**	—	**	—
Threat of violence	***	***	***	***
Verbal abuse	*	***	—	***
Tied up/blindfolded	**	***	**	—
Use of weapons				
Firearms	**	***	***	*
Noxious substances, e.g. CS gas	**	*	***	—
Knives or other sharp instruments	***	*	*	*
Blunt objects, e.g. bats, fists	***	***	*	***
Effect of trauma on others				
Managers and colleagues	**	***	**	**
Family	**	***	***	**

Key: *** High risk; ** Medium risk; * Low risk; – No significant risk.

traumatic incidents. Attacks were generally related to robberies and included the employees being kidnapped, threatened with violence, verbally abused, tied up and blindfolded. Assaults were carried out using a wide range of weapons including firearms, bats and fists.

Key stages of the Programme

A systematic approach to dealing with traumatic incidents in the workplace is essential. Table 8.2 illustrates the core Trauma Care

Table 8.2 The core Trauma Care Programme

		Stages of response
Stage −1	Selection, induction training and education	Pre-trauma training to help employees develop the appropriate level of knowledge and skills to deal with a traumatic incident.
Stage 1	Crisis management and diffusing	Immediate personal and organisational needs are met. This may include first aid, personal support, dealing with the police and media. During Stage 1 employees are also given an opportunity to talk about the traumatic incident to a peer or manager and information on debriefing and traumatic stress responses will be given to the employee.
Stage 2	First line debriefing	Recognises the operational and organisational aspects of the trauma and provides an early opportunity for the traumatised employee to make sense of their experience. Provides an opportunity to receive education and information on the nature of traumatic stress and traumatic stress reactions.
Stage 3	Psychological debriefing	A more in-depth debrief where the thinking and emotional aspects of the trauma can be fully explored and an assessment of the ongoing needs undertaken. Training in how to deal with the major trauma responses including arousal, re-experience and avoidance provided.

| Stage 4 | Trauma counselling/ psychiatric care | Where the employee requires further support, a referral for trauma counselling and/or psychiatric care offered. |
| Stage 5 | Follow-up, audit and evaluation | Individual cases are followed up to ensure that progress is maintained and delayed reactions identified. Performance against agreed criteria is carried out (e.g. employee satisfaction data, reductions in sickness absence and medical retirements). |

Programme adopted by the Post Office. This Programme had six main stages, the first stage beginning before the traumatic event and the final stage involved in the audit and evaluation of the total programme. The successful execution of each stage of the programme was important to the success of the subsequent stages.

Stage –1: selection, induction training and education

In Stage –1 each business had the responsibility for assessing all potential employees for their suitability for a job. In high-risk jobs, this involved assessing the candidate's ability to cope with traumatic events. Following selection, a recruit was provided with extensive training and education on how to avoid dangerous or difficult situations. In addition, new recruits were also trained in a range of coping skills that had been shown to help reduce the impact of common reactions to traumatic stress. The implementation of Stage –1 assisted the effectiveness of the overall Trauma Care Programme by reducing the number of employees that were particularly susceptible to trauma following a distressing incident. The Post Office's Trauma Care Programme involved introducing a training programme for managers and employees on the effects of trauma with the aim of ensuring that managers would have the skills to identify employees experiencing post-traumatic stress reactions. Another aspect of the induction training was the clarification of the role of the manager during the post-trauma period. Managers were made personally responsible for ensuring that appropriate levels of support were made available to employees involved in traumatic incidents.

The induction training was supported by a trauma care video that used real experiences of Post Office employees to demonstrate the physical, psychological and social effects of trauma. The video also showed how the employee could develop simple coping skills to reduce the likelihood of long-term post-traumatic disorders. In the video, the support that was available from managers, the business, occupational health and employee support services was described. A range of information leaflets was also developed which included:

- organisational policies and procedures relating to trauma care;
- guidance notes on where to get help;
- advice and information on dealing with the effects of trauma;
- what to do if asked to help the police with their enquiries;
- what would happen when making a court appearance.

Stage 1: crisis management and diffusing (first 24–48 hours)

This stage of the programme was particularly important, as the way in which employees were treated by their manager and colleagues immediately following a traumatic incident had a significant impact on the speed of their recovery. Managers handling the aftermath of a traumatic incident required a number of skills which included the ability to evaluate the situation and anticipate the needs of the employee, to maintain communications, to delegate authority to act and to deal with the stress of the situation. The trauma care training assessed managers' skills and the programme provided checklists to help managers work through what they needed to do to handle the immediate aftermath of a traumatic incident. Following a traumatic experience, most employees were found to welcome an opportunity to talk about what had happened to them with their manager or colleagues. The process of diffusing was an important part of the Trauma Care Programme as it provided an opportunity for the traumatised employee to talk about their experience.

Stage 2: first line debriefing (3–7 days after the incident)

During Stage 2 the emphasis changed from managing a crisis to providing essential psychological first aid for victims. The Post Office's trauma care programmes used fellow employees or peers to deliver the early stages of trauma care. There were two main reasons for this approach. First, managers and peers understand the work undertaken by the victim better than an outsider and therefore have a good understanding of the nature and impact of the traumatic experience. Second, manager or peer debriefers are normally able to contact their traumatised colleagues more quickly than specialised trauma debriefers who may have to be brought in to the area. Around 500 trauma debriefers were trained by the Post Office's organisational counselling psychologist and all undertook two days of training and had to pass an assessment before they were considered competent to undertake a first line debriefing.

The first line debriefing (see Table 8.3) provided the traumatised employee with an opportunity to talk about their traumatic experi-

Table 8.3 The four stages of the first line debrief

Introduction	This is an essential opening phase of the debriefing in which the first line debriefer clearly defines the process and boundaries of the debriefing. In view of the nature of the manager-employee relationship, there is a need to deal with failure to comply with organisational policy. The first line debrief is voluntary and, where an employee is unwilling to be debriefed by a peer or manager, the employee is offered the opportunity to be debriefed by a employee support adviser or occupational health nurse.
Telling the story	The second stage involves telling the story. This is done in a slow, systematic way with the story beginning before the event and ending at the present. The first line debriefing sticks to the facts of the incident; thoughts and feelings are acknowledged but not explored at this stage.
Information	The first line debriefer then moves on to providing information to the traumatised employee. This information is designed to help the employee to return to normal life and prevent the occurrence of secondary problems such as alcoholism or phobias.
Close	In the closing phase the first line debriefer checks that the employee is safe to go home and will ensure that there is someone at home to stay with them. Where necessary, the first line debriefer will arrange for the employee to be taken home and that a colleague is made available to stay with them. The first line debriefer will also arrange to contact the employee again and where further help is needed will organise an appointment for a psychological debrief.

ence in a safe and controlled environment. This experience helped the victim to begin the process of coming to terms with what had happened and to begin the recovery process. The debriefing also provided the first line debriefer with the opportunity to assess whether the employee had a need for further debriefing. The First Line Debriefing Model designed in the Post Office was rather different to other models of debriefing as it did not explore thoughts or feelings but rather worked systematically through the actual traumatic incident, gathering sensory information on what happened (i.e. what was seen, heard, touched, tasted and smelt). Two first line debriefing models were developed for the use of managers and peers. The first was designed for debriefing two employees and the second for debriefing a single employee.

Where there was a group of traumatised employees following a post office hold-up or an attack on a Royal Mail sorting office, a group debriefing was undertaken. This could only be undertaken by a trained occupational health nurse or employee support adviser.

Stage 3: psychological debriefing

Following the first line debriefing, employees might require a deeper level of debriefing. In this case, the first line debriefer or manager would refer the employee to a trained psychological debriefer. The psychological debriefing used in the Post Office was designed for use with individual employees (Tehrani and Westlake 1994) and undertaken by a trained psychologist, counsellor or other health professional. In the psychological debriefing, the story of the traumatic incident is gone through three times. In the first telling of the story the facts are elicited, in the second, the thoughts connected to those facts are established and then finally the feelings evoked by the facts and thoughts are described. This gradual unfolding of the trauma story has the effect of reducing the emotional responses to the traumatic event. The psychological debriefing is undertaken in a single session with a follow-up session. Employees who show no signs of recovery following a psychological debriefing and follow-up session are referred for a medical assessment by their GP or an occupational health physician.

Stage 4: trauma counselling and psychiatric care

Where an employee is not recovering from the effects of a traumatic event, the occupational health physician would make the decision on the needs of the employee. This would usually involve consulting the employee's GP. Where the problem is seen as psychological, the employee may be referred to a trauma counsellor. The Post Office did not undertake trauma counselling internally and therefore referrals were made to an external counselling organisation. Following counselling or psychiatric interventions, employees were 'followed up' and where necessary rehabilitation programmes developed for them.

Stage 5: follow-up, audit and evaluation

All employees who had experienced a traumatic incident were followed up at 3-, 6- and 12-month intervals following the incident. This was to ensure that the employee was continuing to progress and had not suffered a delayed trauma response. The follow-up also provided evaluation data on the success of the Trauma Care Programme as an intervention for supporting victims of trauma.

The Post Office had a number of mechanisms for auditing the quality of the service provided. First, it measured the service against agreed service standard levels. Service standard agreements, which were set up within each business, set out the speed, quality and nature of the services that were to be provided. The service standards approach was part of the total quality working standards adopted by the Post Office. Second, occupational health and employee support services undertook internal audits of case handling and clinical standards to ensure that the performance and competency of the practitioners were monitored, and opportunities for service improvements were identified. Experienced counselling supervisors oversaw all the psychological debriefers. The supervisors were responsible to the organisation for ensuring that the debriefers were working within their level of competency.

The programme evaluation was based on a number of indicators. First, each employee was offered the opportunity to complete a post-incident questionnaire that gathered both qualitative and quantitative data for analysis. Second, the level of sickness absence and medical retirements for employees who experienced a traumatic event were monitored by the Post Office. These were compared with the levels that were the norm prior to the introduction of the Trauma Care Programme.

Initial difficulties

Within the Post Office, there was strong support for the Trauma Care Programme from employees and managers. Not surprisingly, there were some initial teething problems to be overcome before the Programme was totally accepted. These included:

- problems in dealing with the Post Office culture which had a tendency to be authoritarian with the result that a number of traumatised employees felt unable to express their feelings of fear or anxiety and refused to be debriefed;
- managers being unavailable to undertake debriefing because they were affected by the same traumatic incident;
- difficulties in separating the security debriefing from the psychological debriefing;
- a reluctance to be debriefed by an unpopular manager;
- conflicting advice on returning to work from the debriefing manager and the union;
- difficulties in employees returning to the workplace prior to a full return to work.

These issues were resolved through discussion with management. Following the introduction of the Programme the culture of the Post Office gradually changed and employees were more willing to seek emotional and psychological support following a traumatic experience. It was recognised that there would be times when the local manager would not be in a position to undertake a debriefing and therefore a panel of trained managers was introduced to cover for traumatised and other unsuitable managers. Training for union representatives proved successful in ensuring that employees were getting the same advice, and organisational systems were changed where they prevented a gradual return to work.

Many of the debriefing managers were initially concerned that the caring approach required when undertaking debriefing would conflict with their need to manage more difficult employee situations, such as disciplinary meetings. This anticipated conflict between the management role and the caring role did not in fact occur and most managers found that they were able to recognise that debriefing requires skills of caring and control. Reports from management trainees revealed that the skills learnt on the course not only enabled them to undertake first line debriefing but also enabled them to manage other difficult tasks, including performance reviews and dealing with grievance issues, more effectively. Initially some managers thought that their staff would not choose to be debriefed by a line manager. However, this was not found to be the case, as most employees preferred to be debriefed by someone they knew and who understood them and the situation, rather than by an outsider.

The role of senior managers

The Post Office senior managers had an important part to play in introducing the Trauma Care Programme, the most important aspects being the:

- acknowledgement that traumatic incidents could cause harm to employees;
- recognition that the Post Office had a role to play in providing support for victims of trauma;
- provision of the resources necessary to support the introduction and running of the Trauma Care Programme;
- willingness to go through the training themselves.

The organisational acceptance of the role of managers and colleagues in helping employees to recover from traumatic experiences provided the opportunity to bring about changes in the organisation's culture which made talking about feelings in a safe environment acceptable. The introduction of first line debriefing training helped the trainees not only to learn about debriefing but also to raise a wide range of other operational and security issues involved in the operation of the Programme. Senior managers in each of the businesses had given their undertaking that operational issues that had an impact on the safety of the workforce or the effectiveness of the Trauma Care Programme would be addressed. The rapid response and effectiveness of this problem-resolution process was made possible by the priority and importance given to the Programme by the senior management teams.

In 1992, it was thought that a single Trauma Care Programme would be appropriate for use throughout the Post Office. However, as it became apparent that each business needed a programme adapted and adjusted to its own requirements, these were then developed. The ownership of the Programme by employees was helped by each business developing its own support material.

Cost benefit analysis

CASHCO

CASHCO, the first business to adopt a trauma care programme, obtained financial and personal data on the operation of the programme from the CASHCO personnel databases. These contain staff records, including the number of days of sickness absence recorded for employees following a traumatic event. Inspection of the employee records for three years prior to the commencement of the programme showed that employees involved in traumatic incidents took, on average, eight days' sick leave. During the three years following the introduction of the programme, the average number of post-incident sickness absences had fallen from eight to four days, making an average saving of four days per affected employee.

The total cost of the first line debriefing training for CASHCO was £88,300, made up as follows: training courses £40,000; two training videos, £41,300; and the provision of personal security devices for the homes of operational staff, £7,000.

The average level of savings over the three years following the introduction of the programme was £103,000 per annum. The savings were made up of £37,000 from the reduced level of sickness absence following incidents; £56,000 from the reduction in the number of employees needing to be medically retired as unfit for work; and an estimated saving of £10,000 which was non-measurable. This non-measurable saving included the cost of temporary staff covering for the sickness absence of traumatised employees, overtime payments for employees covering the duties of absent colleagues, and recruitment costs for new staff to replace employees who were medically retired or resigned following a traumatic event. The data showed that, even as early as the first year, the programme more than paid for itself. The second and third years provided an overall saving of £200,000. CASHCO anticipated the need to arrange for at least one first line debriefing course per year to train newly-appointed managers. In addition, there was a need for short refresher training courses with an estimated cost of £10,000 per year.

Subscription Services Limited

Subscription Services evaluated its trauma care programme by comparing the number of stress-related sickness absence days for the year before the introduction of the programme with those for one year following completion of the first line debriefing training. It found that there was a reduction of 32 per cent in stress-related sickness absence and medical retirements. This reduction translated into a saving of £115,000 each year after the deduction of the costs of the programme.

In 1996, Subscription Services decided that there was a need to augment the programme with a second programme designed to deal with stress and burnout. The new programme involved educating managers in common stress reactions and coping methods, and trained them to deal with a wide range of job and personal problems which might impact on the well-being of employees. Although not part of the trauma care programme the employee well-being programme was anticipated to provide additional support for enquiry officers.

Discussion

The Post Office Trauma Care Programme can never be complete or perfect and will need to be continually reviewed and improved. The main objective must be to evaluate the Programme based on both the psychological assessments of the victims of trauma and the organisational benefits. Further work needs to be done to evaluate the project on the effectiveness of the trauma care interventions, but some of the tools of evaluation are already in place. In order to satisfy business needs, organisational measurements must be established to assess the value of the change in organisational effectiveness brought about by the Programme.

Chapter 9

Choosing and managing an external provider of post-trauma support[1]

Introduction

For organisations where the incidence of traumatic events is infrequent or the employees are widely dispersed, there are likely to be few advantages in introducing an in-house trauma counselling and debriefing service. However, selecting, managing and auditing an external provider is not a trouble-free process. Organisations need to be aware that the purchasing of an external post-trauma support service on its own may not fully meet all the needs of the organisation or its traumatised employees.

This chapter looks at what an organisation should do when planning to introduce an external service, how to go through the selection process and how to decide what should be included in the service standards agreement and contract. Finally, the chapter looks towards the future and suggests ways in which both purchasing organisations and providers can enhance the quality and effectiveness of the post-trauma support provision to organisations and their employees.

External providers of trauma counselling and debriefing can never take over the organisation's duty of care to protect the health, safety and welfare of its employees involved in a traumatic event in the workplace. It is important that prior to talking to a potential provider of psychological debriefing, the organisation takes the time to undertake an organisational risk assessment. The assessment should examine the nature of the traumatic hazards, the incidence of traumatic exposure and the severity of the impact of the exposure on

1 Based on Tehrani, N. (2002) *Psychological Debriefing, Working Party Report.* Leicester: British Psychological Society.

those involved (Tehrani 1995). In addition, the organisation should consider the role it would like to play in the delivery of the trauma support programme to its employees. The culture of the organisation is an important factor in selecting that role (Tehrani 2000a). Organisations that have developed a people-centred caring culture are more likely to want to be involved in providing support, while task-focused organisations are more likely to be comfortable with a role that manages the process and outcomes.

Selecting a provider

Where to start?

Some organisations considering the need to provide post-trauma support for their employees may already be using the services of an external counselling service or employee assistance programme (EAP). These providers are likely to be offering a range of services from telephone assessment, advice and counselling, to face-to-face counselling, employee seminars and management support. It would perhaps be natural for the organisation to automatically assume that their existing provider would be the best and most logical place to begin when selecting a psychological debriefing and support service. However, the appointment of the existing counselling provider should not necessarily be the automatic response. Psychological debriefing and counselling are specialist skills that require additional training and management and not all counselling services or EAPs will be able to provide the same depth or quality of service required for meeting the needs of employees or the organisation. It is important therefore that organisations look at the full range of trauma support providers before making a choice of which provider best suits the organisation's unique needs (EAPA 1997).

One of the first problems that organisations face when looking for a provider is to identify what is available. There are a large number of potential providers including:

- EAP and counselling services providers who provide trauma debriefing and counselling as one of a range of services;
- regional EAPs or counselling services serving a geographical area of the UK;
- large specialist providers who are solely involved in providing trauma debriefing and counselling;

- individual psychologists and counsellors offering debriefing and trauma counselling.

As there is no central register of psychological debriefers and counsellors, it is difficult for organisations to know whom to contact when seeking a psychological debriefing provider. There are a number of approaches that can be taken to identify potential providers:

- contact other organisations such as banks, rail companies or retailers to ask for the name of their debriefing provider;
- search the internet;
- contact the Employee Assistance Practitioners Association (EAPA);
- contact the British Psychological Society;
- contact the British Association of Counselling and Psychotherapy (BACP).

Writing a tender document

It is important to have a specification of the services your organisation requires, together with comprehensive technical and commercial questionnaires designed to identify the nature of the services that can be provided. Tender documents ensure that the selection process is undertaken fairly and that essential business requirements are fully described. Tender documents are made up of seven sections:

1 instruction to the tenderers on how and when the tender document should be completed and returned to the organisation;
2 specification of the work to be carried out;
3 a technical questionnaire dealing with the standard and quality of the psychological counselling and debriefing;
4 a commercial questionnaire dealing with the nature of the provider's business and business viability;
5 the format for the pricing of the service;
6 a draft agreement;
7 an undertaking of bona fide tendering.

In order to get an idea of what is available it is advisable to send out the tender documents to a number of potential providers. The aim is to get a minimum of five or six completed tenders from which three or four providers can be shortlisted to present their proposals to the organisation.

The selection process

The initial selection process starts with the written tender documents. Each document should be evaluated based on the technical and commercial information provided, together with the costs of the services. It may be helpful for organisations to seek specialist advice on the technical information from an expert in post-traumatic stress. The specialist should be able to explain technical terms and evaluate the quality of the service being offered. The second stage of the selection process should involve a presentation by those providers that were selected to go through to the second stage. However, this should not be a one-way process and the organisation should prepare a series of searching questions to ensure that the provider is capable of providing the quality and style of service the organisation requires (Cape 1991). The organisation may test some of the assertions of the provider by asking for confirming evidence of the statements made (e.g. if the provider tells you that they have available an international 24-hour service, ask for the name and details of a counsellor or debriefer who would be available at one of your overseas locations and satisfy yourself that they are actually capable to do the work as claimed within the stated timescale).

Specification of work to be done

The final specification cannot be written until the organisation and provider have agreed the technical and commercial specifications and the contract details. However, the items listed below give an indication of what should be in the specification. The organisation should give as much information as possible when sending out the tender document.

- What is to be included in the tender (e.g. only debriefing or a range of trauma care interventions, the number of employees)?
- What is the geographical area to be covered (e.g. details of sites, is a nationwide or international service required)?
- What aspects of the trauma care does the organisation want to provide itself?
- How is the service to be accessed, is there to be a gatekeeper or is there free access?
- What are the minimum qualifications and experience of the counsellors and debriefers?

- What other specialist knowledge or skills are required (e.g. cultural awareness, location, languages spoken)?
- What clinical supervision and specialist support should be provided to the debriefers?
- How, and how often, does the provider assess the competence of the counsellors and debriefers?
- What professional development should the counsellors and debriefers undertake?
- What is the nature and scope of the debriefing protocol?
- What counselling model is being used?
- How and when should the provider undertake clinical assessments of the psychological symptoms of the traumatised employees?
- What is the process for referring employees for psychiatric treatment or specialist trauma counselling?
- What is the process for informing the organisation about employees who are suffering from a trauma-related disorder?
- What is to be in the management reports and how often are they provided?
- How does the provider demonstrate that it is meeting appropriate quality of service standards?

The answers to the technical and commercial questionnaires provide some of the details that will eventually form part of the service specification.

Technical questions

Examples of technical questions/requirements are:

- Does the provider have a quality award under BS5750, ISO/EN9000, Investors in People or EFQM? If yes, give details.
- What are the names of the account and clinical managers?
- Who are the key staff and managers involved in this account and what is their level of experience, background and qualifications?
- What is the process by which the organisation can be assured that all the counsellors and debriefers used on this contract meet the requirements set out in the specification?
- Provision of a copy of the psychological debriefing protocol and details on how the elements of the debriefing protocol are delivered.

- Provision of details of the counselling model and a description of how it is delivered.
- How is client satisfaction measured?
- How and when will the counsellor or debriefer measure the level of traumatic stress symptoms or other psychological response to the traumatic incident?
- What process will be used to maintain communication with the organisation?
- Provision of details of the contract performance monitoring systems to be used on this contract.

Commercial questionnaire

The commercial questionnaire looks at the viability of the provider. Examples of commercial questions include:

Period of trading
- How long have you been established?
- How long have you been involved in supplying psychological debriefing services?

Turnover
- Give company turnover and profit for the previous three years directly attributable to the services tendered for.

References
- Supply the names and addresses of five companies, together with a contact name and fax number or email address for whom you have supplied similar services in the last three years.

Insurance
Supply copies of your:
- insurance policy against third party risks;
- employer's liability insurance;
- public liability insurance;
- professional liability insurance for each psychological debriefer of not less than £2 million for any one incident and unlimited in total.

- How are disputes arising from the performance of this contract to be resolved? These proposals should include the frequency of meetings and the level of management involvement.
- How will the service be launched?
- Supply of a copy of the codes of practice under which the organisation operates.
- Submission of a copy of the organisation's quality statement.

The contract

The contract is binding on the organisation and the provider. The contract should include:

- the start and end date of the contract;
- the process for introducing variations to the contract;
- timings and process for pricing reviews;
- the process for making payments;
- confidentiality undertakings for both the provider and the organisation;
- how publicity and the media will be handled;
- process for handling failures in service delivery or service standards;
- contract termination;
- intellectual property ownership;
- indemnity and insurance;
- named representatives for the provider and the organisation.

Auditing

The purchasing organisation has a duty to ensure that its providers of psychological debriefing services provide services that meet the agreed service standards and clinical requirements. Auditing is the way that the purchasing organisation can ensure that it is getting what it has paid for (Sayle 1987). The auditing process involves a review of the efficiency, effectiveness and reliability of the provider's management and operational systems. Auditing is based on objective evidence and should be undertaken by external specialists competent in their audit role.

The auditing process should involve:

- measuring client satisfaction (employee);
- customer satisfaction (organisation);

- compliance with the standards of service delivery;
- audit of the technical/clinical standards.

Audits should be undertaken against the background of the agreed standards described in the service specification and contract.

Satisfaction audit

Client satisfaction can be audited by the use of simple client satisfaction forms that would be distributed to employees undergoing counselling or debriefing. These forms can be returned anonymously and might ask such questions as 'How sensitive to your needs was the counselling/debriefing?', 'How well was the counselling/debriefing handled?', 'Do you feel that the counselling/debriefing was helpful?', 'Was the education material helpful?', 'Would you recommend this service to a colleague?' and 'Did you feel the counselling/debriefing was rushed?' Ideally, the client satisfaction forms should be sent back to the organisation direct as this ensures that full consideration is given to all the comments made.

Customer satisfaction can involve a number of interested groups including the manager of the traumatised employee and the organisational contact. For the manager the satisfaction is likely to include the ease of setting up sessions and the attitude of the counsellor or debriefer towards the organisation and its needs. The organisation should also audit the timing and quality of the management information and additional support provided.

Compliance audit

This part of the audit investigates whether or not the systems are being implemented and meet the agreed standards. This process should:

- assess whether the programme is fully complying with the agreed service specification;
- check that the provider's management systems and records are able to ensure the standard of the service, the training and the supervision of the debriefers;
- verify that the links between the provider and the organisation have been established and are working;
- interview a sample of counsellors and debriefers used in the

contract to ensure that they meet the agreed professional, supervision and continuing professional development specifications;
• interview a sample of employees who have used the service to ensure that the service provided was as set out in the specification.

Clinical audit

The clinical audit needs to be undertaken by a psychologist or counsellor qualified and competent in audit, trauma counselling and debriefing. The audit should:

• assess the appropriateness of the counselling and debriefing session notes, traumatic stress questionnaire results and the actions taken by the counsellor/debriefer;
• interview a random sample of employees who have undergone counselling or debriefing;
• interview a random sample of counsellors and debriefers to assess clinical awareness and competence to undertake a debriefing and to identify where an employee requires specialist treatment;
• assess the appropriateness of the counselling and debriefing protocols including any educational material.

A copy of the audit report that would provide the results of the satisfaction, compliance and clinical audits should be made available to the provider and the organisation. The primary purpose of the audits is to improve the quality of the psychological debriefing service. The report should include positive as well as negative features of the audit and should be discussed by the organisation and the provider in order to improve the service specification and monitoring process (Thomas 1996).

Assessing effectiveness

It is important to ensure that the external provider has put in place a robust evaluation process. This not only ensures that traumatised employees are being carefully tracked, and where necessary referred on for more intensive treatments, but it also protects the organisation from claims of negligence relating to the debriefing treatment.

From an organisational perspective there are two kinds of evaluation. First, there is a clinical evaluation that looks at the outcomes of the counselling and debriefing in terms of the signs and symptoms of post-traumatic stress and ideally compares this with what would have occurred where no intervention had been provided. Second, there is an organisational evaluation of the trauma support. Organisations are generally interested in the:

- reduction in days of sickness absence following a traumatic event;
- satisfaction of employees with the service provided;
- morale and attitude of employees to the organisation and customers;
- levels of medical retirements;
- instances of litigation and claims for compensation.

While it is important to ensure that the trauma support is clinically effective, the economic value in terms of reduced costs of sickness absence and medical retirements, and the improvements that can be achieved in employee morale, can have more influence on how well psychological debriefing is accepted within an organisation.

Discussion

There are many factors involved in the decision on whether to use an external or internal post-trauma support service. The decision may be determined by the size of the organisation, the level of risk and/or the availability of competent practitioners within the organisation. Where an organisation employs a large number of workers and there is a high incidence of traumatic exposure it would frequently be more cost effective to establish an internal trauma support programme than to buy the service from an external provider. The geographical dispersal of employees may also be a factor, particularly when there is a wish to provide crisis management support. If an external provider is the most appropriate option it is important that the organisation ensures that the provider has the specialist competence and qualifications to undertake the trauma care interventions and that audit and evaluation tools are used to ensure the quality of the service.

Summary: Part II

It is difficult to be precise on what constitutes a disaster or crisis. The definition depends on the perspective taken. All disasters overwhelm the resources of the person, organisation or group to cope. Therefore, to the individual concerned the death of a partner or a child in a car crash would be no less disastrous than the death of 20 people on a train or 400 on an aircraft. Organisations need to plan to deal with a wide range of crises – for example, the death of a manager from a heart attack or a disaster caused by a major fire killing and injuring a number of employees. Traditionally, organisations have not been good at addressing 'people issues' in their business continuity plans and employees are often given scant attention by business continuity managers who are more comfortable dealing with computers and floods than with people. The Health and Safety Executive guidelines on undertaking risk assessments provide a template for identifying the risks to employees and can be used by organisations wishing to develop trauma care plans.

Although it is easy to identify the primary victims of a trauma it is sometimes more difficult to be sure how many other people may be affected. The secondary trauma victims will include such groups as the emergency services, friends, first-aiders, colleagues, bystanders, families, counsellors and investigators. It is not sufficient for the organisation to provide support for the primary victims. Although the main emphasis of this book is on psychological support, it is important to recognise that social and practical support may have an even more important role to play. This is particularly true in the immediate aftermath of a disaster.

Organisations also need to be aware of the importance of communication at the time of a disaster. Traumatised employees are particularly vulnerable at these times and the intrusion of the media may make recovery more difficult where employees and their families are exposed to intrusive media coverage. On the other hand, it is important to be aware that communication within organisations and with those most closely involved in the traumatic event may provide important information that can aid recovery.

As time passes, the needs of employees can change. In the early stages it is important that the distressed person is given time to rest. Interventions that begin too early are at best ineffective and at worst harmful. There are four major stages in a trauma programme: crisis management, diffusing, debriefing and trauma counselling. Training is required to deliver these interventions effectively and the skills are not always easy to develop. One of the most important aspects of trauma care is the avoidance of the psychiatric labelling of those involved in the traumatic incident.

As the needs of organisations differ, it is important that trauma care providers are flexible in their approach to introducing trauma care programmes. Although some trauma care principles are critical, others should be adapted to the organisation. For example, in some organisations the first stages of crisis management and diffusing may be undertaken by managers or colleagues, whereas in other organisations this may be the role of an occupational health nurse or counsellor.

One of the interesting differences between organisations and researchers is the relative value each places on their measurements of success. For the researcher, this may be a change in a trauma questionnaire but for the organisation a reduction in sickness absence may be much more persuasive. It is therefore important to make sure that the needs of the organisation and the research are both represented in the evaluation criteria.

Part III

The measurement and assessment of traumatic stress in the workplace

In order to undertake assessments and evaluations of post-trauma interventions there is a need to identify appropriate evaluative tools with which to measure changes in post-traumatic stress symptoms. In Chapter 10, some of the existing tools and techniques for measuring post-trauma symptoms are described together with the difficulties that organisations are likely to face when using these tools. Chapter 11 describes the development of a new psychometric tool designed specially for use with employees affected by traumatic experiences. The new tool is called the Extended Impact of Events Scale (IES-E). The IES-E extended the original Impact of Events Scale (IES) from two to three scales by including items to assess the symptoms of arousal. Arousal is the third of the trio of diagnostic symptoms that make up the criterion for the diagnosis of PTSD. In Chapter 12, the attention moves away from measurement tools to the need for a way to assess and evaluate post-trauma interventions within the workplace. The issues surrounding the current controversy over whether the randomised controlled trial is the only true approach to establishing the effectiveness of treatments is explored and an alternative approach to the randomised controlled trial is suggested. A multiple method of research that involves the use of a range of qualitative and quantitative research tools together with the process of triangulation is suggested as a more appropriate approach to research in the workplace.

Chapter 10

Assessing psychological trauma

Introduction

This chapter describes the development of a range of psychological assessment tools used to measure the psychological impact of traumatic events on people. From the time that post-traumatic stress was first recognised as a psychiatric disorder, researchers have worked on developing instruments to assess the range and magnitude of the post-trauma symptoms (Foa *et al.* 1993; Newman *et al.* 1996). Over time, four groups of trauma assessment tools have emerged. The first measures the nature and features of the traumatic event and the extent to which it meets the Criterion A of *DSM IV* (American Psychiatric Association 1994). The next two groups examine the psychological impact of the traumatic experience on the victim using either structured interviews or self-report techniques. The final group assesses the psychobiological or psychophysiological changes brought about by the traumatic experience.

When traumatic incidents occur in the workplace, the organisation will need to undertake a number of different assessments. For example: What has been the impact on individual employees? What treatments are necessary? How effective are the interventions? Can PTSD be diagnosed clinically? It is unlikely that a single assessment tool could meet all the organisational needs. The more reliable and versatile the assessment tools in monitoring, evaluating and assessing symptoms and interventions, the more attractive the tools will be to the organisation.

Assessment of the nature and features of a traumatic event

The criteria used for defining a traumatic incident require two components to be met. First, the traumatic event must involve actual or threatened death or serious injury, or a threat to the physical integrity of self or others; and second, the person must experience feelings of intense fear, helplessness or horror (see Table 1.1, p. 10). The emphasis placed on the situational features of a traumatic incident as a determining factor for the diagnosis of PTSD has led to the development of a number of questionnaires for assessing the level of traumatic exposure. Some questionnaires have been designed to assess a range of different traumatic experiences (Vrana and Lauterback 1994) while others have been developed to assess the impact of specific traumas such as armed combat (Keane *et al.* 1989), police work (Kopel and Friedman 1999), domestic violence (Shepard and Campbell 1992) and sexual assault (Koss and Gidycz 1985).

Lifetime trauma exposure questionnaires

Research has shown that exposure to traumatic events is a more common experience than was previously thought. In fact, most people will experience at least one incident in their lives that would meet the *DSM IV* criteria for a traumatic experience (Breslau 1998). This finding has resulted in an increased use of lifetime traumatic exposure questionnaires as a means of screening people for their previous history of traumatic exposure. Lifetime trauma exposure questionnaires could be used in organisations as part of a selection process for personnel recruitment to jobs with a high risk of experiencing traumatic events. Some of the better-known trauma exposure questionnaires that are likely to be useful to organisations include the following:

Traumatic Life Events Questionnaire (TLEQ)

Kubany (1995) developed this questionnaire, which examines exposure to 17 traumatic incidents. These include natural disasters, motor vehicle crashes, physical assaults and mugging. After the traumatic events have been recorded, the individual is asked to rate the nature of the experience of the trauma in terms of the magnitude of horror, fear, helplessness and distress caused.

Traumatic Stress Schedule (TSS)

Norris (1990) developed the TSS, which is shorter than the TLEQ and quicker to administer. It involves the person completing a self-report questionnaire, which measures the impact of nine different traumatic events. These include robbery, physical assaults, sexual assaults and the loss of a loved one through an accident, murder or suicide.

Evaluation of Lifetime Stressors (ELS)

Krinsley and Weathers designed the ELS in 1995. This evaluation tool has two parts: first, there is a comprehensive self-report questionnaire and then a structured clinical interview. The results of the questionnaire form the basis of the interview.

Combat Exposure Scale (CES)

This scale was developed for use with the Armed Forces following conflict (Keane *et al.* 1989). The CES is widely used with the original version being standardised on Vietnam veterans. More recently, the scale has been adapted for use with veterans from other conflicts including the Persian Gulf, Somalia and Bosnia.

While traumatic exposure surveys and questionnaires can be used to identify the nature of an individual's exposure to traumatic incidents, these tools will not identify whether the individual was distressed or traumatised by the experience. In some organisations, workers are regularly exposed to events as part of their normal duties that would be extremely traumatic to other people (e.g. military, emergency services, health professionals). It has been shown that in most circumstances emergency workers and the military are able to deal with a range of traumatic incidents without adverse reactions (Friedman 2000a). This level of resilience to exposure to traumatic experiences is explained by the protection afforded to these workers by their mental preparation and training (Mitchell and Everly 1993). In order to assess whether an employee has been adversely affected by a traumatic incident, there is a need to undertake an assessment of the trauma symptoms. This can be done using structured clinical interviews, self-report questionnaires and psychophysiological or psychobiological assessments.

Structured clinical interviews

In clinical settings, where the accuracy of diagnosis is essential, a structured interview is a commonly used assessment technique. Structured interviews not only enable the clinician to diagnose post-traumatic stress, but also provide valuable information which can be used to assist in the development of a treatment plan. The structured interview involves the clinician systematically going through a standardised list of questions designed to assess different aspects of the traumatic stress diagnosis. The structured interview approach has been adopted to reduce diagnostic error by ensuring that all relevant trauma symptoms are fully investigated. Two well-established structured interviews are described below.

Structured Clinical Interview for DSM IV (SCID)

The SCID was developed by Spitzer *et al.* (1990) and is one of the most widely used general psychiatric diagnostic tools. The PTSD element of the SCID (SCID-PTSD) is made up of 19 items and examines in turn all of the PTSD diagnostic criteria. The SCID provides information about the presence of both current and lifetime diagnoses so clinicians can determine whether someone who currently does not meet the *DSM IV* criteria for PTSD may have done so in the past. SCID-PTSD is highly correlated with other PTSD measures (Kulka *et al.* 1990).

CAPS-1 Scale

This scale (Blake *et al.* 1990, 1995) was developed as an expansion of the SCID scale. The CAPS scale is recognised as one of the most accurate and comprehensive tools that are available to assess PTSD (Wilson and Keane 1997). The CAPS-1 was designed to avoid the limitations of other structured interviews by including criteria for assessing both the intensity and frequency of symptoms. In practice, this means that a person who has occasional intense symptoms can meet the diagnostic criteria as can a person who has frequent but less extreme symptoms. The CAPS-1 questions cover the 17 primary PTSD symptoms plus the additional 13 associated items described in *DSM IV*. Each area assessed in CAPS-1 has clear behavioural descriptions to assist in the rating of symptom intensity and frequency. There has been a growing trend to use the SCID scale for a comprehensive diagnostic assessment but to substitute the CAPS-1 for the SCID-PTSD to carry out the PTSD diagnosis (Friedman 2000a).

Unfortunately, structured interviews are time-consuming and can only be undertaken by a qualified psychiatrist or psychologist. Where the need is to screen a large number of individuals following a major incident or disaster, a self-report survey is a more appropriate tool. Self-report questionnaires can be administered and scored by trained practitioners in a fraction of the time required for structured interviewing.

Self-report surveys

Self-report surveys have a number of advantages over structured clinical interviews. These include the avoidance of subjective interpretation of responses by interviewers, the reduced need for qualified clinicians and the reduced cost and ease of administering the survey in comparison with structured interviews.

Penn Inventory

One of the most frequently used self-report surveys is the Penn Inventory (Hammerberg 1992). This questionnaire is made up of 26 items derived from data obtained from combat veterans. The Penn Inventory has been adapted for use with a wider range of trauma victims, however, it has been criticised for its reliability in assessing post-traumatic stress in female and non-veteran groups (Norris and Riad 1997) and for its inability to discriminate between symptoms of traumatic stress and depression.

The Purdue PTSD Scale-Revised (PPTSD-R)

This scale (Lauterbach and Vrana 1996) is based on the *DSM IV* criteria with 17 items each assessing a feature of the *DSM IV* diagnostic criteria. The scale was developed using the experiences of undergraduates who had been exposed to a range of traumatic incidents. Responses are scored on a five-point scale for frequency of occurrence. In studies undertaken to assess the reliability and validity of this scale there were high correlations with other post-trauma scales and a low correlation with scores on questionnaires measuring anxiety or depression.

Mississippi and Revised Civilian Mississippi Scales

The Mississippi Scale (Keane *et al.* 1988) and the Revised Civilian Mississippi Scale (Norris and Perilla 1996) are widely used self-assessment scales. The Mississippi Scale was designed for combat veterans while the revised scale was developed for a wide range of trauma victims. The items are scored on a five-point scale, which assesses diagnostic features of *DSM*. Although the reliability data on the original scale is good, the reliability data for the revised civilian version is not yet available.

Impact of Events Scale (IES)

The IES (Horowitz *et al.* 1979) is one of the earliest self-report measures for post-traumatic stress, and assesses re-experience and avoidance symptoms. There are 15 items in the scale: 7 assess re-experience and 8 avoidance symptoms. The items are scored on a four-point scale that relates to the frequency of occurrence of the symptom. The IES has been shown to discriminate between trauma-tised groups and non-traumatised groups of subjects (Alexander 1993; Bryant and Harvey 1996). It has the advantage of being quick to administer and of having wide application in a range of trauma situations. The major disadvantage is that it fails to assess arousal – a major group of trauma symptoms.

Self-report questionnaires have been criticised due to the transparency of the items, which may lead to victim response bias (Lyons and Keane 1992). In addition, the specificity of self-report questionnaires makes comparison between victim groups difficult (Weathers *et al.* 1997).

Assessment and the reactivation of trauma symptoms

Problems can be encountered when using structured interviews and self-report questionnaires. The process of asking questions about a traumatic experience is often distressing to the person being assessed and trauma victims frequently find themselves re-experiencing their traumatic incident with the result that post-trauma symptoms that may have been absent for months or years are reactivated. It is not surprising therefore that many victims of traumatic experience dislike and avoid trauma assessments (Fowlie and Alexander 1992; Litz *et al.* 1992). The distress caused by the assessment process can lead the trauma victim to record higher levels of trauma symptoms in the assessment than they would normally experience in everyday life. This effect can result in significant distortions in the recording of symptoms (Briere 1997).

Psychophysiological and psychobiological assessments

In recent years, there has been a growth in techniques to assess traumatic exposure by measuring biological changes. Psycho-physiological assessment typically involves measuring changes to heart rate, blood pressure, muscle tension, skin conductance and peripheral temperature. Most psychophysiological tests involve the presentation of standardised or personalised reminders of potentially traumatic experiences while measuring one or more physiological response. For example, a victim of a road traffic crash may have their blood pressure and heart rate measured while they are exposed to a series of photographs of crashed vehicles. Studies using individually tailored scripts have reported increased skin conductance, heart rate and electromyogram waves in PTSD subjects when compared with subjects without PTSD (Orr *et al.* 1995). More recently, there has been an increasing interest in the psycho-biological assessment of traumatic stress. Biological studies have shown that PTSD is characterised by a progressive sensitisation of biological systems, in particular the hypothalamic-pituitary-adrenal system (Yehuda 1998). The changes that occur following a traumatic event are very different to those found in individuals suffering from other forms of chronic stress or depression (Yehuda *et al.* 1995). Although psychophysiological and psychobiological assessment tools reduce the likelihood of re-traumatising vulnerable trauma victims, there are a number of limitations to their use, including the requirement for medical equipment and trained medical technicians to undertake the assessments. Therefore these techniques are only likely to be used with individuals who are suspected of suffering from PTSD and not for screening new individuals or as a normal part of a trauma care programme.

Organisational need to measure traumatic stress

In the past ten years, there has been progress in the development of reliable and valid traumatic stress assessment tools, however these developments have not yet addressed the needs of organisations. Clinician-administered interviews, despite their accuracy of diagnosis, are not appropriate for general use in the workplace, as they are time-consuming and can only be administered by a trained clinician. More useful to organisations are self-report questionnaires, which take between 10 to 15 minutes to complete, and are relatively easy to score and evaluate. However, apart from the armed services, there is a lack of questionnaires designed specifically for use with employees.

In organisations, there is a need to identify vulnerable employees and to provide the appropriate level of information and care for them. In order to achieve these objectives, organisations need to have access to measurement tools that:

- predict individuals who are likely to experience PTSD;
- establish background levels of post-traumatic stress in the workforce;
- monitor the rehabilitation of traumatised employees;
- evaluate the effectiveness of specific traumatic stress interventions;
- monitor the effectiveness of trauma care programmes;
- provide clinical evidence of the severity of post-traumatic stress suffered by an employee.

In all but the last item in this list, self-administered questionnaires are likely to be the measurement of choice for organisations due to their flexibility, cost and speed of administration. However, when clinical evidence is required for compensation claims or in considering the best way to handle a complex trauma case, the structured clinical interview may be a more appropriate tool. The failure to develop post-traumatic stress measurement tools which are appropriate for use in organisations has resulted in a general failure to evaluate the effectiveness of trauma care programmes (Rick *et al.* 1998b).

Discussion

The different tools that are available to assess different aspects of traumatic stress should not be regarded as competing but rather as meeting different, specific needs. There is a clear need for organisations to undertake assessments of those roles that carry a risk of exposure to traumatic incidents. Part of this involves ensuring that selection and recruitment processes identify applicants that have a predisposition to develop post-traumatic stress. Following a traumatic incident, the use of a specially designed questionnaire or survey which identifies employees who were exposed to particularly distressing or horrendous experiences would be useful in ensuring that attention is given to those employees in greatest need. A simple self-report questionnaire can be used by the organisation to identify those employees who have developed post-traumatic stress responses and to monitor their recovery. Although most employees would be expected to recover from their experience, a few may go on to develop PTSD. For these employees the use of structured clinical interviews or psychophysiological or psychobiological assessments may be appropriate. However, these more complex assessments would normally be undertaken outside the working environment.

Chapter 11

Developing a trauma scale for organisations[1]

Introduction

Organisations need to be able to assess the magnitude and range of the psychological harm suffered by employees exposed to a traumatic event at work. This assessment will enable them to meet their duty of care by identifying which employees require psychological help and to make sure that appropriate psychological support and treatment is provided. Organisations also need to be able to monitor employees at intervals following the incident to identify any delayed trauma responses and to track the effectiveness of the treatment and rehabilitation programme. In this chapter, the development and validation of a traumatic stress questionnaire, the Extended Impact of Events Scale (IES-E) is described. The IES-E was created for use with traumatised employees and is an extension to the Impact of Events Scale (IES) (Horowitz *et al.* 1979), taking the 15 items from the original scale and adding 8 new items to measure arousal symptoms. Four studies are described in which the structure, reliability and discriminant validity of the extended scale are established. The studies use data gathered from traumatised employees who had been exposed to a range of traumatic incidents including armed raids, serious threats and physical assaults.

Impact of Events Scale (IES)

In 1979, Horowitz published a short self-report measure for measuring the levels of symptoms following exposure to a traumatic stressor

1 (Based on Tehrani, N., Cox, T. and Cox S. (2002) Assessing the Impact of traumatic incidents: the development of an extended impact of events scale, *Counselling Psychology Quarterly*, 15(2): 191–200. www.tandf.co.uk

(Horowitz *et al.* 1979). This scale was the IES and had been created using the clinical observations of the typical responses of individuals who had suffered a traumatic experience. The statements by these victims of trauma to describe their symptoms were gathered and analysed. Horowitz found that the responses fell into two clusters. One described a range of intrusive thoughts and feelings such as 'pictures of it kept popping into my mind' and the other described avoidance behaviours such as 'I stayed away from reminders'. The reliability of the IES was tested using a test-retest procedure and the reliability was found satisfactory with coefficients of .87 for re-experience and .79 for avoidance. A later validation study (Zilberg *et al.* 1982) showed that the IES discriminated between individuals with post-traumatic stress and a control group which consisted of patients with anxiety. The IES was also found to be sensitive to changes in clinical status over time.

Since its development the IES has been used in a wide range of settings including natural disasters (Anderson and Manuel *et al.* 1994), car crashes (Jeavons 1998), sex abuse (Thompson *et al.* 1995) and with firefighters (McCarroll *et al.* 1995). Due to its versatility, validity and speed of administration, the IES has become one of the most popular questionnaires used to measure post-trauma reactions. Unfortunately, the IES has a major limitation in that it focuses on only two of the three diagnostic criteria for PTSD: re-experience and avoidance. The third criterion, arousal, is not measured. This failing has led many researchers to augment the IES with other question-naires such as the General Health Questionnaire (GHQ) (Goldberg 1978), the Symptoms Checklist-90-R (SCL-90-R) (Derogatis 1983) and the Hospital Anxiety Depression Scale (HADS) (Snaith and Zigmond 1994) as a means of gaining data on psychophysiological arousal. It would seem appropriate therefore to consider the possibil-ity of extending the IES scale to include items that test the presence of arousal rather than rely on other psychometric tests. In response to this, Weiss and Marmer (1997) developed a revised IES question-naire (IES-R). Marmer selected additional items by analysing other traumatic stress scales rather than taking the naturalistic approach used by Horowitz in the development of the original scale. While most of the items selected by Marmer for the IES-R were related to arousal, one item measures dissociation, a symptom not associated with arousal in *DSM IV*. Therefore, the decision was taken to extend the IES questionnaire using a similar method to that used by Horowitz and to adhere to the symptoms described in *DSM IV*.

The first study reports on the psychometric evaluation of the extended version of the IES (IES-E) using exploratory factor analysis (EFA) and related techniques. This study largely concerns the structure of an IES extended to include items related to arousal. The study tested for two models of trauma response, the first based on a single general factor and the second on three specific factors. The second study tested the ability of the IES-E to discriminate between subjects reporting highly memorable positive and negative life events.

Study 1: factor analysis of IES-E data from stressful work incidents

Subjects

The subjects in the first study were drivers or crew members of a security transportation organisation that handled cash and other valuable items. The subjects had all been involved in and formally reported a traumatic event at work during 1993/4. A range of incidents with different levels of severity had been reported and 170 questionnaires were distributed, of which 105 were returned satisfactorily completed (response rate 62 per cent). The final sample was predominantly male (n = 93) and ages ranged from 20 to 60 years with the sample being evenly distributed between the two boundaries.

Procedure

The names of employees who had formally reported traumatic incidents were obtained from the personnel department. Each employee was sent a letter explaining the purpose of the study and requesting their cooperation in the prompt completion of the IES-E, which was enclosed. The letter also emphasised the confidential nature of the study and reminded employees of the additional sources of help that were available for those who wanted further counselling or support.

Measures

The questionnaire was divided into two sections. The first collected basic demographic information and information on the nature of the incident and its severity – for example, whether firearms were involved or the employee had suffered any physical injuries. The IES-E was in the second section of the questionnaire and consisted of the original IES with eight additional items that had been identified as the most commonly reported descriptions of arousal symptoms provided by traumatised employees. These items were then checked against the items used by Horowitz *et al.* (1979) and for theoretical validity against *DSM IV*. The additional items selected were: 'I feel down and depressed for no reason', 'I experience wide mood swings', 'I experience tenseness in my body', 'I am irritable with others', 'I have a tendency to avoid others', 'I jump or get startled by sudden noises' and 'I try to avoid situations or places'. Both the IES and the additional items were scored using a five-point Likert-type scale, tapping frequency of occurrence. The scores ranged from 0 (never) to 4 (most of the time).

Results

The IES and the additional items were combined into an extended IES-E and submitted to an exploratory factor analysis (EFA) (Ferguson and Cox 1993). The EFA process involves three stages: pre-analysis checks, factor extraction and factor rotation.

Pre-analysis checks

One of the most important means of achieving a stable factor structure is to have a large enough sample. The size of sample required is determined by the number of variables and factor saturation (Kline 1986). Here the requirement is for a sample size of at least 100. This criteria was met as there were 105 employees in the study.

The appropriateness of the correlation matrix for factor analysis was established using the Kaiser-Meyer-Olkin (KMO) test of sampling adequacy and the Bartlett test of Sphericity (BS). The KMO is conducted to establish whether the associations between the variables in the correlation matrix can be accounted for by a smaller set of factors (Ferguson and Cox 1993). A minimum value of 0.5 is required (Dziuban and Shirkey 1974). The BS is conducted to test the null hypothesis that no relationships exist between any of the variables. A significant test statistic (based on Chi square) indicates that there are discoverable relationships in the data. The data conformed to pre-analysis checks. The results of the KMO and BS tests were 0.89 and 1307.98 (p = 0.001) respectively. These results indicate that there is a correlation matrix that is appropriate for factor analysis.

Factor extraction and rotation

Of the many available heuristics for determining the number of factors to be considered, the Kaiser 1 heuristic (K1) was used. The K1 extracts as many factors as there are eigenvalues greater than 1. Eigenvalues provide an estimate of the amount of variance associated with a factor. Table 11.1 presents the K1 summary of eigenvalues greater than 1 and identifies three factors.

The existence of three factors was confirmed by the Scree test (Cattell 1966) and a three-factor model solution was finally accepted following principal components analysis with oblique rotation.

Three factors were extracted from the unrotated solution with a strong first factor that suggests the presence of a general higher-order factor. This was confirmed by the presence of substantive correlations between the three factors. The scale composition and factor loadings on the IES-E are presented in Table 11.2.

The three-factor model was considered further using an oblique rotation. In this model, the analysis showed that one of the original IES items, 'I avoided letting myself get upset when I thought about it or was reminded of it', had moved from the avoidance dimension to the intrusion dimension. The internal reliability of the three scales was assessed using Cronbach's alpha (Cronbach 1951) and was found to be high (see Table 11.2).

Table 11.1 A summary of the eigenvalues

Factor	Eigenvalue	% of var.	Cum. %
1	12.38	53.8	53.8
2	1.97	8.6	62.4
3	1.27	5.5	67.9
4*	0.97	4.2	72.2

* Rejected as the eigenvalue is less than 1.

Table 11.2 Summary of the loadings from the oblique factor rotation

Factor	Statement	Factor 1	Factor 2	Factor 3	Alpha value
Avoidance	I felt as if it had not happened or was not real.	0.81			0.91
	I tried not to think about it.	0.81			
	I tried not to talk about it.	0.75			
	My feelings about it were kind of numb.	0.64			
	I stayed away from any reminders.	0.53			
	I tried to remove it from my memory.	0.52			
	I was aware that I still had a lot of feelings about it, but I did not deal with them.	0.47		−0.45	
Arousal	I felt down or depressed for no reason.		0.92		0.92
	I experienced wide mood swings.		0.86		
	I experienced tenseness in my body.		0.83	0.47	
	I was irritable with others.		0.83		
	I had a tendency to avoid other people.		0.79		
	I jumped or got startled by sudden noises.		0.76		
	I avoided situations or places.		0.57		
Re-experience	I thought about it when I did not mean to.			−0.80	0.93
	Pictures about it popped into my mind.			−0.73	
	I had waves of strong feelings about it.			−0.69	
	I had dreams about it.			−0.59	
	I had trouble falling asleep or staying asleep.			−0.55	
	Other things kept making me think about it.			−0.51	
	Any reminder brought back feelings about it.	0.42		−0.49	
	I avoided letting myself get upset when I thought about it or was reminded of it.			−0.46	

Descriptive statistics for the three factors

The variables that comprised the three-factor scales were then summed to produce three variables: avoidance, arousal and re-experience. Descriptive statistics were then calculated for these three variables (see Table 11.3). The correlations of the three variable scales are shown in Table 11.4.

This data offers two types of model: the first based on a (global) trauma reaction measure and the second involving specific measures of avoidance, arousal and re-experience. The emergence of three factors from the IES-E highlights the need for an additional dimension to the original IES – one that measures the arousal symptoms commonly found following a traumatic incident.

Study 2: discriminative validity of the IES-E

This study compared the scores of subjects on the IES-E when recalling a major life event of either a positive or negative nature, which had occurred during the last year.

Subjects and procedure

Respondents were asked to recall the most significant major life event that had occurred over the last year and rate it as either positive or negative. Once subjects had identified and rated a life event,

Table 11.3 Descriptive statistics for arousal, re-experience and avoidance

Factor	Mean	N	Std Dev	Kurtosis
Arousal	8.0	105	6.1	20.0
Re-experience	12.7	105	9.6	27.0
Avoidance	6.9	105	6.8	21.0

Table 11.4 Correlation matrix for the three variable scales

Factor	Arousal	Re-experience	Avoidance
Arousal	1.00		
Re-experience	0.70	1.00	
Avoidance	0.64	0.80	1.00

they were asked to complete the IES-E. None of the subjects had formally reported a stressful work-related event in the previous year. A total of 103 subjects took part in Study 2: 52 recalled negative events and 48 recalled positive events. The ages of the subjects ranged from 21 to 60 years. There were 35 male subjects and 63 female subjects (5 were missing). This sample roughly matched the age of the subjects in Study 1 although in this study there was a higher proportion of female subjects.

Analysis

A series of independent sample t-tests were carried out to compare the means of the two groups for each scale. The results showed that positive events could be distinguished from negative events in terms of all the IES-E dimensions (see Table 11.5). There was no evidence of age or gender effects.

The use of the IES-E in the workplace

Since its development the IES-E has been used in a number of organisations to assess the magnitude of employees' responses to traumatic incidents and later as a way of evaluating the effectiveness of organisational and psychological interventions in the rehabilitation process (Walpole 2000; Tehrani et al. 2001). The IES-E has proved to be acceptable to employees, being easy to understand and quick to complete and score. On average the IES-E takes seven minutes to complete and can be scored in around one minute. When used in a

Table 11.5 Summary of the results of independent t-tests of the three dimensions and general factor

Factor	Event	Mean	Std Dev	t-value	df	2-tail sig.
General factor	Positive	14.9	12.6	−9.3	96	0.001
	Negative	41.2	15.1			
Avoidance	Positive	2.0	2.7	−13.8	92	0.001
	Negative	13.9	5.3			
Arousal	Positive	2.3	3.7	−7.6	96	0.001
	Negative	10.0	6.0			
Re-experience	Positive	10.7	8.6	−4.5	98	0.001
	Negative	17.9	7.3			

pre-debriefing educational session it provides a language and framework that helps the traumatised employees recognise that the responses they are experiencing are normal following a traumatic incident. When used as an evaluation tool, the IES-E allows trauma practitioners to assess the progress of their clients, enabling trauma programmes to be evaluated. Where organisations have used the IES-E for making initial assessment of trauma symptoms it has been found that the data can also help in the design of individual treatment programmes (Tehrani *et al.* 2001).

Discussion

The first study confirmed the IES-E as a three-dimension scale providing a comprehensive measurement of post-trauma reactions consistent with the symptomatology described in *DSM IV*. While the factor analysis supported the Horowitz *et al.* (1979) sub-dimensions of intrusion and avoidance, one item from the IES moved from the avoidance scale to the intrusion scale. It is not possible to say why this occurred but this movement might be due to cultural differences in how the item was interpreted. Horowitz used American subjects while this study involved British subjects. The factor analysis confirmed that the additional items introduced into the IES formed a new dimension measuring arousal symptoms that was statistically distinct from the avoidance and intrusion dimensions.

The second study established the discriminant validity of both the measurement models deriving from the IES-E. The IES-E was shown to distinguish between major positive and negative life events on all three dimensions and on the global trauma scale.

It is interesting to note that the scores from the respondents in Study 2 were generally higher than those found from the respondents in Study 1. A number of possible reasons for this difference can be suggested. First, many traumatised individuals use avoidance as a way of dealing with their experience and therefore the depressed scores were a result of avoidance. Second, victims of work-related stressful events may suppress their responses because of social or organisational pressures, particularly in relation to career development or job security. Third, it is possible that a workforce that is trained to deal with traumatic incidents may not be traumatised by events which would cause extreme distress in untrained individuals.

Although some work has begun on testing the IES-E in organisations it is necessary to undertake more evaluations of the tool, testing its acceptability to trauma victim groups, practitioners and organisations.

Chapter 12

Difficulties of evaluating post-trauma interventions in organisations

Introduction

The questions 'Does it work?' and 'Is it better than other interventions?' are central to evaluation research and of great importance to organisations providing health care programmes for their employees. There is a major difference between evaluation research and other forms of research, in that evaluation research has the needs of consumers as its primary focus (Dane 1990). In post-trauma care there are a number of individuals and groups of consumers with an interest in whether the current interventions of trauma care management, debriefing and trauma counselling can provide any benefit. Each group will have opinions on the measurements of success criteria to be used to test the effectiveness of the intervention programme. In this chapter, the success criteria of a number of interested consumers will be examined, together with the existing methods of evaluating post-trauma interventions. Some of the challenges in undertaking post-trauma research in organisations will be described including the problems of dealing with organisational change, a lack of resources and short timescales. The current state of research into trauma counselling and debriefing is described together with some suggestions on what might be done to resolve the current difficulties.

What is success?

The introduction of evidence-based practice (EBP) as a means of helping practitioners and their clients to make decisions on which type of treatment is most effective, and for which people, has increased interest in the evaluation of psychological interventions (Department of Health 2001). The aim of a clinical assessment is more than looking at an intervention in isolation; rather, it seeks to measure the value of the intervention within the wider context of a total service or approach (Robson 2001). Although much evaluation research has been involved in looking at the outcomes of specific interventions, it is important to remember that an evaluation has two areas of focus: process and outcome. Process evaluations involve examining such things as the promotion, communication, procedures and training that take place as part of the intervention or programme. An understanding of process is a vital part of any evaluation, as without this the true findings of the evaluation may be obscured or misunderstood. The second area of evaluation is outcomes. The outcome is the extent to which the intervention or programme met its stated objectives. While outcome evaluations are important, emphasis should be placed on the evaluation of the organisational processes, such as the methods of recording of traumatic incidents, the timing of interventions, involvement of managers and support of victims of traumatic events. It is possible that organisational processes hold the key to the success or failure of organisational care programmes (Griffiths 1999). The recognition that there may be different and sometimes competing outcome objectives to the evaluation of trauma care makes the planning and agreement of the nature of the clinical evaluations important. Trauma care programmes will have a number of groups of interested parties who will want to know what is evaluated and a view on what kind of success criteria they would see as appropriate. Some of these groups are:

- Trauma victims and their families
- Victim's managers
- Organisations
- Unions
- Practitioners (psychologists, counsellors and debriefers)

- Trauma service providers
- Researchers
- Health trusts
- Lawyers
- Government agencies
- Department of Health

It is highly unlikely that the interests of each group will be the same. In most evaluation exercises, some groups will be pleased and others critical of the process and outcome findings (Berk and Rossi 1990).

For organisations, the success criteria for a trauma care programme might be:

- appropriateness of the programme for the organisation;

- levels of user satisfaction;
- reductions in sickness absence and medical retirements;
- quality of the training materials;
- quality of the professional support;
- cost benefits of the programme.

In contrast, researchers interested in undertaking clinical assessment would be looking for outcomes such as reductions in symptoms. To be acceptable to these researchers, the results would have to be obtained using the principles of a true experimental design involving the use of randomised controlled trials. Foa *et al.* (2000b) describe the features of a well-controlled study as one that involves:

- clearly defined target symptom or syndrome;
- measures with good psychometric properties to measure symptom severity;
- blind evaluators to prevent expectancy and demand bias;
- trained assessors;
- treatment programmes that are replicable and specific;
- unbiased random assignment to treatment conditions;
- the use of treatment adherence ratings.

As the evaluation of a trauma care intervention can be undertaken against a number of different criteria, it is possible that an intervention will have a positive evaluation against one set of criteria and a negative evaluation against another. It is therefore important to establish an agreed set of criteria for the organisation and the researchers before the evaluation is undertaken.

How can success be measured?

Clinical success can be measured in a number of ways. Humphris (1999) described a continuum of ways to gather evidence. This ranged from quantitative to qualitative methods (see Figure 12.1). However, for some researchers the only acceptable model of research is the randomised controlled trial, with all other approaches being regarded as inferior (Eccles *et al.* 1998). Unfortunately, in the real world, the laboratory standards of experimental control are rarely possible and therefore other methods of evaluation are required to take account of the more complex organisational environment.

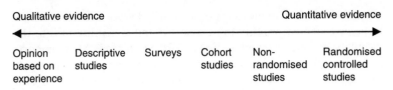

Figure 12.1 The continuum of evidence (Humphris 1999)

Randomised controlled trials

The most commonly published research literature on evaluating the effectiveness of psychotherapeutic interventions uses randomised controlled trials and standardised psychometric questionnaires. Randomised controlled trials are regarded as the research gold standard and involve two main elements. First, the selection of a random sample of subjects is taken from a known population. The random selection process allows the use of well-established statistical methods in making generalisations from the findings from the sample to the whole population. Second, the random allocation of subjects to different experimental conditions allows for an indication of causal relationships. Unfortunately, it is difficult to achieve representative samples from a known group or to randomly allocate subjects to different experimental conditions. This is particularly true when the subjects are traumatised employees. There are also considerable legal and ethical problems for organisations in allocating employees to working conditions that will randomly traumatise them and then randomly assigning those traumatised employees to treatment or non-treatment groups.

Quasi-experiments (non-randomised controlled studies)

In response to these 'real life' problems, alternative experimental approaches have had to be developed to the overly strict controlled trial conditions. These solutions have to recognise the limitations of working in organisations and employ less stringent requirements for the allocation and sampling of subjects. Fortunately, there are alternative research designs known as quasi-experiments (QEs) which have been derived from the work of Campbell and Stanley (1963). Campbell and Stanley describe QEs as 'a research design involving an experimental approach but where random assignment to treatment and compression groups has not been used'. The QE is valuable because it allows a hypothesis to be tested, cause and effects to be investigated, validity to be assessed and generalisations to the populations and different settings to be attempted. Most importantly, the QE is suitable to be undertaken outside a laboratory setting. Despite the attraction of this approach many researchers regard the QE as second best (Judd *et al.* 1991) and only to be considered if a controlled trial is impossible. Cook and Campbell (1979) reject this attitude, preferring to compare and contrast the relative advantages and disadvantages of controlled trials and QEs.

Two QE designs are particularly useful in organisations:

- Pre- and post-testing of experimental and comparison groups selected on some other basis rather than random assignment. In this design, care is taken to select the two groups based on at least two matching variables (e.g. pre-score, exposure to trauma, age).
- Interrupted time series design, in which a number of matched experimental groups are treated with the same intervention at different points in time. Measurements are made on regular occasions during the whole period. The measurements involve all groups, allowing inter-group, comparisons to be made both within and between groups, before and after the experimental intervention.

Surveys

The main difference between a survey and an experiment is the fact that surveys lack any interventions designed to bring about a change. The typical survey aims to be passive in that it seeks to describe and analyse an existing state of affairs. The survey examines a sample of individual responses not in their own right but as a means to gaining an understanding of the population from which they are drawn. Surveys may be used to find out how employees view a trauma care programme within an organisation. They may identify stress hazards within the organisation (Cox and Griffiths 1999) or the incidence of whole-life exposures to traumatic experiences (Breslau 1998). Surveys provide evidence that is easy for business managers to understand, and because of the ease of collection may involve large numbers of participants. Surveys can collect three kinds of information (Dane 1990): a) facts, including demographic features such as age, sex, education; b) opinions, such as individual preferences, feelings or intentions; and c) behaviours, such as how much alcohol is drunk a week.

Cohort studies

Cohort studies take groups of individuals and study them over a period of time. These studies can be retrospective or prospective. In retrospective studies, the subjects are asked to recall information from the past. One example of a retrospective study involved the interview victims of violent crime and examination of their current levels of emotional affect (Davis and Friedman 1985). Prospective studies require the researchers to decide upon the evidence that they are going to collect from a particular group of subjects. An example involved survivors of civilian attacks. These individuals were examined for their level of dissociation immediately after the attack. The group was then tracked for a period of six months. The result showed that those suffering dissociation had a higher level of PTSD than those who did not dissociate (Shalev *et al.* 1996).

Case studies

In the past, case studies were considered as 'soft options' only useful for generating ideas that could then be tested by more rigorous experimentation (e.g. Campbell and Stanley 1963). However, this view is changing and case studies are beginning to be seen by some as a bedrock of scientific investigation (Bromley 1986). Case studies have a potential to contribute to knowledge and understanding which is highly relevant to therapeutic practice (McLeod 1994). They involve the study of groups of individuals and programmes as well as single individual cases. The value of case studies as opposed to large-scale experimental studies is that they:

- provide information that is immediately applicable to the therapeutic relationship;
- are well suited to make sense of the processes of change;
- are flexible and can accommodate situations where the researcher may not have or may not wish to have control over the behaviour of the subject of the study or little control over the amount or type of data being collected (McLeod 1994).

Case studies can be used to explore, to describe and to explain

(Yin 1994), and are most useful when 'how' and 'why' questions are being asked, particularly when the experimenter has little control over events. There are a number of different types of case study, ranging from qualitative narrative case studies to single case quantitative studies. In narrative case studies the story told by the traumatised person is analysed using qualitative techniques to elicit and analyse the descriptive account (Yalom 1989). Single case experiments are used to evaluate therapeutic change using the case study approach (Scott and Stradling 1992a). Single case quantitative studies use quantitative techniques to trace changes that take place during individual therapy over the duration of the therapeutic process (Hill *et al.* 1983).

Opinion based on experience

The use of expert panels and clinical experience takes a rather lowly place in the hierarchy of evidence accepted by the Department of Health (Eccles *et al.* 1998). The problem with clinical experience and practice is that it may not relate to whole populations but only to the people or situations that the clinician has experienced. Where a panel of experts meet to form a consensus there can be some major pitfalls. It is sometimes found that consensus is that of the loudest voice, the hidden agenda or economic advantages rather than one that supports a particular view (Humphris 1999). One area where the use of expert opinions has had an important part to play is the diagnostic criteria developed for PTSD in *DSM IV* (American Psychiatric Association 1994). The criteria for post-traumatic stress were initially established through debate. The debate was then followed by field studies undertaken by an expert group of clinicians under the direction of a lead professional and under the auspices of the American Psychiatric Association.

Difficulties in undertaking research in organisations

Carrying out experiments in organisations is almost impossible, and even carrying out QEs may be too much to ask (Griffiths 1999). Even when research is possible, it requires the researcher to have a range of skills not always taught in academic courses on research design and methods. When undertaking research in organisations it is important for researchers to understand that there needs to be a balance of benefit between the research and the operation of the business. Researchers who are only comfortable working in the pure environment of the laboratory are unlikely to be happy working in the constantly changing world of the business manager. Researchers need to recognise that the purpose of the organisation is not to provide the researcher with an interesting working environment conducive to the research. Instead, the researcher should recognise that he or she is privileged to have an opportunity to undertake action research in the real world. Robson (2001) provides some advice for researchers working in organisations which includes the need for:

- sensitivity to the environment in which the study is to take place;
- flexibility in your approach to research;
- ability to sell the research ideas to the organisation;
- ability to sell the findings of the research;
- adoption of research methods suitable for the organisation;
- a high level of communication and interaction skills.

In research relating to trauma interventions, it is possible that the researchers and the business managers will be looking for different outcomes. The researcher may wish to establish whether a particular intervention can be demonstrated to bring about a reduction in post-trauma symptoms using a recognised clinical measurement tool. Business managers are more likely to be interested in the levels of employee satisfaction recorded by users of trauma care programmes and want to know whether the programmes have brought about a reduction in the levels of sickness absence.

Current research into trauma

Considerable effort has gone into researching the outcomes of trauma debriefing and counselling. However, little research has been published on trauma counselling and debriefing taking place within organisations. This may be because of the current emphasis on randomised controlled trials as the only research methodology acceptable in systematic reviews of research (Wessley et al. 1998). Recently there have been serious criticisms of the systematic reviews for failing to assess the quality of the controlled trials involved in their meta-analysis: 'If the raw material is flawed then the conclusions of the systematic review cannot be trusted' (Juni et al. 2001). This issue is particularly important in the case of post-traumatic stress and psychological debriefing. In making a judgement on the quality of a controlled trial, a number of common deficiencies have been identified (Pocock 1983):

- inadequate definition of eligible subjects;
- inadequate definition of treatment schedules;
- inadequate definition of methods of evaluation;
- lack of appropriate control group;
- failure to randomise subjects to alternative treatments;
- lack of objectivity in subject evaluation;
- failure to use blinding techniques (when appropriate);
- too few subjects.

Dyregrov (1998) identified a large number of methodological flaws in the studies reported in the Cochran Report on debriefing (Wessley *et al.* 1998) and these concerns have been acknowledged in the recently produced guidelines on evidence-based practice (EBP) records (Department of Health 2001). This supports the notion that controlled trials may not always be the best approach to dealing with complex issues such as post-traumatic stress and that more effort should go into developing alternative approaches to research methodology.

A way forward

The problems that face researchers and organisations remain. How do we know that what we are doing works? It would appear that the answer does not lie with a purist approach to research as might be suggested in the Cochran Report. Rather, the evidence suggests that there should be more work undertaken on trying to develop a range of experimental tools designed to work alongside each other in a multiple method approach. Such tools can include a range of qualitative and quantitative designs. The decision on which tools should be used should be based on their utility and effectiveness in dealing with the issues in real-world settings rather than on some notion of experimental superiority. One of the ways that this multiple method approach can be achieved is through the technique of triangulation. This provides a mechanism by which separate pieces of evidence from different sources can be brought together as a means of improving the effectiveness of the study and the level of confidence in the findings (Wilson 1999). Using this approach, evidence would need to be gathered from at least three different domains, the results from one source of evidence providing a means for testing another source of evidence. If two sources give the same results then, to some extent, they cross-validate each other.

Discussion

Despite the current debate, trauma care programmes adopted by organisations meet a number of needs. First, they enable the organisation to deal with the traumatic event in a systematic way, ensuring that the needs of employees and of the business are met. Second, they demonstrate an organisational commitment to employees and their well-being. Third, they provide an opportunity for employees to share their experiences with their peers in order to increase awareness and build a shared understanding of the meaning of the incident to the working team. Finally, they help the organisation to identify those employees that need additional help. It is difficult to know exactly where trauma care is going in the future. It seems strange that researchers have given so much emphasis to certain elements of trauma care programmes such as debriefing, rather than examining the benefits of an integrated trauma care approach. Perhaps there is a need for organisations to be more involved in telling the academic world what they regard as success criteria. In this way, a balance can be achieved between the clinical and the organisational benefits of a trauma care programme. Despite some limitations there are clear indications that organisational debriefing is an effective and valued part of trauma care programmes. Demands for the withdrawal of this approach without considering the positive evidence gathered in organisational settings are premature and may lead to countless employees suffering psychological symptoms unnecessarily.

Summary: Part III

It is important to have assessment tools to produce reliable and valid information to support the use of psychological interventions. A large number of assessment tools have been developed for use with victims of post-traumatic stress. These tools can be used to measure the nature and magnitude of the traumatic exposure and assessments range from a detailed structured interview undertaken by a clinician to a simple self-report questionnaire handed out and completed by a large number of trauma victims.

Despite the number of tools, none had been developed for use with employees. This was a concern for organisations that required a measurement tool to help in the identification of employees who required special care or support. Organisations were also interested in anything that would help them select employees who would be resilient to the impact of traumatic exposure in those roles where total elimination was not possible.

Ideally, the organisations wanted a self-report tool which was simple for the employees and which would not require a psychologist to interpret. This need resulted in the development of a new questionnaire that was an extension of an existing one which was highly regarded by researchers into post-traumatic stress. The problem with the original questionnaire, the IES, was that it only measured two of the three diagnostic features of post-traumatic stress. Therefore, the IES had to be augmented with other questionnaires in order to measure the missing feature, arousal. In order to identify the additional items the statements of employees describing their symptoms following a traumatic event were taken and tested to identify those that formed a new factor alongside the intrusion and avoidance symptoms that made up the IES. Once the new items were found, it was necessary to undertake a number of other tests to ensure that the new scale provided results that would be reliable and valid. The IES-E has been used extensively in research ever since it was developed and has played an important part in evaluating the work described in Part IV of this book.

Although there is a recognition of the importance of well-controlled studies it is clear that in organisations the pure research models are much less easy to use. This is particularly true in research into disasters in the workplace. By definition, disasters are not events that can be easily predicted and therefore research has to be undertaken under real-world conditions. This means that it is not often possible to use the gold standard of experimentation, the randomised controlled trial. What is possible is a combination of different tools and approaches to research including, wherever possible, the randomised controlled trial or QEs. However, the use of surveys and descriptive studies also has merit, particularly when they form part of a range of measures taken to demonstrate the effects of an intervention. It could also be argued that in their desire to meet the requirements of an experimental protocol, some experimenters have distorted the situation to such an extent that the results have little relationship to what occurs in real life.

Part IV

Organisational research – case studies

Part IV brings together four case studies that have been undertaken using the principles described in the earlier parts of this book. The first two chapters examine the nature of the traumatic experience and identify the types of event that have the most impact. In the first chapter, the traumatic experience is acute, often lasting for less than three minutes, in which time a raider armed with a shotgun, knife or baseball bat threatens the employee with the aim of carrying out a robbery. In the second chapter, the traumatic attack is bullying. Bullying is by definition a long-term or chronic attack which involves an abuse of power and which frequently lasts for months if not years. Chapter 13 describes the effects of being held in an armed raid or being held hostage by criminals intent on robbery. The experiment was designed to ascertain the extent to which personal and situational factors determine the levels of post-traumatic stress experienced by the victim. Chapter 14 challenges the view that post-traumatic stress is confined to people who are exposed to acutely traumatic events such as fires, accidents and crime. The chapter looks at the experiences of over 150 occupational health nurses, counsellors and personnel professionals in order to identify the incidence of bullying and then to find out how exposure to bullying affects these professionals.

The second two chapters deal with the post-trauma care interventions used following two major disasters that occurred in the UK. A contrast is drawn once more between interventions that are used to deal with acute and chronic post-traumatic stress. Chapter 15 describes the acute interventions that were provided in support of supermarket employees who became involved in caring for the victims of a major rail crash. The interventions involved a group debriefing and follow-up of employees. In Chapter 16, the traumatic event was the explosion of a terrorist bomb outside an office block in Manchester. However, in this case the interventions took place two and a half years after the incident with employees who had developed chronic post-traumatic stress symptoms. In this chapter, the trauma counselling approach is described together with some of the other activities that were developed to support these employees. In Chapters 15 and 16 evaluations were undertaken which assess the effectiveness of the interventions in reducing the trauma symptoms.

Chapter 13

The Post Office – identifying the causes of acute post-traumatic stress

Introduction

People exposed to a traumatic event exhibit a variety of responses. Some develop a post-traumatic disorder, while others, having experienced a similar horrifying event, go on to live a life free of psychological distress (McFarlane and de Girolamo 1996). This difference in an individual's response to traumatic experiences suggests that there are differences in personal vulnerability to traumatic stressors (Yule 1999; Ullman and Filipas 2001). However, despite these individual variations in post-trauma responses, epidemiological studies show that some traumatic events cause a higher incidence of PTSD independent of other factors (Resnick *et al.* 1993; Kessler *et al.* 1995; McFarlane and Yehuda 1996). Following a traumatic exposure the availability and quality of post-trauma support and counselling has an impact on the speed of recovery (Perry *et al.* 1992). Taken together it is clear that post-traumatic stress responses are complex and are affected by at least three different groups of factors: a) personal, social and demographic differences; b) features of the traumatic incident; and c) post-trauma support. This study has been designed to examine some aspects of these three factors.

Personal, social and demographic differences

Recent research has revealed a number of predisposing factors that increase the likelihood of PTSD occurring after a traumatic exposure (Briere 1997; Lauterbach and Vrana 2001). An epidemiological study (Breslau and Davis 1992) which took place within an urban community found that 39 per cent of the members of that community had experienced one or more events that were consistent with Criterion A for the diagnosis of PTSD (American Psychiatric Association 1994). An assessment of the psychological well-being of this traumatised group found that nearly 24 per cent had developed PTSD. The Breslau and Davis study showed that women were four times more likely to develop chronic PTSD than men. In a study that looked at the impact of sexual assault and domestic violence however, it was found that men were more likely than women to develop post-trauma reactions (Briere *et al.* 1995). Therefore, it is possible that the differences in the proportions of men and women that experience post-traumatic symptoms may be due to the fact that women are more likely to be exposed to a sexual attack than men. The influence of age on the development of PTSD has not been widely studied, however there are some indications that age may be a factor in the development of this disorder (McCahill *et al.* 1979). For many years, it was assumed that young children did not understand the nature of traumatic experiences and therefore did not develop post-traumatic stress (Joseph *et al.* 1997). Recently it has been established that young children do respond to trauma, although the manifestation of their response may be different to that of adults (Yule *et al.* 1999). The diagnostic criterion in *DSM IV* recognises this difference between children and adults and describes the post-trauma symptoms of both adults and children. It has been suggested that the elderly and the young may be at greater risk of developing post-traumatic stress than people in their middle age (Raphael 1986). It has not been established whether any increased incidence of post-traumatic stress in the young is due to a lack of mental preparation or training to deal with traumatic exposure and which provides some protection against traumatic stress. It is possible that in the elderly the increased levels of post-traumatic stress might be due to a rekindling of responses to earlier traumatic experiences. Social relationships including family situation and support have been shown to be important factors in the development of post-traumatic stress (Briere 1997).

Perhaps the most extensively researched vulnerability factor has been the impact of a previous history of psychiatric illness (McFarlane 1992). Where a victim of a traumatic event has suffered anxiety or depression in the past, there is an increase in the likelihood of post-traumatic stress. A number of studies have examined this relationship between mental health and post-traumatic stress. A study by Mayou *et al.* (1993) looked at victims of road crashes and found that people with a previous history of an emotional disorder were more likely to develop PTSD than those without a similar psychiatric history. An investigation of Australian firefighters (McFarlane 1988a) found that the major predictors were the firefighter's neuroticism scores and a family history of emotional disorder. However, McFarlane's findings have been challenged (Scott and Stradling 1992a) as not necessarily applying to victims of all types of traumatic situation.

Situational factors

Many of the studies that have looked at situational factors relating to post-traumatic stress have related to war, disasters or sexual abuse and not situations that are commonly found in the workplace. In the sinking of the cruise ship *Jupiter*, 50 per cent of the passengers suffered chronic PTSD (Boyle *et al.* 1995) and in the case of the Buffalo Creek disaster, 59 per cent of victims experienced PTSD (Green *et al.* 1992). In contrast, the rate of PTSD in volunteer firefighters exposed to a severe bush fire was much lower at 16 per cent of those exposed (McFarlane 1988a). There have been few studies which have examined the psychological effect of violence at work, particularly violence that is of such an intensity as to result in post-traumatic stress. A scale of traumatic situations was constructed (Green 1993) and identified a number of situational factors which were related to an increased incidence of post-traumatic stress. The situational factors included witnessing the death of another person, actual injury to self, witnessing the injury of another person and a threat to one's own life. McFarlane and Yehuda (1996) reviewed the data from a range of traumatic situations involving violence and found the incidence of PTSD was substantially higher in people who had experienced a personal attack, a threat to life or a physical injury. A study of victims of bank robberies (Miller-Burke *et al.* 1999) found that the level of threat to personal safety and the use of an offensive weapon were related to a higher level of post-trauma symptoms.

Interactions between personal and situational factors

The notion of what constitutes a traumatic event is less straightforward than might be suggested by reading *DSM IV*. Recent research has shown that the extent to which an event is traumatic is determined by an interaction between the magnitude of the traumatic event and a range of victim risk factors (Breslau 1998). This interactionist view is likely to result in a more accurate assessment of the vulnerability of individuals to develop post-traumatic stress (Briere 1997). However, it is also important to recognise that this interaction may be mediated by post-event variables such as level of social support, resources, and post-trauma debriefing and counselling.

Post-trauma support

The presence of personal and social support following a traumatic episode has been shown to improve the psychological outcome (Buckley *et al.* 1996). Yet despite the generally positive relationship between support and recovery there are some studies that show high levels of social support can *increase* the incidence of post-traumatic stress symptoms (Solomon and Smith 1994). Debriefing is one of the most commonly used post-trauma interventions. There has been an active debate on the effectiveness of debriefing over the past few years, based on largely anecdotal testimony on the benefit of post-trauma debriefing and the lack of controlled studies that assess the benefits of this type of intervention (Tehrani 1998a). Random controlled studies into debriefing have shown it to be linked to an increase in post-traumatic stress symptoms (Bisson *et al.* 1997) or to provide no benefit (Hobbs *et al.* 1996; Brewin *et al.* 1998). However, these studies have been criticised on the grounds of their poor methodology (Dyregrov 1998). Added to the difficulties of establishing whether counselling and debriefing are helpful, concerns have also been expressed about the use of in-house counselling and support services (West and Reynolds 1995). Some researchers have demonstrated that where employees fear stigmatisation for seeking psychological support there is a lower uptake of these services (Sibicky and Dovidio 1986). A recent Appeal Court ruling (*Hatton v. Sutherland and others* 2002) said that it would be unlikely that organisations would be found negligent in meeting their duty of care if they employed counsellors and debriefers to support their employees. It is likely therefore that organisations would see the provision of counselling as a way of avoiding expensive litigation.

The following study was designed to assess the impact of personal and situational risk factors in the development of post-traumatic stress and examines the utilisation and perceived helpfulness of post-trauma support. The study was undertaken within the naturalistic setting of the workplace and was designed to be within the constraints set by the organisation. The main objectives were to provide the organisation with information on the operation of its trauma care programme and help in identifying employees who might be most vulnerable to post-traumatic stress.

Method

This study examines the post-traumatic impact of an armed raid on security van drivers. The subjects were all employed by CASHCO, the part of the Post Office involved in the transportation of high-value goods. Each employee underwent extensive training designed to increase awareness of the security equipment and procedures for reducing the risk of robbery and provide them with skills in how to behave should they become the victim of an armed raid. In addition, all the staff had been made aware of the range of psychological responses to a traumatic event including armed raids (Tehrani 1995). The employees' managers had undertaken a two-day training course on post-traumatic stress, first line debriefing and post-trauma management (Tehrani 2000b). This course included a competency assessment. The occupational health professionals and welfare officers had also been trained in psychological debriefing (Tehrani 1998b). One year following the introduction of a trauma care programme, all the employees exposed to an armed raid were sent a post-incident questionnaire. The types of traumatic incident included during this period were 'across the pavement' raids, hijackings, hostage-taking and threats of violence. The post-incident questionnaire also collected personal information together with information on the severity of the raid, the nature of the threat and any injuries sustained. In addition, the utilisation of post-trauma care and its perceived helpfulness were recorded. The employees completed the IES-E, which provided a measure of the current intensity of their post-trauma symptoms.

Subjects and procedure

The number of employees identified as having been involved in raids during the qualifying period was 170. Each was sent a questionnaire (see Appendix A). A letter written by the CASHCO's director of personnel accompanied the questionnaire, and explained that the purpose of the questionnaire was to improve the quality of the trauma care programme. The employees were assured that personal information would be kept confidential and only statistical data would be provided to the organisation. Of the 170 questionnaires, 101 were returned, a response rate of 59 per cent. Prior to the distribution of the questionnaires, it had been agreed with CASHCO that where an employee was suffering from traumatic stress symptoms, additional support and counselling would be offered, funded by the organisation.

Measures

The post-trauma questionnaire was designed for this group of employees and was fully discussed with representatives of the organisation to ensure ease of completion and relevance to the employees. The questionnaire sought information about the employee and features of the traumatic event. Each employee also provided contact details including their name, home address and home telephone number. This data was used to identify and contact employees where additional counselling or support was required.

Personal information

The employees provided information on their gender, age, marital status, children, living companions and history of anxiety and depression.

Situational information

The employees provided information on the incident that had occurred during the qualifying period. The situational features were taken from the descriptions provided by the organisation's security department as typical of armed raids. These descriptions included whether the employee had been: a) physically attacked; b) had physical injuries; c) was threatened with violence (whether guns, knives, sticks, bats or gas were involved); d) if a gun was fired; e) if there was verbal abuse; and f) if the employee was alone or with others. The questions required the employee to tick a yes/no response box.

Use of IES-E

The trauma symptoms were assessed using the IES-E (see Chapter 11). The employees were asked to identify which of the statements were true for them during the past fortnight. The scale indicated frequency rates that ranged from 0 for 'never experienced' to 4, 'experienced most of the time'. The data from the IES-E has three subscales of avoidance, arousal and re-experience, the sum of which provided a global score or general factor.

Post-trauma support

In this section of the questionnaire, the employees identified the support they had sought and received following the raid. This support included talking, debriefing, counselling and personal support. For each source of support, the employee was asked to indicate the helpfulness of the support received. The questionnaire allowed the employees to provide additional comments where there was a wish to clarify the reason for a particular response.

Results

IES-E scores

The IES-E scores for each of the employees were calculated and analysed, and the 'boxplot' shows the mean scores and deviations (see Figure 13.1). In the boxplot, 50 per cent of the scores are represented by the boxes with the full range of scores being indicated by the lines and whiskers.

Scores of 14 for arousal and avoidance, 22 for re-experience and 50 on the general factor were regarded as having achieved 'caseness' for that trauma symptom. Inspection of the data indicated that 33 per cent of employees achieved caseness for arousal, 16 per cent for avoidance, 23 per cent for re-experience and 26 per cent for the general factor. These results indicate that in this group of traumatised employees arousal was the most commonly experienced post-trauma symptom.

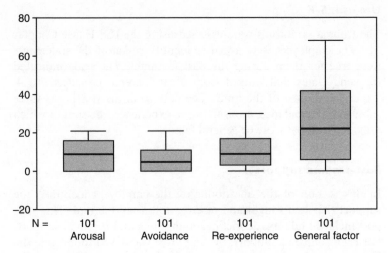

Figure 13.1 Employee scores on IES-E scale showing the mean and range

Personal risk factors

As the data collected in this part of the study is categorical (i.e. based on whether a personal characteristic is present or not) the analysis was undertaken using Chi square analysis (χ^2), Phi coefficient (ϕ) and odds ratios (ORs). These techniques are useful in determining the presence or absence of an association between two nominal variables within a group of subjects. However, while these statistical tools establish the existence of a statistical association, they do not give any indication of the strength of that association. From the data it was found that of the 101 employees, 95 were males and this bias in the sample was consistent with the actual numbers of male and female employees undertaking this work. Slightly over half the employees were married and 64 per cent had children. Almost 20 per cent had been treated for anxiety or depression in the past. The age range was fairly evenly distributed between the four age bands with 26 employees being in their twenties, 28 in their thirties, 23 in their forties and 24 in their fifties and over. Table 13.1 shows the personal features of this group of employees.

The results of the analysis are shown in Table 13.2. These indicate that a previous history of anxiety and depression is related to the occurrence of arousal, re-experience and the general factor for post-trauma symptoms. It was also found that employees who had a pre-

Table 13.1 Numbers of employees in each personal category

Response	Married	Parents with children	Living with others	Previous anxiety/ depression	Takes regular exercise	Eats regular meals
Yes	57	64	88	17	63	81
No	43	36	9	82	38	20

Table 13.2 The increased risks of experiencing post-trauma symptoms when personal factors are present

Personal factor	Arousal	Avoidance	Re-experience	General factor
Anxiety/depression	p≤	p≤	p≤	p≤
χ^2	0.001	0.894	0.001	0.001
φ	0.001	0.370	0.001	0.001
95% confidence range	1.8–12.4	0.5–4.2	2.0–11.1	2.0–11.9
Increased risk (OR)	**4.8**	**1.5**	**4.7**	**4.9**
Parents of children	p≤	p≤	p≤	p≤
χ^2	0.007	0.097	0.19	0.063
φ	0.009	0.117	0.26	0.081
95% confidence range	1.1–1.9	1.0–1.7	0.9–1.6	1.0–1.7
Increased risk (OR)	**1.5**	**1.3**	**1.2**	**1.3**
No regular exercise	p≤	p≤	p≤	p≤
χ^2	0.820	0.083	0.003	0.244
φ	0.49	0.094	0.002	0.369
95% confidence range	0.7–2.0	0.9–2.7	1.5–3.7	0.7–2.1
Increased risk (OR)	**1.2**	**1.6**	**2.4**	**1.3**

vious history of anxiety or depression were almost five times as likely to experience caseness levels of arousal, re-experience and the general PTSD factor. In addition, being a parent was associated with arousal (OR 1.5). On the other hand, it was found that employees who took regular exercise experienced less re-experience symptoms (OR 2.4) than those employees who did not exercise regularly. None of the other variables had a significant association with any of the IES-E scales.

Situational risk factors

As with the personal risk factors, the statistical method used to explore the relationship between situational factors and post-trauma symptoms involved a Chi square analysis (χ^2), Phi coefficient (ϕ) and ORs. In this part of the study the association between physical injury, threats and weapons used and the incidence of post-traumatic stress symptoms are examined. Table 13.3 illustrates the nature of the traumatic situations experienced by the employees. The table shows that 58 per cent of the subjects were threatened with personal violence and 42 per cent suffered physical injury during the raid. The raiders physically attacked 34 per cent of the subjects and 73 per cent of subjects were threatened with a gun. However, guns were only *fired* on 13 per cent of the occasions. Baseball bats were used in 18 per cent of raids and noxious substances such as ammonia or CS gas were used in 13 per cent of raids. Knives were only used in 3 per cent of raids. In 12 per cent of the raids, more than one type of offensive weapon was employed.

Of the eight situational factors, only three were found statistically associated with a caseness score on the IES-E. These were gun fired, noxious substance and physical attack. No significant association with the IES-E scales was found for physical injury, threat of violence, or the presence of guns, bats or knives (see Table 13.4).

The χ^2 analysis indicated that the firing of a gun was strongly associated with all the IES-E factors. Where a gun was fired, employees were 11.3 times more likely to experience high levels of re-experience, 6.1 times more likely to experience avoidance symptoms and 3.3 times more likely to experience arousal than those who had not experienced a gun being fired. The presence of a gun at the scene of an incident was not found to be associated with significant levels of post-trauma symptoms as measured by the IES-E. However, the presence of noxious substances was associated with 3.3 times the level of arousal compared with situations where such were not present. Physical attacks were found to be associated with high scores on the general factor of the IES-E. Interestingly, where there was a physical attack or the presence of a noxious substance there was *lower* risk of avoidance and re-experience respectively.

Table 13.3 The percentage exposure to violence, threats and offensive weapons during armed raids

Physical injury	Threat of violence	Physical attack	Gun present	Gun fired	Bat	Noxious substance	Knife
42%	58%	34%	73%	13%	18%	13%	3%

Table 13.4 The significance of the χ^2, ϕ and risk tests for the presence of situational factors and the incidence of post-trauma symptoms

Situational factor	Arousal	Avoidance	Re-experience	General factor
Gun fired	p≤	p≤	p≤	p≤
χ^2	0.02	0.01	0.001	0.001
ϕ	0.017	0.001	0.001	0.001
95% confidence range	1.1–9.0	2.4–16.0	3.4–37.7	2.7–30.7
Increased risk (OR)	3.3	6.1	11.30	9.13
Gun involved (but not fired)	p≤	p≤	p≤	p≤
χ^2	0.23 (ns)	0.15 (ns)	0.15 (ns)	0.33 (ns)
ϕ	0.32	0.16	0.17	0.16
95% confidence range	0.9–1.6	1.0–1.7	0.9–1.7	1.0–1.7
Increased risk (OR)	1.1	1.3	1.2	1.2
Noxious substance	p≤	p≤	p≤	p≤
χ^2	0.022	0.877 (ns)	0.39 (ns)	0.95 (ns)
ϕ	0.017	0.44	0.49	0.09
95% confidence range	1.1–9.3	0.5–5.1	0.14–2.5	0.9–6.4
Increased risk (OR)	3.3	1.5	0.61	2.4
Physical attack	p≤	p≤	p≤	p≤
χ^2	0.88 (ns)	0.52 (ns)	0.82 (ns)	0.041
ϕ	0.337	0.80	0.49	0.045
95% confidence range	0.7–2.2	0.7–2.2	0.7–2.2	1.0–2.9
Increased risk (OR)	1.3	0.91	1.2	1.76

Summary of personal and situational results

The significant relationship between a previous experience of anxiety or depression and a higher incidence of post-trauma symptoms is not particularly surprising. First, it is possible that the factors that caused the original anxiety or depression will not have been resolved, leaving the employee more vulnerable than other employees to the impact of a traumatic exposure. Second, the anxiety and depression may indicate a pre-existing lack of psychological coping skills. Third, it is possible that the employees with a history of anxiety or depression may have had less effective supportive relationships and therefore may have had less personal help in dealing with the aftermath of the trauma.

The finding that the parents of children are prone to arousal symptoms might be due to the special relationship the parents have with their children. A common comment from employees when describing their traumatic ordeal was that at the time of the traumatic events the faces of their children came to their minds. This experience was usually accompanied by a fear that they might never see their children again.

The odds ratio (OR) indicated that employees with a previous history of anxiety or depression were almost five times as likely to experience post-traumatic stress symptoms as those with no history of anxiety and depression. Being a parent had a weaker indicator of the risk of post-traumatic stress symptoms, with the likelihood being around 1.4 times as great as someone with no children. These results would suggest the need to be aware of the increased vulnerability of employees with these personal factors.

The situational factor results provided no evidence to indicate that the presence of a gun, knife or baseball bat at the scene of a robbery was a strong indicator of an increased risk of post-traumatic stress. However, there was strong evidence that the firing of a gun was associated with each of the IES-E scales. Other attacks such as the use of gas were found to be associated with a higher level of arousal but this association is not found in any of the other IES-E scales. A physical attack was associated with a high score on the general scale of the IES-E. These results would indicate that special care should be taken with employees with a history of anxiety and depression who are involved in incidents where guns are fired. It would also be appropriate to recognise that parents and people who have been exposed to gas or have been physically attacked may require additional support.

Utilisation of post-trauma support: its perceived helpfulness

CASHCO introduced a post-trauma care programme for employees involved in armed raids. The programme was designed to provide first-line debriefing by a manager or peer for all employees. Where an employee required more help, a referral was made for psychological debriefing from the occupational health or welfare services. Employees with more serious post-trauma symptoms were referred for trauma counselling by the occupational health or welfare service or the employee's GP. It was not compulsory for employees to attend any part of the trauma care programme, however employees were encouraged to make use of the services and a record was made of those employees who refused support. Inspection of the post-trauma scores on the IES-E suggests that one year following their traumatic experience a third of employees still had post-trauma symptoms indicative of post-traumatic stress.

Talking about the raid

Talking about a traumatic experience as a way of making sense of it has been shown to aid recovery (Tedeschi and Calhoun 1995). Of the 101 subjects involved in an armed raid, 84 reported talking to at least one person following the raid. Table 13.5 indicates the frequency of talking to a range of potential 'listening groups'. Some employees spoke to more than one type of listener. The mean helpfulness scores were calculated for each type of listener where 2 was very helpful and 0 not at all helpful.

The mean perceived helpfulness scores show that welfare was regarded as the most helpful followed by occupational health and the employee's partner. However, these perceptions of helpfulness were not associated with lower levels of post-trauma symptoms.

Debriefing

Debriefing was offered to all the subjects and 80 per cent were debriefed at least once. Debriefing was available from a number of sources. Managers and colleagues had undertaken a model of debriefing designed specially for the organisation (Tehrani 2000b) and a more advanced model of debriefing was offered by occupational health (Tehrani and Westlake 1994). The model adopted by welfare was based on that developed by Mitchell (Mitchell and Everley 1993). Subjects also gained access to debriefing via their GPs, but the nature of this debriefing is unknown. Table 13.6 shows the source of the debriefing undertaken by the employees. Most were debriefed by their manager, occupational health or a colleague. The mean helpfulness scores were calculated for each group, where 2 was very helpful and 0 not at all helpful. The helpfulness results showed that occupational health and colleague debriefings were perceived as being most helpful and welfare debriefings the least helpful. Table 13.6 also shows that managers undertook the largest proportion of debriefing sessions, followed by occupational health, colleagues and then welfare. Only seven employees went to their GP for debriefing.

Table 13.5 Groups talked to by subjects following an armed raid and the mean helpfulness score

	Partner	Family	Friends	Colleagues	Manager	Occupational health	Welfare	Union
Number	51%	28%	38%	56%	43%	27%	13%	21%
Helpful?	1.42	1.28	1.21	1.26	1.20	1.52	1.75	1.14

Table 13.6 Sources of debriefing and perceived helpfulness

	Manager	Occupational health	Colleagues	Welfare	GP
Total	67%	33%	17%	16%	7%
Helpful?	1.00	1.27	1.24	0.88	1.14

Table 13.7 Trauma counselling and perceived helpfulness

	Occupational health	GP	Other
Total	26%	7%	5%
Helpful?	1.2	1.2	1.37

There were no significant associations between debriefing, the helpfulness of debriefing and post-trauma symptoms.

Post-trauma counselling

Where there was a need for further support, trauma counselling was offered. This was accessed through occupational health or the employee's GP. Thirty-one per cent of employees sought counselling and some accessed counselling from more that one source. Table 13.7 shows the percentage of employees provided with trauma counselling. The mean perceived helpfulness score was calculated with 2 being very helpful and 0 being not at all helpful.

When the associations between counselling and post-trauma symptoms were examined, it was found that no significant differences existed between the employees who went for post-trauma counselling and those that did not.

Other support

Thirty-six of the subjects accessed other forms of support. Most was provided by occupational health and managers. The sources of support and the mean perceived helpfulness are shown in Table 13.8.

The most helpful support came from sources outside the programme. The organisation, managers and occupational health were also seen as helpful. The welfare service and Post Office solicitors were regarded as relatively unhelpful. There were no significant

Table 13.8 Number of employees seeking support and the perceived helpfulness

	Organisational	Manager	Occupational health	Welfare	Solicitors	Other
Total	11%	19%	22%	9%	9%	10%
Helpful	1.27	1.26	1.27	0.80	0.78	1.5

correlations between the helpfulness of support and trauma symptoms.

Summary of post-trauma support results

Overall, employees who had gone through a traumatic experience found the post-trauma care that was provided to be helpful. All employees talked to someone, the most popular being partners, colleagues and managers. However, employees found talking to the welfare officer or occupational health nurse the most helpful. These results are not surprising as the employees would need to make an appointment to talk to welfare and occupational health professionals which would not be the case with their partner, colleagues or manager. In normal circumstances, the trauma care programme offered all traumatised employees a debriefing with their manager or a colleague. Where the employee was found to be particularly badly affected by an incident a referral would be made for an occupational health debriefing. This resulted in the highest proportion of debriefings being undertaken by managers and colleagues. Employees were helped more by being debriefed by a colleague than by their manager. This finding was influenced by the nature of the employee's relationship with his or her manager. Employees also found the debriefing by occupational health nurses more helpful than the debriefing by the welfare officers. This may have been because these two services used different debriefing models and the employees found the occupational health model more helpful. Following the traumatic event around a fifth of employees sought additional support. Most was provided by their manager or occupational health. The support from occupational health, their manager and from the organisation was seen as the most helpful, and the support from the company solicitors and the welfare service the least helpful. The higher scores for helpfulness for occupational health and managers may have been due to the employee education that had occurred in the organisation regarding the trauma care programme. The education described the support that was available from the manager, organisation and occupational health, and this was not the case for the welfare service or the solicitors.

Discussion

This study should be considered in the context of an organisation introducing a new trauma care programme. In the early stages following the introduction of the programme, it was organisationally unacceptable to introduce an elaborate evaluation programme as part of the post-trauma procedures. The organisation wanted to know two things: what would the programme cost and what were the potential savings? Until these questions were answered, it was not possible to undertake any further research. The successful results of this business evaluation (reported in Chapter 8) allowed the organisation to move forward. Having established that the trauma care programme was meeting business needs, the present study was approved by senior managers. The study made it possible to identify some personal and situational risk factors associated with an increased incidence of post-traumatic stress. This information was valuable to the organisation as not only did it help in the refinement of the selection procedures for CASHCO crews, it also helped to identify those employees that may have needed additional help following a traumatic exposure. Unfortunately, there were some limitations to the study. It was not possible to identify whether talking, debriefing or counselling helped to reduce post-traumatic stress symptoms as no psychometric testing had been carried out immediately following the traumatic event and before any interventions took place. However, the data did provide an insight into the perceived helpfulness of these interventions to the employees. The study demonstrated some of the difficulties and benefits of undertaking research within an organisational setting.

Chapter 14

Workplace bullying – a source of chronic post-traumatic stress?

Introduction

In recent years, there has been an increasing interest in the impact of interpersonal conflict at work. The expression of this conflict can result in physical or psychological violence and victimisation. Although physical violence and threats of violence have been widely studied within the field of traumatology, this is not the case with psychological victimisation, mobbing or bullying. Indeed the criterion for diagnosing post-traumatic stress does not include the behaviours which would be regarded as bullying (Ravin and Boal 1989). Despite the lack of formal recognition of bullying as a cause of post-traumatic stress, practitioners and researchers working with victims of bullying recognise the similarities between their symptoms and post-traumatic stress (Scott and Stradling 1992a; Weaver 2000; Tehrani in press).

In this study, 165 care professionals (CPs) were surveyed to establish the incidence of bullying and the observation of bullying occurring in their place of work. Each CP completed a survey that included the IES-E. In the survey the nature of the bullying was recorded as well as the CP's opinion on the quality of the support available within the organisation. From the data gathered the patterns of symptoms were compared with those of employees involved in armed raids.

What is workplace bullying?

Bullying in the workplace has received increasing attention over the past decade, however a number of different names have been given to bullying. Einarsen (1999) described mobbing, emotional abuse, harassment, mistreatment and victimisation as part of the same phenomenon as bullying. He described bullying as the 'systematic persecution of a colleague, subordinate or superior, which, if continued, may cause severe social, psychological and psychosomatic problems for the victim'. Leymann (1990) described bullying behaviours as common in everyday life, and suggested that they only become bullying when they occurred on a regular basis with the aim of causing humiliation and harm. Leymann suggests that the bullying behaviour itself may not be the cause of the problems for the victim but that the real harm is caused by:

- frequency of the behaviours;
- situation in which they occur;
- power gap between the victim and the perpetrator;
- lack of an escape;
- victim's attribution of the offender's intentions.

Bullying is therefore by definition a chronic rather than an acute form of abuse with similarities to domestic violence (Roberts 2000) and the constant exposure of emergency and health service workers to violent and distressing situations (Violanti and Paton 1999).

Bullying and psychological well-being

Workplace bullying has been shown to have a negative impact on employee well-being (Niedl 1996; Zapf et al. 1996; Rayner and Cooper 1997). There is evidence that bullying is related to increased levels of anxiety and depression (Hoel 1999; Bond et al. 2001), poor mental health (Zapf et al. 1996) and post-traumatic stress (Field 1996; Leymann 1990). The formal diagnosis of post-traumatic stress requires the victim to experience, witness or be confronted with an event that involves actual or threatened death or serious injury to their physical integrity or to the physical integrity of others. Under most circumstances, bullying is unlikely to meet this criterion. However, despite the fact that the exposure to bullying behaviours is not regarded as a traumatic experience, the post-traumatic stress symptoms observed in victims of bullying are similar to those found in victims of rape (Dahl 1989). Indeed, the symptoms found in a group of bullied employees were found to be more severe than those of train drivers who had run over people on the rail track (Malt et al. 1993). A study by Leymann and Gustafsson (1996) looked at 64 victims of bullying who attended a clinic specialising in the treatment of victims of psychological trauma including victims of armed raids, industrial accidents and serious car crashes. When the bullying victims were assessed on a range of diagnostic questionnaires, 92 per cent were found to have PTSD. In a discussion of these findings, Leymann and Gustafsson said the magnitude of the symptoms in bullied employees was higher than in train drivers who had run over suicidal individuals and were similar to those of raped women.

Research questions

The present study looks at the nature and impact of bullying in the workplace. The questions asked in the study are:

* What is the incidence of bullying in caring professions?
* Are the symptoms of victims of bullying similar to those experienced by victims of physical trauma?

Method

Subjects

The study sample consisted of 165 CPs who had attended training courses or conferences relating to occupational psychology in the two-year period between 2000 and 2002. Each person attending the training or conference was given a short questionnaire and asked to complete and return it by the end of the session. Emphasis was placed on the importance of all those attending the sessions completing the questionnaire whether or not they had experienced or observed bullying in the qualifying period.

The questionnaire

The questionnaire collected demographic information on age, sex and employment status. The respondents were also asked if they had experienced or observed bullying in the past two years. Three questions identified whether the bullying had involved discrimination on the grounds of race, sex or disability. There was an opportunity to identify which of 11 common forms of bullying behaviour had been experienced or witnessed, and whether the bullying had been reported. There were two questions relating to the quality of support provided by the organisation and finally the IES-E scale of post-trauma symptoms (see Appendix B).

Results

Demographics

The age range of the group was normally distributed with the average age of 42 years. In the group 48 per cent were managers and of these the largest proportion were male (60 per cent). In the group it was found that 67 had been bullied, 113 had observed bullying taking place and 43 had neither been bullied nor had they observed bullying occurring to others.

Frequency of bullying

Table 14.1 shows the frequency of bullying and observations of bullying. The results show that most of the CPs who had been bullied were aware that others were also being bullied. Over a third of the group were not being bullied, however they were aware that other people were being bullied. Around a quarter of the CPs had not been bullied and were unaware of any bullying taking place.

These results suggest that women are bullied more frequently than men. However, the results were strongly influenced by status. In this group, more of the managers were male rather than female. In the non-manager group men were bullied more frequently than women (45 per cent and 41 per cent respectively). In the manager group, 43 per cent of female managers and only 30 per cent of male managers perceived themselves as being bullied during the past two years. The relationship of the person identified as the bully was similar for male and female CPs (see Table 14.2), with the major source of bullying being a manager.

Some bullying involved discrimination relating to sex, race or disability. In this group of employees, 16.1 per cent recorded sexual discrimination, 8.4 per cent racial discrimination and 9.6 per cent physical or disability discrimination.

Table 14.1 Frequency of being bullied and observing bullying in male and female subjects (n = 167) during the past two years

% frequency	Total bullied	Total observed bullying	Bullied & observed bullying	Bullied but not observed bullying	Not bullied but observed bullying	Not bullied & not observed bullying
Male	36.4%	63.6%	27.3%	10.9%	34.5%	27.3%
Female	42.0%	69.0%	36.6%	6.3%	32.1%	25.0%

Table 14.2 Sources of bullying for CP group

	Manager	Peer/non-manager	Customer/client
All employees	55.7%	27.5%	9.0%
Male employees	52.1%	29.1%	7.3%
Female employees	57.1%	26.8%	9.8%

Types of bullying

A wide range of behaviours have been identified as bullying (Hoel and Cooper 2000). Of the behaviours recorded in this survey the most prevalent were unfair criticism, intimidation, unpleasant personal remarks, public humiliation and malicious gossip. The results for male and female subjects were broadly similar, however women experienced more bullying as unfair criticism, while men identified more ganging up and physical attacks (see Table 14.3).

Not everyone who is bullied feels able to report the bullying to their manager, and three main reasons have been used to explain this under-reporting. First, a concern that their complaint would not be taken seriously, second, because the manager was the bully and third because of a belief that reporting the bullying would make the situation worse (Rains 2001). In this study, a higher percentage of bullied men reported the bullying event to their manager than bullied women. The reasons recorded for not reporting the bullying were: a) the manager was the bully (84.4 per cent); b) it would have made

Table 14.3 Incidence of bullying behaviours

Bullying behaviour	All employees	Men	Women
Unfair criticism	59.9%	52.7%	63.4%
Intimidation	58.1%	56.4%	58.9%
Unpleasant personal remarks	47.3%	43.6%	49.1%
Public humiliation	43.1%	38.2%	45.5%
Malicious gossip	37.1%	38.2%	36.6%
Being ignored	34.1%	30.9%	35.7%
Threats	31.1%	30.9%	31.3%
Ganging up	27.5%	32.7%	25.0%
Physical attack	9.6%	14.5%	7.1%
Hiding or taking personal property	9.0%	14.5%	6.3%

matters worse (46.9 per cent); or c) it would not have been taken seriously (15.6 per cent).

The quality of support to employees was assessed using a five-point scale where 1 was very good and 5 very poor. The mean score for training to deal with bullying was 3.63 and the quality of the support was rated at 3.59. The scores on the IES-E questionnaire indicated that 36 of the 67 employees who had been bullied and 4 of the employees who had not been bullied but had observed bullying had high levels of symptoms of post-traumatic stress. These levels were consistent with a diagnosis of PTSD.

Risk factors for bullying

The Chi squared analysis revealed that there were significant risks identified for some of the bullying behaviours, the most serious being threats which were associated with significantly higher levels of arousal, avoidance, re-experience and the general factor. Being ignored or 'sent to Coventry' was found to be associated with high levels of arousal and high scores on the general factor. Being bullied by a manager was associated with high levels of arousal. The results are illustrated in Table 14.4.

Table 14.4 Bullying behaviour and post-trauma symptoms

Bullying behaviour	Arousal	Avoidance	Re-experience	General factor
Threats	$p\leq$	$p\leq$	$p\leq$	$p\leq$
χ^2	0.003	0.044	0.001	0.001
ϕ	0.003	0.05	0.001	0.001
95% confidence level	1.23–2.76	1.0–2.2	1.4–3.1	1.4–3.03
Risk (OR)	**1.8**	**1.5**	**2.12**	**2.10**
Ignored (sent to Coventry)	$p\leq$	$p\leq$	$p\leq$	$p\leq$
χ^2	0.038	0.079	0.059	0.009
ϕ	0.049	0.10	0.077	0.010
95% confidence level	1.02–2.13	0.94–1.99	0.99–2.11	1.15–2.37
Risk (OR)	**1.4**	**1.3**	**1.4**	**1.65**
Manager was bully	$p\leq$	$p\leq$	$p\leq$	$p\leq$
χ^2	0.009	0.192	0.189	0.146
ϕ	0.013	0.27	0.257	0.199
95% confidence level	1.09–1.6	0.92–1.36	0.93–1.39	0.95–1.4
Risk (OR)	**1.3**	**1.1**	**1.1**	**1.1**

Incidence of post-traumatic stress in the bullied

Taking the individual scales from the IES-E, it was found that there were higher numbers of employees who achieved caseness for avoidance (25.7 per cent) than for arousal (23.4 per cent), the general factor (21.6 per cent) or re-experience (18 per cent). Taking all the symptoms together, 9 per cent of employees achieved caseness in the four symptoms. These results suggest that around one in ten of the employees had experienced post-traumatic stress symptoms.

Differences between victims of bullying and armed raids

The scores on the IES-E for the subjects in this study were then factor analysed using the same process as had been used in the development of the IES-E (see Chapter 11). The factor extraction indicates that there were two factors with eigenvalues of greater than 1 (see Table 14.5); the third factor had an eigenvalue of less than 1. The new analysis was then compared with the original IES-E and it was found that while the avoidance factor remained, the factors of arousal and re-experience had collapsed into a single factor (see Table 14.6). The internal reliability of the three scales was then assessed using Cronbach's alpha and the reliability was found to be strong (see Table 14.7). These findings indicate that for victims of bullying the symptoms of arousal and re-experience are more closely associated than in victims of armed raids.

Discussion

This study has shown that in the previous two years 40 per cent of the CPs had been bullied and 68 per cent had observed bullying taking place. These results are high when compared with the study by Hoel and Cooper (2000) in which it was shown that 24.5 per cent

Table 14.5 Summary of eigenvalues

Factor	Eigenvalue	% of var.	Cum.%
1	14.84	64.51	64.51
2	1.27	5.51	70.02
3	0.95	4.1	74.16

Table 14.6 Summary of loadings from the oblique factor rotation

Avoidance	Factor 1	Factor 2
I felt as if it hadn't happened or was not real		0.640
I tried not to think about it		0.871
I tried not to talk about it		0.838
My feelings about it were kind of numb		0.655
I stayed away from any reminders		0.679
I tried to remove it from my memory		0.630
I avoided letting myself get upset when I thought about it or was reminded of it		0.654

Arousal	Factor 1	Factor 2
I felt down or depressed for no reason	0.686	
I experienced wide mood swings	0.719	
I experienced tenseness in my body	0.676	
I was irritable with others	0.718	
I had a tendency to avoid other people	0.667	
I jumped or got startled by sudden noises	0.701	
I avoided situations or places	0.659	

Re-experience	Factor 1	Factor 2
I thought about it when I did not mean to	0.724	
I experienced feelings of self-blame or guilt	0.739	
Pictures about it popped into my mind	0.773	
I had waves of strong feelings about it	0.751	
I had dreams about it	0.831	
I had trouble falling asleep or staying asleep	0.787	
Other things kept making me think about it	0.778	
Any reminders brought back feelings about it	0.788	
I was aware that I still had a lot of feelings about it but did not deal with them	0.615	

Table 14.7 Summary of the results of Cronbach's alpha

Factor	Alpha value
1	0.97
2	0.91

of employees had been bullied and 45.2 per cent observed bullying in the past five years. The study by Rayner (1997) showed that 53 per cent of employees had been bullied at some time in the past. Several reasons might explain these results. First, it is possible that CPs are more vulnerable to being bullied than other groups of employees. Second, CPs are likely to be approached for advice and support from employees who have been bullied during the course of their work. Third, CPs are more aware of bullying and therefore more likely to label bad behaviours as bullying than other groups. Fourth, it is possible that this was a biased sample. However, the issue of bias was partly addressed by the fact that the response rate for the CPs was 100 per cent of those given the questionnaire and was representative of the CPs surveyed.

The study showed that over half the perpetrators of bullying were managers and a third were non-managers or peers; these results were broadly in line with other research. Although women appeared to be bullied more frequently than men, most of this difference was accounted for by two factors. First, non-managers are bullied more than managers and second, more men were managers than women. However, some gender differences were observed within the manager and non-manager groups as female managers and male subordinates had experienced slightly higher levels of bullying than their opposite gender colleagues.

Of the 67 CPs that had been bullied in the past two years it was found that 44 per cent were experiencing caseness levels of PTSD symptoms based on the general factor of the IES-E. However, when these results were examined in more depth it was found that the symptoms clustered rather differently to those of victims of acute trauma exposure. More specifically, in victims of bullying the symptoms of arousal and re-experience had formed a single cluster with avoidance remaining as a separate cluster. This finding is not totally unexpected as similar results have been found in the complex PTSD symptoms of battered women and victims of childhood abuse (Resick 2001). There are a number of explanations why victims of bullying may experience re-experience and arousal symptoms more often than victims of other traumatic experiences. The first comes out of the fact that bullying is a very personal attack. The trauma involved in fires, accidents and armed raids is impersonal, and the major features of the traumatic experience situational. In these situations, it is possible to show that the objective characteristics of the event are strongly related to PTSD symptomatology (Kemp *et al.*

1991). However, in bullying and domestic violence the trauma is personally motivated with the subjective distress having a greater influence on the incidence of PTSD (Kilpatrick *et al.* 1985). A second explanation is that, for most people, bullying is a private event. The bullied person will try to hide their feelings and distress while in the presence of the perpetrator. Consequently, the hidden negative emotions associated with feelings of powerlessness, distress and helplessness become strongly associated with a wide range of work-related situations through a process of conditioning. Finally, bullying may continue for prolonged periods, which may result in a state of 'learnt hopelessness' (Alloy *et al.* 1990). Long-term exposure to bullying without a means of escape allows for a higher level of conditioning to be established. In turn this can lead to strong conditioned associations to be formed where exposure to an environmental or cognitive trigger can elicit re-experiences in the form of dreams and flashbacks together with associated high level of arousal.

Little research has been undertaken on the impact of prolonged or chronic trauma perpetrated in a working or personal relationship. It would appear that there are some differences in the magnitude and interrelationship between groups of symptoms which can differentiate acute and chronic victims of trauma, but more needs to be done to identify the mechanisms that are involved in the development of post-traumatic stress in a range of situations.

Chapter 15

The Paddington rail crash – how to deal with a crisis[1]

Introduction

This chapter looks at how an organisation handled an unexpected disaster and how the existing policies, procedures and systems were able to meet the needs of the crisis and the ongoing support of the workers. Chapters 6 and 8 looked at some of the requirements of a trauma care programme. In this chapter, the emphasis is on the support provided for a group of supermarket employees involved in offering emergency refuge and support to hundreds of distressed and injured passengers from a train crash. The trains had collided in a cutting next to the supermarket's car park and most of the passengers escaping from the trains were taken to the supermarket's coffee bar prior to being moved to hospital or sent home. The interventions with the employees are described, together with the evaluation process and results. Unlike planned research, disaster research takes place at a time of considerable anxiety and therefore has its focus on the protection of life, health and well-being. Yet, despite the difficulties, procedures were put in place that helped to identify the employees in greatest need of support. The activation of the trauma care programme also took some of the burden of support off the shoulders of managers whose main emphasis was caring for the employees while trying to maintain the operation of the business.

1 Based on Tehrani, N. Walpole, O. Berriman, J. and Reilly, J. (2001) A special courage: dealing with the Paddington rail crash, *Occupational Medicine*, 5(2): 93–9, by permission of Oxford University Press.

Background

In the study, a supermarket chain that had introduced a trauma care programme to deal with a range of violent incidents including armed raids, physical attacks and verbal abuse found itself faced with a major disaster. Convinced of the value of trauma care in supporting distressed and traumatised employees, the trained occupational health professionals decided that they should use their trauma management and debriefing skills to help the staff involved.

The rail crash

On 5 October 1999, at one of the busiest times of the day on the British rail network, two commuter trains packed with passengers crashed into each other a few minutes outside the mainline Paddington railway station in London. A number of carriages were severely damaged in the impact and resultant fire destroyed large sections of the train. The crash occurred at Ladbroke Grove on a section of track overlooked by blocks of flats, a supermarket and a railway bridge. Some of the first people on the scene were employees of the supermarket. These employees not only provided ladders to help passengers climb up from the track to the safety of the supermarket's car park but also provided immediate first aid, emotional support and comfort. The supermarket's employees handled this major disaster with efficiency and a level of human kindness that was acknowledged by passengers, bereaved families and the wider community. The Sainsbury's supermarket occupational health team and management had identified that where employees were faced with incidents that exposed them to actual or potential death or serious injury there is a need to provide immediate and ongoing support. Following the Paddington crash it was decided that the supermarket's violence at work policy and procedures (Sainsbury's 1997) should be activated by the store and by the occupational health service. A small team of occupational health advisers was present in the store on the day of the incident and remained on site throughout the following week. During the initial period, informal diffusing and identification of the employees involved in the rescue was undertaken. The atmosphere in the store during this early stage was highly emotional. It took over two weeks for the tracks to be cleared. During this time, the employees faced the constant attention of the media and the families of victims were constantly visiting the store to thank the employees for their support and try to find someone that could make some sense of what had happened. Outside, the emergency services, investigators and engineers were using cranes and heavy lifting gear to locate the bodies of the deceased passengers and remove the burnt-out carriages. The disaster remained front-page news and the main item on the television, hence constantly confronting the employees with a reminder of what had happened.

Interventions

Crisis management

In the early stages of the disaster, the employees were fully involved in trying to provide support to the distressed and injured passengers. Initially there was some confusion over what had happened and the store remained open, but quickly it became apparent that this was a major incident. The first problem that faced the employees was how to get down to the level of the track as the track was in a deep cutting. Some noticed that some builders' vans were passing, persuaded them to stop and used the ladders to help some of the passengers up to the car park and then over to the store's coffee bar. Very quickly, the coffee bar had been changed into a reception centre where passengers could be assessed and provided with cups of tea and food. All the employees worked together to provide the support and mobile phones were offered to allow the passengers to telephone their families to say that they were safe. During the initial stages of the disaster it was not possible for the members of the occupational health trauma team to get to the store as the access roads were full of emergency vehicles. The store manager supported his staff by keeping the media at bay and by offering first aid support and refreshments to passengers and rescuers. The next day the occupational health nurses began the process of assessing the needs of the employees. Everyone present on the day of the crash was spoken to informally and provided with an opportunity to speak in private where this was requested. During this stage the store manager became a focal point, bringing everyone together to thank them for their courage and bravery.

Group debriefing

One week after the crash all the employees exposed to its aftermath were invited to a group debriefing session and twelve attended. The session began with the employees completing the IES-E (Tehrani *et al.* 2002) and the Goldberg Anxiety & Depression Scale (Goldberg *et al.* 1988). The assessments were undertaken to identify employees who may be experiencing high levels of trauma symptoms and to decide whether a group debriefing would be the best route forward. Following the assessment, the employees took part in a short educational session on post-trauma stress. During the session, they had an opportunity to ask questions about their own symptoms and responses, and to gain clarification on some of the common post-traumatic stress symptoms. Following the education an outline of the purpose and process of group debriefing was given. The employees were then offered an opportunity to take part in such a debriefing (Tehrani 1995). All the employees opted to take part.

The group debriefing process

The debriefing process, which had been developed over a number of years, was based on learning that had taken place in a number of organisations. Unlike the models that had been developed by Mitchell and Everly (2001) and Dyregrov (1997) this model concentrated on the facts of the story with acknowledgement rather than exploration of thoughts or feelings. The structure of the group debriefing model is shown in Figure 15.1. The debriefing team was made up of three members, the lead debriefer, the peer debriefer and the supporter, each having a different role and responsibilities. The group debriefing process consisted of five stages. The first stage was the introduction

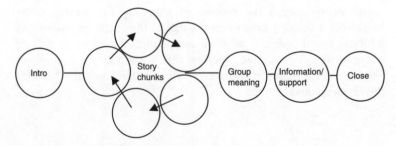

Figure 15.1 The group debriefing process

in which the lead debriefer introduced the members of the debriefing team and their roles and described the debriefing process. At this point current trauma symptoms in the group were acknowledged. The lead debriefer then explained that the debriefing would be dealing with the things that had happened during the incident and emphasised the importance of recognising the sensory aspects of the experience. The group was then told that the session was voluntary and that all personal information revealed would be kept confidential. The group was told that normally the session would last between one and a half to two hours. At this point, the employees had an opportunity to ask questions and leave the session if they wished. In the second stage of the debriefing the lead debriefer asked each person in turn for their name and what they had been doing before the incident. The peer debriefer then summarised what had been said. The first employee to become aware of the disaster was then encouraged to give the first part of their story. This was then added to by the second person to arrive on the scene and so on until everyone was included. In this way the whole story was built up, each segment being taken in small chunks, ensuring that everyone had said as much as they wished about what had happened. At regular stages, the peer debriefer summarised what had been said and identified gaps and discrepancies until the whole jigsaw of the story was pieced together.

During the third stage of the process the aim was to help the group establish a 'group meaning'. The lead and peer debriefers worked together with the group to reflect on what had been said in the debriefing. Gradually a group meaning emerged that acknowledged the nature of the event and the part everyone had played in helping the train passengers. At the end of this process, the group meaning that had been identified was 'this was a distressing incident but the group stuck together and did its best'.

In the information and support stage, symptoms were discussed and hints on coping given. Lifestyle information was provided together with information on ongoing support. The debriefing was then closed with a focus on the future arrangements for referrals. The support debriefer role was to be a gatekeeper and to debrief the debriefers.

The debriefing allowed the employees to examine in detail what had happened during the day of the crash, to fill gaps in the story, check understanding and share knowledge. Of particular significance were the changes in attitude that occurred during the debriefing.

At the beginning of the process the participants talked about those things that they would have liked to have done to help others but did not do. At the end of the debriefing they were recognising the positive things that they had achieved individually and as a group. This process allowed the group to create the shared understanding that they had worked together as a team and despite their fears had helped a lot of passengers deal with a traumatic event.

Following the group debriefing, six employees requested individual sessions. These handled a number of personal problems relating partly to the crash and partly to personal situations that had been made worse by post-trauma symptoms. In these sessions, further support was given in order to enhance coping skills and build resilience.

Follow-up

Four months after the crash, the debriefed employees completed the trauma questionnaire for a second time. They also completed a survey that assessed the quality of support provided to them. To obtain information on the effectiveness of the debriefing the manager of each of the employees was asked to complete a questionnaire. The questionnaire assessed the level of performance of the employee in the period immediately following the crash against their current performance. The questionnaire also compared the level of employee sickness absence in a three-month period in the year prior to the crash with the same period following the crash. A representative of the store's management team provided feedback on Sainsbury's violence at work policy and procedures.

Results

Trauma questionnaires

The results from the IES-E showed that at the time of the group debriefing the mean scores for the three major traumatic stress symptoms were arousal (15.8), avoidance (18.3) and re-experience (24.2). These scores indicate a high level of post-trauma symptomatology (Tehrani *et al.* 2002). The mean scores on the Anxiety & Depression Scale were anxiety (6) and depression (4.8) which is a level at which employees would have a 50 per cent chance of having a clinically important disturbance (Gamm *et al.* 1990).

Four months after the debriefing a second administration of the questionnaires indicated a significant reduction in the symptoms measured by the IES-E and Goldberg (see Table 15.1). Four months after the rail crash only one employee had scores on the IES-E and anxiety and depression scales which suggested there were still high levels of post-traumatic stress reactions. Two employees had a caseness level score for depression.

Employee survey

The survey showed that all the employees in the store on the day of the crash became actively engaged in helping injured passengers from the trains. The survey looked at the way the store handled the situation, helpfulness of the support, helpfulness of the debriefing, helpfulness of counselling and other comments.

All the employees expressed the view that the store had handled the situation well. The only criticism was that the store manager might have closed the store earlier and kept it closed longer. However, it was recognised that the store manager worked hard to protect the employees from exposure to the intrusion of the press and media.

Around 60 per cent of the employees recorded that they had received personal support in the first few days following the crash. Everyone who had been given help found this early support valuable. The main reasons given by the employees for their positive responses were that the support provided them with reassurance that their reactions and feelings were normal. The proactive support also meant that they were able to speak to someone outside their family and friends. The group debriefing was also reported as helpful by all

Table 15.1 Paired samples test comparing scores before and after debriefing

Symptom	Mean scores		Mean Diff.	Std dev	Std Error	T score	Significance
	Before	After					
Anxiety	5.9	3.1	2.8	2.6	0.8	3.74	0.003**
Depression	4.8	2.2	2.6	2.2	0.6	4.08	0.001**
Avoidance	18.3	9.7	8.6	3.9	1.1	7.7	0.000**
Arousal	15.8	6.3	9.6	7.8	2.2	4.3	0.001**
Re-experience	24.4	9.3	15.0	7.0	2.0	7.5	0.000**

** significant at >005 level.

the employees. Employees recorded three areas in which they found the trauma care programme helpful. First, they were helped by having the common symptoms of traumatic stress explained to them. Second, they found it very helpful to listen to their colleagues' experiences of the rescue of the train passengers. Third, they valued spending time with others involved in dealing with the disaster.

Following the debriefing, seven employees asked for trauma counselling. The counselling was seen as positive by all the employees, the main reasons being that it provided an opportunity to talk to someone from outside the organisation and a chance to deal with personal issues in private. The provision of individual training in relaxation was also highly valued, as was the personal advice on how to deal with post-trauma symptoms. Overall, the employees reported that they felt much better and that they had been well looked after. It was also recognised that the trauma care programme was valuable and needed.

Manager survey

The Manager survey assessed seven areas of the employees' performance: 1) performance on job; 2) timekeeping; 3) approach to work; 4) ability to concentrate; 5) attitude to customers; 6) relationship with colleagues; and 7) cheerfulness. In addition, comparisons were made with the number of days of absence recorded in the first quarter of 1999 (seven to nine months before the crash) and the corresponding quarter in 2000 (two to four months following the crash). The performance indicators showed that all the employees demonstrated an improvement in performance between November 1999 and April 2000 (see Table 15.2), with the greatest improvement being in their cheerfulness, ability to concentrate and performance on the job. The managers assessed the performance of most of the employees as excellent or very good in April 2000. There was a reduction in the level of sickness absence between the first quarter of 1999 and 2000. In the group of 12 employees 14 fewer days absence were recorded in 2000 than had been recorded in 1999.

Manager feedback

The store's management team had not only to manage the health and well-being of their staff but also had to run a retail operation. Some of the managers were actively involved in the rescue of injured

Table 15.2 Managers' assessment of employee performance

Performance area	Av. improvement	T score	Sig.
Performance on job	0.50	2.6	0.033*
Timekeeping	0.38	1.0	0.351
Approach to work	0.25	1.5	0.170
Ability to concentrate	1.25	3.99	0.005**
Attitude to customers	0.25	1.53	0.170
Relationship to colleagues	0.38	1.16	0.29
Cheerfulness	1.5	5.61	0.001**

* P < 0.05
** P < 0.01

passengers and had their own well-being to consider. The management team recorded their gratitude for the opportunity to use the occupational health team to deal with the psychological impact of the crash on the staff. In disasters the task of managing the recovery often requires the introduction of specialist teams, each with its own roles and responsibilities (Flin 1996). The operational impact of the crash on the store was enormous. Many of the roads in the area were closed or had restricted movement due to the needs of the emergency vehicles. This made it difficult for the store to get its lorries through with essential supplies to replenish its shelves. The press and others working at the scene required feeding and many used the facilities of the store. Regular customers found it difficult to get to the store through the emergency services' cordons. Many of the families and friends of the injured and bereaved visited the store to thank employees and to buy flowers to place at the scene or to write in the condolence book. The store's first aid materials had been exhausted in helping the rail crash victims and needed restocking. The store's managers felt that they were lacking in the necessary knowledge and expertise to deal with the impact of the disaster on the workforce. The managers also believed that the employees would not wish to talk to them about very personal problems.

Discussion

There are few organisations where there is a total absence of traumatic events, be they physical or psychological. There is a clear need for organisations to respond appropriately to all forms of trauma in order to protect the psychological well-being of employees. With an increasingly complex and technological world, the likelihood of organisations having to deal with large-scale disasters is growing. Although many organisations have introduced trauma care programmes, few have undertaken evaluations of these programmes that meet the rigour required by academic researchers. Despite this lack of evaluation, organisations and employees appear to have a high level of satisfaction with the effectiveness of this support in helping the recovery process.

The current debate raises a number of important questions:

- To be successful is it enough to show that a trauma care programme meets organisational expectations (e.g. is highly valued by the users and reduces levels of sickness absence)?
- In order to evaluate trauma care programmes, is it ethically and morally acceptable to withhold interventions from some employees in order to 'prove' that debriefing or some other aspect of the trauma care programme is effective?
- Can we trust the validity and reliability of clinical assessment tools designed for use in hospitals or laboratory settings when used with employees in the workplace?

Chapter 16

The Manchester bomb – trauma counselling and long-term support

Introduction

Fortunately, most people who have been exposed to a traumatic event will experience a short period of distress and then go on to live their lives free from haunting memories (Van der Kolk and McFarlane 1996). However, this is not always the case. In this chapter, employees whose workplace was destroyed by an IRA bomb were followed up two years after the incident. All had returned to work and appeared to be coping well, despite occasional problems on Bonfire Night or when there was a fire alarm test. Yet, beneath the surface many of these employees were living and coping with high levels of psychological symptoms. In this chapter the interventions undertaken to support this group of employees is described together with the outcomes. The outcomes indicated that the interventions had brought about a significant improvement in the employees' psychological well-being and quality of life.

The bomb

On Saturday 15 June 1996 just after 11 a.m., the IRA detonated a bomb in a vehicle parked next to the Arndale Centre in Manchester. The police had been given a telephone warning at around 9.30 a.m. and the suspect van was identified 15 minutes later. The shops and offices in the surrounding area were evacuated and the area cordoned off. Longridge House, a regional office of the Royal Insurance Company, was within the cordoned area and 35 employees and two security guards were on duty. As the area was being cleared, these employees became aware that they were becoming isolated within the cordoned area. A number of staff left the office to pick up breakfast rolls and noticed the cordons but were allowed back into the area by the police. A security guard asked a police officer what was happening and the officer said that the staff should stay in the building and that the police would keep them informed. The security guards then told the staff this. At around 10.30 a.m. a helicopter began circling overhead. At 11.10 a.m. there was a controlled explosion at which time many of the employees believed that the danger was over. Seven minutes later the main bomb exploded close to Longridge House causing significant damage to the building and the surrounding area. Within Longridge House, ceilings had fallen down and windows had been blown in, furniture had been dislodged and there was a gaping hole in the external walls. As a result of the blast, employees had suffered broken bones, cuts and other injuries but miraculously no one had been killed. After the explosion, firefighters entered the area and it was obvious that they did not expect to find anyone still within the cordon. The firefighters helped the employees out of the building but it took some time for arrangements to be made to take the injured to hospital. Some of the injured staff had to wait for more than 20 minutes before they had any medical attention. The employees were extremely shocked by what had happened to them and most left belongings in the building. This became a cause for concern as these belongings included house keys, cheque books and other personal items. Initially the company was not allowed access to the building, however when access was made possible the personal belongings were recovered and returned to the employees.

Initial support

Fortunately, the Royal Insurance Company had in place a well-developed crisis management plan and process. As the news of the bomb emerged, the company's crisis response came into operation. The crisis management team for the site initially focused its efforts on trying to establish who had been present at the time of the explosion, and whether they had been injured. This proved to be more difficult than expected as the bomb blast had destroyed the out of hours register and the injured employees had been dispersed between different hospitals in the city. It was not until the following Tuesday that everyone present on that day had been accounted for and contacted.

The trauma support plan was used to support the employees. After the initial contact everyone apart from those confined to hospital was invited to gatherings in a nearby hotel. In these gatherings they were provided with information and psychological support. The immediate trauma support was delivered by a group of trauma counsellors and included group debriefing, which provided the employees with an opportunity to share their experiences. At this time the employees who were having ongoing difficulties were offered the opportunity of individual counselling. The impact of the bomb on the employees is shown in Table 16.1.

There was a higher proportion of women at work on the day of the bomb. On average the female employees took more time off work than the male employees and also had more counselling. After two years, more male employees had left the organisation, however the most common reason for leaving the company for both male and female employees was a promotion opportunity.

Soon after the explosion, the organisation went through a merger and there was a considerable amount of change. Two years after the bomb there was a review of the way the company had handled the disaster. The review showed that although there were some areas where improvements could be made the organisation had handled the disaster well, both commercially and for its employees. It was therefore a surprise to the organisation when it learnt that several of its employees were still having significant psychological problems. It was found that despite having returned to work and apparently working normally, many employees were also coping with phobias, panic attacks and other trauma-related symptoms. As soon as the organisation became aware of the nature and magnitude of these problems, it decided that there was a need to address the employee difficulties and to introduce a programme of support.

Table 16.1 Impact of the Manchester bomb on employees

	Male	Female	Total
Present on day	11	24	35
Average number of days off work sick	20.8	44.4	37
Took up offer of counselling organised by company	2	10	12
Av. no. of counselling sessions provided by company*	1.5	5.3	4.6
No. still with company 2 years after bomb	7	21	28

* Some employees arranged their own counselling.

Dealing with chronic trauma

The first step was to assess the size of the problem. Royal & SunAlliance (R&SA) (previously Royal Insurance) provided a briefing on the handling of the initial incident and some background on the employees involved. From this briefing, it became clear that the senior manager who led the crisis management team at the time of the bomb and who was still in post was highly regarded by all the employees.

Seminars were arranged to which the employees were invited, including two that had left the company but who were still working in Manchester. The seminars were held in October 1998 and were attended by 16 people. They began with an introduction by the senior manager and personnel manager, after which a presentation was given that looked at stress and post-traumatic stress and described the differences between the two. During the presentation, there were questions from the participants and a recognition of the trauma symptoms being described.

After the presentation, everyone completed a short traumatic stress questionnaire and a stress questionnaire. The questionnaires were very helpful as they allowed everyone to talk about the symptoms that they were still experiencing. It was reassuring for many of the participants to realise that they were not the only ones who were having difficulties with panic attacks or being upset by loud noises.

After the questionnaires were completed, there was an open forum providing an opportunity for the participants to talk about their feelings. A feeling of anger emerged towards the people who had planted the bomb, together with feelings of frustration that the bombers had not been caught and that even if they were caught nothing could be done to make up for what they had suffered on that day. There was almost equal anger against the police for their failure to clear the building before the bomb went off. Finally, there was anger against the media, who the employees believed had mis-reported the bombing by continually underplaying the plight of the Royal Insurance employees who were the only people actually within the cordoned area at the time of the explosion.

Guilt was expressed by some employees who believed they could have done more to help their injured colleagues. However, those who had been injured also had the opportunity to reassure their colleagues that they did not feel that they had not been cared for during the incident.

Many of the staff described classical symptoms of anxiety; these included panic attacks, phobias and hyperarousal. All the participants said that they wanted to get on with their lives, but that this was difficult. Participants described how every time a child burst a balloon, a firework exploded, a van was parked on double yellow lines or police cordons were seen, the old feelings of fear and anxiety returned.

After the seminar the questionnaire data was analysed. The mean scores on the IES-E and Goldberg scales are shown in Table 16.2. An inspection of the individual scores showed that of the 16 employees who attended the seminars 7 met the criteria for post-traumatic stress, 10 had high levels of anxiety and 8 high levels of depression. As high levels of anxiety and hyperarousal were a common feature for most of these employees, a half-day relaxation training session was organised to provide them with a range of relaxation skills. These included the use of progressive relaxation, diaphragmatic breathing, meditation, visualisation, sensible eating and exercise (Davis *et al.* 1995).

All the employees were offered trauma counselling. Nine employees who had attended the seminar accepted this offer together with two additional employees who had not attended the seminars but who had recognised that they were having problems relating to the bomb. Of the 11 employees who came for counselling 8 had symptoms indicating high levels of post-traumatic stress.

Trauma counselling

The approach to the trauma counselling employed cognitive behavioural techniques (Scott and Palmer 2000) together with narrative therapy (White 1995) and psychobiological education. The counselling was made up of three parts: assessment, understanding the symptoms and then increasing coping skills and resilience. While

Table 16.2 Mean scores and standard deviations for IES-E and Goldberg scales*

Symptom	Avoidance	Arousal	Re-experience	Anxiety	Depression
Mean score	12.4	13.2	16.9	4.7	2.9
Std Dev.	3.9	4.9	7.2	2.4	2.1

* The cut-off score for avoidance and arousal is 14 and for re-experience 22. For anxiety the cut-off is 5 and for depression 3.

each session was made up of the three elements, the balance between them changed as the sessions progressed. Each of the sessions lasted around two hours and they typically took place once a fortnight for the first two or three sessions and then monthly.

First session: what happened?

In the first session, the employee described what they could recall from the day of the explosion. They described what they were doing during the morning and then what happened when the bomb went off, in the immediate aftermath and during the next few days. Particular emphasis was given to their sensory experiences at these times. In many of the employees, there were strong elements of irrational guilt and shame. The irrational thinking was explored and gently challenged. The session then looked at current symptoms which were explained with reference to the psychobiological impact of traumatic stress (see Chapter 2) and simple coping skills were offered as ways of dealing with these symptoms.

Second session: what can help you?

The second session began with a review of the first session and an examination of any changes in symptoms that had taken place during the intervening period. A full personal history was then taken. This identified where there were pre-existing problems and enabled the identification of the coping skills that the employee had developed previously. The process of externalisation that was used during this stage allowed the previous problems not to be seen as intrinsic to the employee but rather as things that *happened* to them. Externalisation changed statements such as 'I am an alcoholic' to 'You are someone who abuses alcohol' or 'I am a depressive' to 'You are someone who is sometimes affected by depression'. During this process negative life events are looked at in another way so that someone who has had an unhappy childhood would be asked 'What is it about you that helped you to survive this?' By the end of the session the employee had begun to understand that they had a lot of skills which could be used to help them and that they did not have to be a victim of their symptoms. At the end of the session, further information was given on trauma symptoms that had been described during the session. Where necessary additional training in coping skills was offered.

Middle sessions: handling the symptoms

As with the earlier session, the middle session began with a review of the progress since the previous session and identification of any symptoms. Where symptoms continued a process of controlled visualisation was used. During this process, the employee was put through a short process of relaxation. They then imagined facing the situations in which they were having problems, for example walking past a parked van or passing a police cordon. The visualisation was based on the employee's own experiences and was introduced slowly allowing the employee to stop the process and go through the relaxation script again should the story become too distressing. This visualisation process was run through a number of times until it stopped causing any emotional disturbance. The employee was then asked to run through the process one more time. This time they were asked to look around themselves at each stage of the story. During this visualisation, they were to notice as many other ordinary things as possible, such as people going about their business, animals, buildings or the weather. Most employees found that there were some rather funny or unusual things happening, such as dogs pulling their owners along, balloons floating in the air or children eating ice cream.

Closing session: moving on

As the employees improved, targets were set for the future. Employees who had been experiencing panic attacks were able to go into shops, cinemas and aircraft where once this had been impossible. As the numbers of panic attacks and phobic responses fell, the emphasis changed to helping the employee gain confidence in their new skills. Employees were also encouraged to identify others who would provide them with support should they have any difficulties in the future. At the final session, employees completed the IES-E and the Anxiety & Depression Scale.

Results

The IES-E scores for employees who attended the trauma counselling and those who chose not to attend were compared. The results (see Table 16.3) showed that the group that had attended the counselling had higher levels of arousal and re-experience symptoms on the

Table 16.3 Comparison between the scores of the group of employees who chose to be counselled and those who did not prior to the commencement of counselling

Symptoms	Mean difference	T score	Significance	95% confidence interval
Arousal	−5.65	−2.83	0.012	−9.88 to −1.42
Avoidance	−0.87	−0.45	0.659	−4.98 to −3.24
Re-experience	−9.03	−3.17	0.006	−15.06 to −2.99
Gen. factor	−15.55	−3.35	0.004	−25.37 to −5.73
Anxiety	−3.19	−3.40	0.004	−5.19 to −1.20
Depression	−1.22	−1.16	0.262	−3.45 to 1.14

IES-E questionnaire and higher levels of anxiety prior to the counselling. However, their avoidance and depression scores were not significantly different.

The scores for the employees who were counselled and those who were not counselled six months after the completion of all the counselling were then calculated (see Table 16.4). These scores showed that there was now no significant difference between the scores of the employees who did not require counselling and those that required counselling. The results also showed that the mean scores for the counselled employees were now lower than those for their non-counselled colleagues.

The final analysis looked at the changes that had taken place in the employees who had been counselled. The results showed a significant improvement in the post-trauma symptoms found in the counselled group but not in the non-counselled group (see Table 16.5).

Table 16.4 Comparison between the scores of the group of employees who chose to be counselled and those who did not, after the completion of counselling

Symptoms	Mean difference	T score	Significance	95% confidence interval
Arousal	0.55	0.25	0.804	−4.04 to 5.13
Avoidance	4.12	1.46	0.164	−1.87 to 10.11
Re-experience	2.53	0.98	0.342	−2.95 to 8.01
Gen. factor	7.19	1.30	0.212	−4.53 to 18.92
Anxiety	0.84	0.81	0.428	−1.36 to 3.05
Depression	1.69	1.95	0.070	−0.152 to 3.53

Table 16.5 Comparison between the before and after scores for employees who were counselled and those who were not

Symptoms	Mean difference		T score		Significance		95% confidence interval	
Counselled?	Yes	No	Yes	No	Yes	No	Yes	No
Arousal	6.91	0.71	5.90	0.918	0.0001	0.40	4.3 to 9.52	−1.2 to 2.6
Avoidance	5.27	0.29	3.63	0.141	0.005	0.89	2.0 to 8.51	−4.7 to 5.3
Re-experience	12.27	0.71	6.90	0.431	0.0001	0.68	8.3 to 16.2	−3.3 to 4.8
Gen. factor	24.45	1.71	8.62	0.715	0.0001	0.50	18.2 to 30.8	−4.2 to 7.6
Anxiety	4.18	0.14	7.15	0.149	0.0001	0.89	2.9 to 5.5	−2.2 to 2.5
Depression	1.91	−1.00	4.01	−1.145	0.002	0.20	0.9 to 3.0	−2.7 to 0.7

At the end of the period, the post-trauma scores for the employees who had been counselled were less than for those who had not required counselling. None of the counselled employees had scores that would indicate the presence of PTSD.

Discussion

The results showed that the employees who were counselled experienced a significant reduction in their post-trauma scores. Their scores at the end of the counselling were lower than those of their colleagues who did not receive counselling. These results would suggest that the counselling was effective in reducing the post-traumatic stress.

This study could be criticised on a number of grounds:

- there was not a random allocation of subjects to counselling;
- the interventions were not of a common duration;
- the interventions varied according to the needs of the employee.

While it would have been experimentally more acceptable to randomly assign these employees to the counselling and non-counselling groups, this would not have been morally or organisationally acceptable. It would not have been reasonable to continue the counselling beyond the time that it was beneficial as this would have had the effect of building dependency rather than empowering the employee to use their own support resources. The intervention, although using the same techniques, was adapted to meet the needs of the individual employee.

Postscript

After the counselling had been completed the area of Manchester where Longridge House had once stood and which had been screened off while the area was redeveloped, was opened up. A new Marks and Spencer store had been built on the site of the office block. This provided an opportunity to help the employees to go back to the place of their trauma over three years earlier. R&SA contacted Marks and Spencer and made arrangements for the employees to be taken into the store after hours in order to deal with any remaining traumatic memories.

The exercise was planned with the aim of helping the employees to:

- accurately remember the past;
- prepare themselves for returning to the site;
- become totally aware of the sensory information from the present;
- deal with the emotions and memories that may emerge when being re-exposed to familiar sights.

On the evening of the visit, the 12 employees and four supporters met together and talked about the old building. They looked at plans of the building to help them remember in detail the location where they had worked and the position of other buildings in relation to Longridge House. The group then walked to the site. There were some emotions shown at this stage but this did not prevent the group walking around the site noting the changes that had taken place. All the time the employees were walking around the new store they were being refocused on the new structures and things that they were experiencing in the present. When the members of the group regained their sense of calm, they entered the building. First they were given some refreshments and when they felt ready they moved into the store. The group walked to a place where they were able to look out of windows onto scenes very similar to those they would have seen from their office windows in Longridge House. During this time, the employees were being constantly asked to describe what they were seeing and to notice the things around them in the store. After a period of about an hour, the employees appeared to be calm and more relaxed. The following day, two of the employees who had found the visit to the store particularly difficult asked to be taken to the store a second time. They wanted to make sure that they would be able to go there again on their own and felt that they would like a little more practice. A day later they reported that they had managed to walk around the store on their own.

Summary: Part IV

The four case studies that make up Part IV demonstrate what can be achieved when working in organisational settings. The first two were designed to try to identify the impact of two types of traumatic experience on workers. In the first, the employees were crew members working in cash carrying vans. All had been exposed to an armed raid. The results of the study showed that there were personal and situational factors which appeared to make the incidence of post-traumatic stress more likely. These included a history of anxiety or depression and being a parent. There were also some situational factors which were associated with higher levels of post-traumatic stress. These were where a gun was fired, or they were threatened with gas or a physical attack. This study supports much of the previous work in this area and suggests that where any of these factors are present the organisation should take special care of the employee.

The second study looked at the impact of a chronic form of trauma: bullying. While bullying is not accepted as a situation which meets the criteria for a traumatic event it does have the potency to cause similar symptoms. This study showed that although victims of bullying had the trauma symptoms of re-experience, avoidance and arousal the relationship between these symptoms was rather different in that victims of bullying were much more likely to have symptoms of arousal and re-experience co-occurring. These are important findings and indicate that there is no reason why post-traumatic stress interventions should not be used effectively to help victims of bullying.

The third and fourth studies involved the delivery and evaluation of post-trauma interventions. In the first, the employees were experiencing the acute trauma of a very recent traumatic exposure. They were provided with immediate diffusing and then with group debriefing and trauma education. In this study the debriefing was successful in helping the employees recover from their ordeal and return to work. The scores on the IES-E showed that four months after the traumatic exposure the employees had experienced a significant reduction in their trauma symptoms and that their performance at work had improved. The final study looked at the needs of a group of employees who had been exposed to a major trauma two and a half years earlier. By this time, the symptoms were well established and for many of the employees had altered their lives for the worse. Most of the employees avoided the part of the town where they had worked at the time of the explosion. Panic attacks, phobias and communication difficulties were common features. However, all these symptoms had gone unnoticed by managers and all the employees were working normally with no significantly different levels of sickness absence to their colleagues. The use of a simple trauma counselling model, which was adapted to the needs of the individual employee, was used to help these chronically traumatised employees address their post-trauma symptoms. The results of this intervention allowed the employees to return to normal functioning and even to return to the place where the bomb was detonated.

Part V

Conclusions and future directions

This book has been developed over a period of eight years. Each stage has used the foundations created in an earlier stage of its development. The key difference between this research and much contemporary trauma research is that this has been undertaken within the workplace. The complexity of the working environment has not been regarded as a problem but rather as a reality that needed to be recognised and worked with.

This final part of the book reviews the work undertaken, identifying gaps and areas for further research. Taking its two aspects, research and practice, the study is reviewed in order to demonstrate the way in which these approaches have complemented and supported each other. Finally the book closes with a recognition that future research in the area of workplace trauma must address the need to develop new ways to undertake research and practice in the real world if it is to adequately respond to the needs of the traumatised employee and the organisation.

Chapter 17

Conclusions and future directions

Introduction

This book combines scientific research with the qualitative findings of a practitioner. These two aspects of investigation have been brought together in such a way that the one enriches the other. Although traumatic stress has only been recognised for around 20 years, it has now been acknowledged that extreme stress brings about changes in psychological and physiological functioning. The changes that occur following exposure to traumatic events are different in nature to those that occur in response to the normal stress of daily living (Shalev 1996).

The workplace as the theatre in which the traumatic experience is played has been largely under-researched. This lack of recognition is surprising given that the number of people exposed to life-threatening events in the workplace is over 1.5 per cent of the working population each year (Health and Safety Executive 1999a). This book addresses this gap in knowledge by looking at trauma and traumatic stress from the perspective of the organisation and the employee. As a result of the work involved in the development of the book, new organisational approaches to managing traumatic stress in the workplace were created and tested in addition to the development of new post-trauma measurement tools and interventions.

This study brings to the fore the need for a more creative way of dealing with psychological problems within the workplace. The need for a process focused on solving the real problems facing organisations and employees is identified. This new approach will need to capture verbal expressions and numerical analysis and then use them in conjunction with each other as a means of establishing working hypotheses based on sparse and complex data.

In this, the final chapter, it is useful to review these two themes in order to identify where other work in this field may lie.

Practice

The historical development of the construct of traumatic stress illustrates the value of balancing systematic clinical observations with scientific research. Without the recorded observations of early clinicians and historians such as Kardiner (1941) and Marshall (1944) there would not have been the rich source of material on which hypotheses could be formed and tested. This observational approach was used in Chapter 3 in which the testimony of trauma victims was collected and systematically analysed to illustrate the changing phases of the peri-traumatic and traumatic responses. The recording of statements made by individuals following a traumatic exposure was of great value in the identification of the additional items used to augment the IES (Horowitz et al. 1979) and create the IES-E. Interestingly, Horowitz had used the same observational process when developing the original IES measure.

The testimony of the victims of traumatic stress and the statutory legislation and guidance were helpful in the development of the organisational models of trauma care. Again, a balance had to be achieved between the needs of organisations to meet their duty of care towards their employees and the need to identify what was appropriate in different organisations. It was fortunate that during the course of these studies opportunities arose that allowed the development of trauma care programmes in a wide range of different types of organisation. These organisations included members of the communications, emergency services, retailing and insurance industries. Careful listening to management and employees in each organisation showed the very different histories, cultures and ways of handling problems that existed. Although it might have been simpler to enforce a common approach to dealing with traumatic events on these organisations, this would not have recognised their unique character and needs. The guidance presented in Chapter 6 takes this learning and the supporting literature to propose a working approach to traumatic stress. This model was then illustrated in Chapter 8 where the problems associated with introducing such a model are identified.

The development of post-trauma interventions and the timing of their utilisation have largely been established by practitioners.

Practitioners have developed models they believe work and typically fail to formally evaluate them. Three post-trauma interventions were developed in support of this research (Tehrani and Westlake 1994; Tehrani 1995). These were a group debriefing, individual debriefing and diffusing models. These models were developed for use within a working environment, recognising the value of involving the organisation, managers and peers of those who had been exposed to a traumatic event. The models were developed using the knowledge gained from 20 years of experience in undertaking counselling and trauma therapy within organisations and were informed by personal research, psychological theory and the available literature on post-traumatic stress.

Research

Practice without the rigour of critical evaluation rarely takes knowledge forward. This study has used the tools currently available to test and evaluate the organisational and individual interventions that had been developed. The use of a wide range of evaluative measures was a feature of this research and this is illustrated in Chapter 8 where the introduction of trauma care programmes was evaluated based on reductions in sickness absence, medical retirements and stress-related sickness absence. However, these findings were only part of the story in that the equally important qualitative feedback from the employees who had used the service also reported their satisfaction with the support that they had received.

An important aspect of the study was the development of a new measurement tool. The original IES (Horowitz et al. 1979) only provided a measure of two of the three features of post-traumatic stress. In order to remove the necessity for augmenting the IES with another questionnaire to provide information on the missing feature (arousal), new items were identified from clinical work. However, having identified a number of possible items these needed to be tested to ensure that the introduction of the new items did not upset the validity and reliability of the original items but added the new dimension of arousal. The testing of the items and the questionnaire using traditional psychometric techniques showed that the new items established the new factor satisfactorily. The analysis of data from traumatised employees showed that the new scale was a valid and reliable tool that could identify people who had suffered a negative life event.

The new scale (IES-E) was then used in four studies as a means of gathering information on the impact of traumatic exposure and on the effectiveness of post-trauma interventions.

In Chapter 13 the aim was to identify factors which might predispose employees to develop traumatic stress following exposure to a life-threatening event. Using the IES-E it was possible to identify a number of personal and situational factors which increased the likelihood of high levels of post-traumatic stress symptoms. This was a useful finding as it allowed the organisation to put in place additional support for employees where the risk of developing symptoms was higher.

The question that then arose was whether people who suffered personal attacks that were less violent or acute than an armed raid or train crash could also develop traumatic stress. In Chapter 14, the study looked at victims of chronic bullying who were assessed using the IES-E. The results were interesting on a simple level where there was clear evidence to show that bullying was linked to symptoms. However, factor analysis of the results from the bullied subjects revealed that the relationship between the three factors was different to those found in victims of armed raids. This finding is interesting in terms of whether bullying causes traumatic stress or another similar disorder. The finding also raised questions on studies that use trauma questionnaires to assess subjects exposed to distressing situations, such as stillbirth and domestic violence, without first ensuring that the questionnaire retains its psychometric properties with these subjects.

Chapter 15 took the work undertaken in Chapter 8 a stage further. In Chapter 8 the evaluation of the trauma care approach could only be achieved on the basis of a cost benefit analysis. However, the development of the IES-E enabled the model of trauma care adopted by Sainsbury's to be evaluated clinically using the IES-E and organisational outcome measures. As with most disasters, the main aim of post-incident support is to assist the victims of the traumatic event as quickly as possible. This study demonstrated the benefit of the group debriefing process and how the organisational trauma care programme achieved its business objectives. The results of the psychological assessments demonstrated a dramatic reduction in post-traumatic stress symptoms over a three-month period. The organisational measures also showed that the workforce returned to work, had lower levels of sickness absence than during the previous year and delivered a high level of customer service within a relatively short period of time.

The final study in Chapter 16 looked at the long-term impact of a traumatic exposure. Incredibly, it was found that two years after a traumatic event a high proportion of employees were still experiencing significant levels of traumatic stress symptoms. A model of trauma counselling that had been developed as part of this study was used to provide support for these employees. The effectiveness of the intervention was then tested using the IES-E. Again it was found that the intervention resulted in a reduction of symptoms to a level which allowed normal functioning. The major finding from this study was the recognition that people can continue working while experiencing high levels of traumatic stress. Yet, despite the length of time that these symptoms had been affecting the employees, with appropriate counselling, the symptoms could be reduced in a relatively short period.

Bringing research and practice together

There exists within psychology a creative tension between theory and practice. On the one hand, the diagnosis and treatment of traumatic stress owes much to the painstaking observations, practical experience and reflective practice of trauma clinicians. On the other hand, the rich theories on the nature and determinants of trauma have been derived from general psychological concepts, refined and modified by the empirical testing and academic critique of trauma theorists.

The distinction between theory and practice is, in many ways, a straw man, as there is considerable overlap between the two (Anderson 1998). The creative cycle (see Figure 17.1), illustrates the

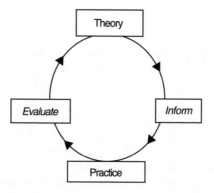

Figure 17.1 The creative cycle

relationship between theory and practice in the process of increasing knowledge. Ideally, robust research should influence best practice, while observations from practice should influence the direction of research. To achieve a creative dynamic, theory should inform practice and practice should validate theory. A recurring theme throughout this book is the need to maintain communication and connections between theory and practice. Connections occur when theoretical principles are stated in predictive and measurable forms and practice uses measurement tools capable of providing the quality of feedback which can refine or redefine theory. Instead of each being dissected out, both should be considered as part of a vibrant and living whole.

Unfortunately, much of what is possible in trauma research is being lost as a result of the fixed attitudes of some researchers and practitioners. Rausch (1974) describes the position of the practitioner as someone who 'rejects the traditional model of statistical research because it has no value to him'. This is perhaps not surprising when one considers the publication of journal articles, which have shown a substantial decline in contributions from 31 per cent 30 years ago to around 5 per cent in 1997 (Anderson 1998). It is believed by many researchers that the laboratory approach is the ultimate scientific method and that the less precise and controlled methods of field observation are merely preludes to scientific study (Goldman 1978). The result is that small-scale studies, regardless of their merit, are excluded from systematic reviews because they fail to use random controlled trials (Rose and Bisson 1998). The current tendency to separate research from practice is unhelpful and should be challenged by researchers and practitioners.

The future

There are a number of areas in which the work undertaken in this book might be taken forward. First, although a basic model of organisational trauma care has been developed, the relative importance of the elements of a trauma care programme require further evaluation. This needs to look at both the outcome and the processes involved in trauma care programmes. The outcome analysis would be used to see how closely each programme meets its objectives while the process analysis would be concerned with a systematic survey of what actually occurs in the programme. This information would help researchers and practitioners identify the critical elements of the programme and ensure that where deviations from the original protocol or outcomes occur these are investigated and appropriate action taken.

Second, research into therapeutic interventions such as debriefing and counselling has traditionally been undertaken using groups of subjects and has involved looking at changes in central tendencies. It would be interesting to contrast this approach with a case study approach in which detailed accounts are taken from a number of traumatised employees. The research could then focus on identifying the antecedents, contextual factors, perceptions and attitudes of the individual to a particular aspect of the traumatic experience. This data could then be used to identify which of the factors affected the outcome of trauma debriefing or counselling.

Finally, while it has been widely accepted that traumatic stress questionnaires are transferable, research undertaken in this book suggests that the impact of different types of traumatic event may not be the same. There is a need for comparative studies to identify whether different traumatic stressors lead to different responses. Specifically, does lower-level chronic trauma such as bullying, domestic violence and emergency service work have different symptom profiles to the acute trauma of a major rail crash, armed raid or rape?

More generally it is hoped that in this field there will be closer working between researchers and practitioners. The practitioner can and should undertake research in the settings in which they work. Research is more useful and alive when it deals with current problems and current situations. Too much psychology seeks to establish universal laws of human behaviour where none are to be found. Cronbach (1975), in viewing psychology as a whole, makes the point that:

> Too narrow an identification with science has fixed our eyes upon an inappropriate goal. The goal of our work is not to amass generalisations atop which a theoretical tower can some-day be erected . . . The special task of the social scientist in each generation is to pin down the contemporary facts. Beyond that, he shares with the humanistic scholar and the artist in the effort to gain insight into contemporary relationships, and to realign the culture's view of man with present realities. To know man as he is, is no mean aspiration.

Appendix A: Post-incident questionnaire (CASHCO)

People react in different ways to traumatic incidents. We want to make sure that the support we provide is helpful to you. This questionnaire is part of the way that we achieve this. All the personal information you provide will be kept confidential.

Name		Today's date	
Home address			
Home phone no.		Work phone no.	
Age years		Male	Female

Feelings about the raid

Below are a number of comments made by people after stressful events. Please check the list and tick ✔ the column that is true for you during the past fortnight.

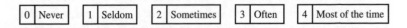

| 0 | Never | 1 | Seldom | 2 | Sometimes | 3 | Often | 4 | Most of the time |

Statement		0	1	2	3	4
F01	I thought about it when I did not mean to					
F02	I avoided letting myself get upset when I thought about it or was reminded of it					
F03	I tried to remove it from my memory					
F04	I had trouble falling asleep or staying asleep					
F05	I had waves of strong feelings about it					
F06	I had dreams about it					
F07	I stayed away from any reminders					
F08	I felt as if it hadn't happened or wasn't real					
F09	I tried not to talk about it					
F10	Pictures about it popped into my mind					
F11	Other things kept making me think about it					
F12	I was aware that I still had a lot of feelings about it but did not deal with them					
F13	I tried not to think about it					
F14	Any reminder brought back feelings about it					
F15	My feelings about it were kind of numb					

Other symptoms

Statement		0	1	2	3	4
A01	I had problems falling or staying asleep					
A02	I felt down or depressed for no reason					
A03	I jumped or got startled by sudden noises					
A04	I had a tendency to avoid other people					
A05	I was irritable with others					
A06	I experienced wide mood swings					
A07	I experienced feelings of self-blame or guilt					
A08	I avoided some situations or places					
A09	I experienced tenseness in my body					

Support following the incident

Talking

I have talked to	Yes/No	Very helpful	Helpful	Not helpful
Partner				
Family				
Friends				
Colleagues				
Manager				
Occupational health				
Welfare				
Union				
Other				

Debriefing

I have been debriefed by	Yes/No	Very helpful	Helpful	Not helpful
Manager				
Colleague				
Occupational health				
Welfare				
Other e.g. GP				

Support

I have had support from	Yes/No	Very helpful	Helpful	Not helpful
Organisation				
Manager				
Occupational health				
Welfare				
Solicitor's office				
Other e.g. GP				

Other comments

Thank you for completing the questionnaire. Please send it in the envelope provided.

Appendix B: Bullying survey

This survey has been designed to find out how much stress is caused by bullying in the workplace. The questionnaires are completed and returned anonymously so that the strictest confidentiality can be assured.

Are you a

1   Manager ☐   Non-manager ☐

2 Personal details

Age	Under 26 yrs		26–35 yrs		36–45 yrs		46–55 yrs		Over 55 yrs	

3 | Male | | Female | |

Bullying and harassment at work

Please tick the boxes that apply to you	**Yes**	**No**
4	Have you been bullied or harassed in the past two years?		
5	Do you know anyone else who has been bullied in the past two years?		

If your answers to Q4 and Q5 are no, complete Q27 and Q28 on p. 238 (quality of support), then return the questionnaire.

6	Did the bullying involve a manager?		
7	Did the bullying involve a non-manager?		
8	Did the bullying involve a customer or member of the public?		
9	Was the bullying or harassment related to a physical characteristic or disability?		
10	Was the bullying or harassment related to race?		
11	Was the bullying or harassment related to sex or sexual orientation?		

If you have personally experienced bullying or have witnessed others being bullied, which of the following happened?	Yes	No
12	Unpleasant personal remarks		
13	Intimidation		
14	Hiding or taking personal property		
15	Ganging up		
16	Physical attack		
17	Malicious gossip		
18	Bad language		
19	Threats		
20	Public humiliation		
21	Being ignored or 'sent to Coventry'		
22	Unfair criticism		

If you have experienced or witnessed bullying	Yes	No
23	Did you report it to your manager?		

If you didn't report the bullying what was the reason?

24	I did not think it would be taken seriously		
25	My manager was the bully		
26	It would have made things worse		

Quality of support

Indicate the quality of the support you have been given by your employer		Very Good	Good	OK	Poor	Very poor
27	Training or counselling to deal with stress, bullying and harassment	1	2	3	4	5
28	The way your employer deals with bullies and harassers	1	2	3	4	5

Stress questionnaire

Spend a moment or two thinking about the bullying you experienced or witnessed. Indicate how often the following things have occurred during the past month by ticking ✔ the appropriate box.

0	Never		1	Seldom		2	Sometimes		3	Often		4	Most of the time

(please see questionnaire on opposite page)

Statement			0	1	2	3	4
29		I felt as if it hadn't happened or wasn't real					
30		I tried not to think about it					
31		I tried not to talk about it					
32		My feelings about it were kind of numb					
33		I stayed away from any reminders					
34		I tried to remove it from my memory					
35		I was aware that I still had a lot of feelings about it but did not deal with them					
36		I felt down or depressed for no reason					
37		I experienced wide mood swings					
38		I experienced tenseness in my body					
39		I was irritable with others					
40		I had a tendency to avoid other people					
41		I jumped or got startled by sudden noises					
42		I avoided some situations or places					
43		I thought about it when I did not mean to					
44		I have experienced feelings of self-blame or guilt					
45		Pictures about it popped into my mind					
46		I had waves of strong feelings about it					
47		I had dreams about it					
48		I had trouble falling asleep or staying asleep					
49		Other things kept making me think about it					
50		Any reminder brought back feelings about it					
51		I avoided letting myself get upset when I thought about it or was reminded of it					

References

Abueg, F.R., Drescher, K.D. and Kubany, E.S. (1995) Natural disasters, in
F.M. Dattilio and A. Freeman (eds) *Cognitive-Behavioural Strategies in
Crisis Intervention*. New York: Guilford Press.

Alexander, D.A. (1993) Stress among body handlers: a long-term follow up,
British Journal of Psychiatry, 163: 806–8.

Alexander, D.A. and Klein, S. (2001) Ambulance personnel and critical incidents – impact of accident and emergency work on mental health and
emotional wellbeing, *British Journal of Psychiatry*, 178: 76–81.

Alloy, L.B., Kelly, K.A., Mineka, S. and Clements, C.M. (1990) Comorbidity in anxiety and depressive disorders: a helplessness-hopelessness perspective, in J.D. Maser and C.R. Cloninger (eds) *Comorbidity in Anxiety
and Mood Disorders*. Washington, DC: American Psychiatric Press.

Altman, J., Brunner, R.L. and Bayer, S.A. (1973) The hippocampus and
behavioural maturation, *Behavioural Biology*, 8: 557–96.

American Psychiatric Association (1952) *Diagnostic and Statistical Manual
of Mental Disorders*, 1st edn. Washington, DC: American Psychiatric
Association.

American Psychiatric Association (1968) *Diagnostic and Statistical Manual
of Mental Disorders*, 2nd edn. Washington, DC: American Psychiatric
Association.

American Psychiatric Association (1980) *Diagnostic and Statistical Manual
of Mental Disorders*, 3rd edn. Washington, DC: American Psychiatric
Association.

American Psychiatric Association (1994) *Diagnostic and Statistical Manual
of Mental Disorders*, 4th edn. Washington, DC: American Psychiatric
Association.

Anderson, K.M. and Manuel, G. (1994) Gender differences in reported
stress responses to the Loma Prieta earthquake, *Sex Roles*, 30: 725–33.

Anderson, N. (1998) The practitioner-researcher divide in work and organisational psychology, a keynote presentation at the British Psychological
Society Occupational Psychology Conference, Eastbourne.

References 241

Andersson, A.L., Bunketorp, O. and Allebeck, P. (1997) High rates of psychosocial complications after road traffic injuries, *Injury*, 28(8): 539–43.

Arata, C.M., Picou, J.S., Johnson, G.D. and McNally, T.S. (2000) Coping with technological disaster: an application of the conservation of resources model to the Exxon Valdez oil spill, *Journal of Traumatic Stress*, 13(1): 23–40.

Armstrong, B. (2000) Multiple stressor debriefing, in B. Raphael and J.P. Wilson (eds) *Psychological Debriefing: Theory, Practice and Evidence*. Cambridge: Cambridge University Press.

Armstrong B., O'Callahan, W. and Marmar, C.R. (1991) Debriefing Red Cross disaster personnel: the Multiple Stressor Debriefing Model, *Journal of Traumatic Stress*, 4(4): 581–93.

Bailly, L. (2003) Psychodynamically orientated intervention strategy for early reactions to trauma, in R. Orner and U. Schnyder (eds) *Reconstructing Early Intervention After Trauma – Innovations in the Care of Survivors*. Oxford: Oxford University Press.

Beale, D. (1999) Monitoring violent incidents, in P. Leather, C. Brady, C. Lawrence, D. Beale and T. Cox (eds.) *Work Related Violence – Assessment and Intervention*. London: Routledge.

Berk, R.A. and Rossi, P.H. (1990) *Thinking About Programme Evaluation*. London: Sage.

Bisson, J., Jenkins, P., Alexander, J. and Bannister, C. (1997) A randomised controlled trial of psychological debriefing for victims of acute burn trauma, *British Journal of Psychiatry*, 171: 78–81.

Bisson, J., McFarlane A.C. and Rose S. (2000) Psychological debriefing, in E.B. Foa, T.M. Keane and M.J. Friedman (eds) *Effective Treatments for PTSD*. New York: Guilford Press.

Blake D.D., Weathers, F.W., Nagy, L.M., Kaloupek D.G., Klauminzer, G., Charney, D.S. and Keane, T.M. (1990) A clinician rating scale for assessing current and lifetime PTSD: the CAPS-1, *Behaviour Therapist*, 13: 187–8.

Blake D.D., Weathers, F.W., Nagy, L.M., Kaloupek D.G., Gusman, F.D., Charney, D.S. and Keane, T.M. (1995) The development of a clinician administered PTSD scale, *Journal of Traumatic Stress*, 8: 75–90.

Bond, L., Carlin, J.B., Thomas, L., Rubin, K. and Patton, G. (2001) Does bullying cause emotional problems? A prospective study in young teenagers, *British Medical Journal*, 323: 4804.

Boyle, S., Bolton, D., Nurrish, J., O'Ryan, D., Udwin, O. and Yule, W. (1995) The Jupiter sinking follow up: predicting psychopathology in adolescence following trauma, in W. Yule, W. (ed.) *Post Traumatic Stress Disorders Concepts and Theory*. Chichester: Wiley.

Brady, C. and Dickson, R. (1999) Violence in health care settings, in P. Leather, C. Brady, C. Lawrence, D. Beale and T. Cox (eds) *Work Related Violence – Assessment and Intervention*. London: Routledge.

Breslau, N. (1998) Epidemiology of trauma and post-traumatic stress disorder, in R. Yehuda (ed.) *Psychological Trauma*. Washington, DC: American Psychiatric Press.

Breslau, N. and Davis, G.C. (1992) Post traumatic stress disorder in an urban population of young adults: risk factors for chronicity, *American Journal of Psychiatry*, 149: 671–5.

Breslau, N., Davies, G.C. and Anderski, P. (1997) Sex differences in post-traumatic stress disorder, *Archives of General Psychiatry*, 54: 1044–8.

Breuer, J. and Freud, S. (1955) Studies on hysteria, in J. Strachey (ed.) *The Standard Edition of the Complete Psychological Works of Sigmund Freud*, vol. 2. London: Hogarth Press.

Brewin C., Andrews, B. and Rose S. (1998) A preventative programme for victims of violent crime, *Journal of Traumatic Stress*, 11: 4.

Briere, J. (1997) *Psychological Assessment of Adult Post-traumatic States*. Washington, DC: American Psychiatric Association.

Briere J., Elliott, D.M., Harris, K. and Cotman, A. (1995) Trauma symptom inventory: psychometrics and association with childhood and assault trauma in clinical samples, *Journal of Interpersonal Violence*, 10: 387–401.

Brom, D., Kleber, R.J. and Defares, P.B. (1989) Brief psychotherapy for post-traumatic stress disorder, *Journal of Consulting Clinical Psychology*, 57(5): 607–12.

Bromley D.B. (1986) *The Case Study Method in Psychology and Related Disciplines*. Chichester: Wiley.

Bromet, E.J., Sonnega, A. and Kessler, R.C. (1998) Risk factors for DSM IIIR post-traumatic stress disorder: findings from the National Comorbidity Survey, *American Journal of Epidemiology*, 147(4): 353–61.

Brooks, C. and Cross, C. (1996) *Retail Crime Costs: 1994/1995 Survey*. London: British Retail Consortium.

Brown, J.M. and Campbell, E.A. (1991) Stress among emergency services personnel: progress and problems, *Journal of the Society of Occupational Medicine*, 41: 149–50.

Bryant, R.A. and Harvey, A.G. (1996) Post traumatic stress reactions in volunteer firefighters, *Journal of Traumatic Stress*, 9: 51–62.

Buckley, T.C., Blanchard, E.B. and Hickling E.J. (1996) A prospective examination of delayed onset PTSD secondary to motor vehicle accidents, *Journal of Abnormal Psychology*, 105(4): 617–25.

Calvin, W.H. (1990) *The Cerebral Symphony*. New York: Bantam Books.

Campbell, D.T. and Stanley, J.C. (1963) Experimental and quasi-experimental designs for research and teaching, in N.I. Gage (ed.) *Handbook of Research on Teaching*. Chicago: Rand McNally.

Cannon, W.B. (1927) The James Lange theory of emotion, *American Journal of Psychology*, 39: 106.

Cape, J.D. (1991) Quality assurance methods for clinical psychology services, *The Psychologist*, 4: 499–503.

Caponigro, J.R. (1998) *The Crisis Counsellor*. Southfield, MI: Barker Business Books.

Cattell, R. (1966) *Handbook of Multivariate Experimental Psychology*. Chicago: Rand McNally.

Chappell, D. and DiMartino, V. (1997) *Violence at Work*. Geneva: International Labour Organisation.

Civil Procedures Rules (1998) SI 1998/3132.

Civil Procedures Rules (1999) SI 1999/1008.

Cook T.D. and Campbell. D.T. (1979) *Quasi-Experimental Design and Analysis Issues for Field Settings*. Chicago: Rand McNally.

Cooke, J. (1995) *Law of Tort*. London: Pitman Publishing.

Cox, T. (1990) The recognition and measurement of stress: conceptual and methodological issues, in E.N. Corlett and J. Wilson (eds) *Evaluation of Human Work*. London: Taylor & Francis.

Cox, T. and Griffiths, A. (1999) The nature and measurement of work stress: theory and practice, in J.R. Wilson and E.N. Corlett (eds) *Evaluation of Human Work – A Practical Ergonomics Methodology*, 2nd edn. London: Taylor & Francis.

Cox, T. and Mackay, C.J. (1976) A psychological model of occupational stress, paper presented to the Medical Research Council meeting 'Mental Health in Industry', London, November.

Cox, T., Smewing, C. and Beale, D. (1993) *The Post Office: An Audit of Post Trauma Support Services*. Sutton Coldfield: Maxwell & Cox Associates (internal Post Office report).

Cronbach, L.J. (1951) Coefficient alpha and the internal structure of tests, *Psychometrika*, 16: 297–334.

Cronbach L.J. (1975) Beyond two disciplines of scientific psychology, *American Psychologist*, 30: 116–27.

Cullinan, W.E., Herman, J.P., Helmreich D.L. and Watson, S.J. (1995) A neuro-anatomy of stress, in M.J. Friedman, D.S. Charney and A.Y. Deutch (eds) *Neuro-biology and Clinical Consequences of Stress: From Normal Adaptation to Post-traumatic Stress*. Philadelphia, PA: Lippincott-Raven.

Dahl, S. (1989) Acute response to rape – a PTSD variant, *Acta Psychiatrica Scandinavia*, 80 (sup. 355): 56–62.

Daly, R.J. (1983) Samuel Pepys and post-traumatic stress disorder, *British Journal of Psychiatry*, 143: 64–8.

Dane, F.C. (1990) *Research Methods*. Pacific Grove, CA: Brooks/Cole.

Dansky, B.S., Roitzsch, J.C., Brady, K.T. and Saladin, M.E. (1997) Post trauma stress research in a clinical setting, *Journal of Traumatic Stress*, 10(1): 141–8.

Davis, M., Robbins-Eshelman, E. and McKay, M. (1995) *The Relaxation and Stress Reduction Workbook*. New York: MFJ Books.

244   References

Davis, R.C. and Friedman, L. (1985) The emotional aftermath of crime and violence, in C.R. Figley (ed.) *Trauma and its Wake*. New York: Brunner/Mazel.

Department of Health (2001) *Treatment Choice in Psychological Therapies and Counselling – Evidence Based Clinical Practice Guideline*. London: Department of Health.

Derogatis, L.R. (1983) *The SCL-90-R: Administration, Scoring and Procedures Manual II*. Baltimore, MD: Clinical Psychometric Research.

Donoghue v. Stevenson (1932) AC 562 HL.

Dryden, W. and Yankura, J. (1995) *Developing Rational Emotive Counselling*. London: Sage.

Duckworth, D.H. (1987) Post-traumatic stress disorder, *Stress Medicine*, 3: 175–83.

Dyregrov, A. (1989) Caring for helpers in disaster situations: psychological debriefing, *Disaster Management*, 2: 25–30.

Dyregrov A (1997) The process in psychological debriefings, *Journal of Traumatic Stress*, 10(4): 589–605.

Dyregrov, A. (1998) Psychological debriefing – an effective method? *Traumatology*, 4(2).

Dziuban, C. and Shirkey, E. (1974) When is a correlation matrix appropriate for factor analysis? Some decision rules, *Psychological Bulletin*, 81: 358–61.

EAPA (1997) *UK Guidelines for Audit and Evaluation of Employee Assistance Programmes*. London: EAPA.

Eccles, M., Freemantle, N. and Mason, J. (1998) North of England evidence-based guidelines development project: methods of developing guidelines for effective drug use in primary care, *British Medical Journal*, 316: 1232–5.

Einarsen, S. (1999) The nature and causes of bullying at work, *International Journal of Manpower*, 20(1/2): 16–27.

European Foundation (2000) *Violence at Work: Survey Data on Violence at Work*, www.eurofound.ie.

Falls, W.A. and Davis, M. (1995) Behavioural and physiological analysis of fear inhibition, in M.J. Friedman, D.S. Charney and A.Y. Deutch (eds) *Neurobiological and Clinical Consequences of Stress: From Normal Adaptation to PTSD*. Philadelphia, PA: Lippincott-Raven.

Feinstein, A. and Dolman, R. (1991) Predictors of post-traumatic stress disorder following physical trauma: an examination of the stressor criterion, *Psychological Medicine*, 21: 85–91.

Ferguson E. and Cox, T. (1993) Exploratory factor analysis: a user's guide, *International Journal of Selection and Assessment*, 1(2): 84–94.

Field, T. (1996) *Bully in Sight: How to Predict, Resist, Challenge and Combat Workplace Bullying*. Wantage: Wessex Press.

Figley, C.R. (1985) *Trauma and its Wake*. New York: Brunner/Mazel.

Figley, C.R. (1993), Compassion stress and the family therapist, *Family Therapy News*, February: 1–8.

Findlay v. *MoD* (1994) Sergeant awarded £100,000, *Times* law report, 1 March.

Flannery, R.B. (2000) Debriefing health care staff after assaults by patients, in B. Raphael and J.P. Wilson (eds) *Psychological Debriefing: Theory, Practice and Evidence.* Cambridge: Cambridge University Press.

Flannery, R.B., Penk, W.E., Hanson, M.A. and Flannery, G.J. (1996) The Assaulted Staff Action Program: guidelines for fielding a team, in G.R. VandenBos and E.Q. Bulatao (eds) *Violence on the Job.* Washington, DC: American Psychiatric Association.

Flin R. (1996) *Sitting in the Hot Seat: Leaders and Teams for Critical Incident Management.* Chichester: Wiley.

Foa, E.B. and Kozak, M.J. (1986) Emotional processing of fear. Exposure to corrective information, *Psychological Bulletin*, 99: 20–33.

Foa, E.B., Riggs, D.S., Dancu, C.V. and Rothbaum, B.O. (1993) Reliability and validity of a brief instrument for assessing post-traumatic stress disorder, *Journal of Traumatic Stress*, 6(4): 459–73.

Foa, E.B., Keane, T.M. and Friedman M.J. (2000a) *Effective Treatments of PTSD.* New York: Guilford Press.

Foa, E.B., Soellner, L.A., Feeny, N.C., Meadows, E.A. and Jaycox, L.H. (2000b) Evaluation of a brief cognitive behavioural program for the prevention of chronic PTSD in recent assault victims, paper presented at 'Advancement of Behaviour Therapy' conference, November.

Forster, J. (1969) *The Life of Charles Dickens*, vol. 2. London: J.M. Dent & Sons.

Fowlie D. and Alexander, D. (1992) Collective action following major disaster, *Journal of Forensic Psychiatry*, 3(2): 321–9.

Freckelton, I. (1998) Critical incident stress intervention and the law, *Journal of Law and Medicine*, 6: 105–113.

Freestone, J. and Raab, R. (1998) *Disaster Preparedness – Simple Steps for Business.* Menlo Park: Crisp Publications.

Friedman, M.J. (2000a) *Post Traumatic Stress Disorder – Latest Assessment and Treatment Strategies.* Kansas City, KS: Compact Clinicals.

Frost and others v. *Chief Constable of South Yorkshire Police and others* (1996) Court of Appeal, *Times* law report, 6 November.

Frost and others v. *Chief Constable of South Yorkshire Police and others* (1998) *Times* law report, 4 December.

Gamm, M., Corpe, U. and Wilson I. (1990) The application of a short anxiety and depression questionnaire to oil industry staff, *Journal of the Society of Occupational Medicine*, 40: 138–42.

Gibson, M. (1991) *Order from Chaos: Responding to Traumatic Events.* Birmingham: Venture Press.

Gloor, P. (1992) Role of the amygdala in temporal lobe epilepsy, in J.P. Aggleton (ed.) *The Amygdala: Neurobiological Aspects of Emotion, Memory, and Memory Dysfunction.* New York: Wiley.

Goenjian, A.K., Najarian, L.M., Pynoos, R.S., Steinberg, A.M., Manoukian, G., Tavosian, A. and Fairbanks, L.A. (1994) Posttraumatic stress disorder in elderly and younger adults after the 1988 earthquake in Armenia, *American Journal of Psychiatry*, 151: 895–901.

Goldberg, D., Bridges, K., Duncan-Jones, P. and Grayson, D. (1988) Detecting anxiety and depression in general medical settings, *British Medical Journal*, 297: 897–9.

Goldberg, D.P. (1978) *Manual of the General Health Questionnaire*. Windsor: NFER.

Goldman, L. (1978) *Research Methods for Counsellors: Practical Approaches in Field Settings*. New York: Wiley.

Goodman, L.S. and Gilman, A. (1975) *The Pharmacological Basis of Therapeutics*. New York: Macmillan Publishing.

Gray, J. (1971) T*he Psychology of Fear and Stress*. London: Weidenfeld & Nicholson.

Gray, J.F. (1987) *The Neuro-psychology of Anxiety: An Enquiry into the Functions of the Septo-hippocampal System*. New York: Oxford University Press.

Green, B.L. (1993) Identifying survivors at risk: trauma and stressors across events, in J.P. Wilson and B. Raphael (eds) *International Handbook of Traumatic Stress Syndromes*, pp. 135–44. New York: Plenum.

Green, B.L., Wilson J.P. and Lindy, J.D. (1985) Conceptualising post-traumatic stress disorder: a psycho-social framework, in C.R. Figley (ed.) *Trauma and its Wake*. New York: Brunner/Mazel.

Green, B.L., Lindy, J.D., Grace, G.C., Leonard, A.C., Korol, M. and Winget, C. (1990) Buffalo Creek survivors in the second decade: stability of stress symptoms, *American Journal of Orthopsychiatry*, 1: 43–5.

Green, B.L., Lindy, J.D., Grace, M.C. and Leonard, A.C. (1992) Chronic post-traumatic stress disorder and diagnostic comorbidity in a disaster sample, *American Journal of Psychiatry*, 60: 45–54.

Griffiths, A. (1999) Organisational interventions – facing the limits of the natural science paradigm, *Scandinavian Journal of Environmental Health*, 25: 589–96.

Hale v. *London Underground Ltd* (1993) Health and safety information bulletin 205, 3 January.

Hammerberg, M. (1992) Penn Inventory for Posttraumatic Stress Disorder: psychometric properties, *Psychological Assessment*, 4: 67–76.

Haslegrave, C.M. and Corlett, E.N. (1999) Evaluating work conditions and risk of injury – techniques for field surveys, in J.R. Wilson and E. Nigel Corlett (eds) *Evaluation of Human Work – A Practical Ergonomics Methodology*, 2nd edn. London: Taylor & Francis.

Hatton v. *Sutherland and others* (2002) Court of Appeal, 5 February.

Health & Safety Executive (1990) *Fatal Accidents: A Compilation of Accident Reports which Appeared in Health & Safety Commission Newsletters 1984–88*. Sudbury: HSE Books.

Health and Safety Executive (1993) *The Prevention of Violence to Staff in Banks and Building Societies*. Sudbury: HSE Books.

Health and Safety Executive (1995) *Preventing Violence to Retail Staff*. Sudbury: HSE Books.

Health and Safety Executive (1998) *Five Steps to Risk Assessment*. Sudbury: HSE Books.

Health and Safety Executive (1999a) *Health & Safety Statistics (1998/9)*. Sudbury: HSE Books.

Health & Safety Executive (1999b) *Management of Health & Safety at Work Regulations*. Sheffield: Health & Safety Executive.

Heath, R. (2001) A crisis management perspective of business continuity, in A. Hiles and P. Barnes (eds) *The Definitive Handbook of Business Continuity Management*. Chichester: Wiley.

Heiskanen, M., Aromaa, K., Niemi, H., Suusinen, A. and Siren, R. (1991) *Accidents and Violence 1988*. Finland: Central Statistics Office of Finland, National Research Institute of Legal Policy.

Herman, J.L. (1993) Sequelae of prolonged and repeated trauma: evidence for a complex post-traumatic syndrome (Desnos), in J.R.T. Davidson and E.B. Foa (eds) *Post Traumatic Stress Disorder: DSM IV and Beyond*. Washington, DC: American Psychiatric Press.

Hiles, A. (2001) Developing and implementing the written plan, in A. Hiles and P. Barnes (eds) *The Definitive Handbook of Business Continuity Management*. Chichester: Wiley.

Hiles, A. and Barnes, P. (2001) *The Definitive Handbook of Business Continuity Management*. Chichester: Wiley.

Hill, C.E., Carter, J.A. and O'Farrell M.K. (1983) A case study of the process and outcome of time limited counselling, *Journal of Counselling Psychology*, 30(1): 3–18.

Hobbs, M., Mayou, R., Harrison, B. and Worlock, P. (1996) A randomised controlled trail of psychological debriefing for victims of road traffic accidents, *British Medical Journal*, 313: 1438–9.

Hodgkinson, P.E. and Stewart, M. (1991) *Coping with Catastrophe: A Handbook for Disaster management*. London: Routledge.

Hoel, H. (1999) Workplace bullying: current state of research, *Employee Health Bulletin*, August: 5–8.

Hoel, H. and Cooper, C.L. (2000) *Destructive Conflict and Bullying at Work*. Manchester: UMIST.

Holoday, M., Warren-Miller, G., Smith, A. and Yost, T.E. (1995) A comparison of on-the-scene coping mechanisms used by two culturally different groups, *Counselling Psychology Quarterly*, 8(1): 81–8.

Home Office (1994) *Dealing with Disasters*, 2nd edn. London: HMSO.

Horowitz, M.J., Wilner, N. and Alvarez, W. (1979) Impact of Events Scale (IES): a measure of subjective stress, *Psychosomatic Medicine*, 41(3): 209–18.

Hubel D.H. and Wiesel T.H. (1977) Ferrier lecture: functional architecture of macaque monkey visual cortex, *Procedures of the Royal Society*, 198:1–59.

Hughes, S. (1990) Inside madness, *British Medical Journal*, 301: 1476–8.

Humphris, D. (1999) Types of evidence, in S. Harmer and J. Collinson (eds) *Achieving Evidence Based Practice – A Handbook for Practitioners*. Edinburgh: Balliere-Tindall.

Income Data Services (1994) *Violence Against Staff, Study 557*. London: Incomes Data Services Ltd.

Jaatun, M.G. (1983) Reported communication, in B. Raphael (1986) *When Disaster Strikes: A Handbook for the Caring Professions*. London: Unwin.

Janoff-Bulman, R. (1985) The aftermath of victimisation: rebuilding shattered assumptions, in Figley, C.R. (ed.) *Trauma and its Wake*. New York: Brunner/Mazel.

Jeavons, S. (1998) Predicting who suffers psychological trauma in the first year after a road accident, paper delivered at 'Road Accidents and the Mind', Bristol.

Jenkins, E.L. (1996) *Violence in the Workplace: Incidence, Risk Factors and Prevention Strategies*, DHHS (NIOSH) publication No. 96–100. Washington, DC: US Government Printing Office.

Joseph, S., Williams, R. and Yule, W. (1997) *Understanding Post Traumatic Stress: A Psychosocial Perspective on PTSD and Treatment*. Chichester: Wiley.

Joyce, D. (1989) Why do police officers laugh at death? *Psychologist*, 2(9): 380–1.

Judd, C.M., Smith E.R. and Kidder, L.H. (1991) *Research Methods in Social Relations*, 6th edn. New York: Holt, Rhinehart & Winston.

Juni, P., Altman, D.G. and Egger, M. (2001) Assessing the quality of controlled clinical trials, *British Medical Journal*, 323: 42–6.

Kaitin, K.I., Bliwise, D.L., Gleason, C., Nino-Mucia, G., Dement, W.C. and Libet, B. (1986) Sleep disturbance produced by electrical stimulation of the locus ceruleus in a human subject, *Biological Psychiatry*, 21: 710–16.

Kardiner, A. (1941) *The Traumatic Neurosis of War*. New York: Hoeber.

Keane, T.M. and Wolfe, J. (1990) Comorbidity in posttraumatic stress disorder: an analysis of community and clinical studies, *Journal of Applied Social Psychology*, 20: 1776–88.

Keane, T.M., Fairbank, J.A., Caddell, J.M., Zimering, R.T. and Bender, M.E. (1985) A behavioural approach to assessing and treating post-traumatic stress disorder in Vietnam veterans, in C.R. Figley (ed.) *Trauma and its Wake*. New York: Brunner/Mazel.

Keane, T.M., Malloy, P. and Fairbank, J. (1988) Mississippi Scale for combat related post-traumatic stress disorder: three studies in reliability and validity, *Journal of Consulting and Clinical Psychology*, 52: 85–90.

Keane, T.M., Fairbank J.A., Caddell, J.M., Zimering, R.J.T., Taylor, K.L. and Mora, C.A. (1989) Clinical evidence of a measure to assess combat exposure, *Psychological Assessment*, 1: 53–5.

Kelly, R. (1981) The post-traumatic syndrome, *Journal of Royal Society of Medicine*, 74: 242–4.

Kemp, A., Rawlings, E.I. and Green, B.L. (1991) Post-traumatic stress disorder in battered women – a shelter sample, *Journal of Traumatic Stress*, 4(1): 137–48.

Kenardy, J.A. and Carr, V.J. (2000) Debriefing post-disaster – follow up after a major earthquake, in B. Raphael and J.P. Wilson (eds) *Psychological Debriefing – Theory, Practice and Evidence*. Cambridge: Cambridge University Press.

Kennedy, E. (1991) *Crisis Counselling: The Essential Guide for Non-professional Counsellors*. Dublin: Gill & Macmillan.

Kessler, R.C., Sonnega, A. and Bromet, E. (1995) Post-traumatic stress disorder in the National Comorbidity Survey, *Archives of General Psychiatry*, 52: 1048–60.

Kilpatrick, D.G., Veronen, L. and Best, C. (1985) Factors predicting psychological distress among rape victims, in C.R. Figley (ed.) *Trauma and its Wake*. New York: Brunner/Mazel.

Kline, P. (1986) *A Handbook of Test Construction: Introduction to Psychometric Design*. London: Methuen.

Koch, W.J., Fedoroff, I., Iverson, G., Taylor, S. and Shercliffe, R. (2000) *Malingering and Litigation Stress in Road Accident Victims*. New York: Elsevier.

Kolb, L.C. (1987) A neuro-psychological hypothesis explaining post-traumatic stress disorders, *American Journal of Psychiatry*, 144(8): 989–95.

Kopel, H. and Friedman, M. (1999) Effects of exposure to violence in South African police, in J. Violanti and D. Paton (eds) *Police Trauma – Psychological Aftermath of Civilian Combat*. Springfield, IL: Charles C. Thomas Books.

Koss M.P. and Gidycz, C.A. (1985) Sexual experiences survey: reliability and validity, *Journal of Consulting and Clinical Psychology*, 53: 422–3.

Kosten, T.R., Mason J.W., Giller, E.R., Ostroff, R.B. and Harkness L. (1987) Sustained urinary norepinephrine and epinephrine elevation in post-traumatic stress disorder, *Psychoneuroendocrinology*, 12(1): 13–20.

Krinsley, K.E. and Weathers, F.W. (1995) The assessment of trauma in adults, *PTSD Research Quarterly*, 6: 1–6.

Kubany, E. (1995) The Traumatic Life Events Questionnaire (TLEQ): a brief measure of prior trauma exposure, unpublished scale available from author Pacific Centre for PTSD, Honolulu, Hawaii.

Kulka, R.A., Schlenger, W.E., Fairbank, J.A., Hough, R.L., Marmer, C.R. and Weiss, D.S. (1990) *Trauma and the Vietnam War Generation: Report* on *Findings from the National Vietnam Veterans Readjustment Study*. New York: Brunner/Mazel.

Landsman, I.S., Baum, C.G., Arnkoff, D.B., Craig, M.J., Lynch, I., Copes, W.S. and Champion, H.R. (1990) The psychosocial consequences of traumatic injury, *Journal of Behavioural Medicine*, 13(6): 561–81.

Laufer, R.S., Frey-Wouters, E. and Gallops, M.S. (1985) Traumatic stressors in the Vietnam War and post-traumatic stress disorder, in C.R. Figley (ed.) *Trauma and its Wake*. New York: Brunner/Mazel.

Lauterbach, D. and Vrana, S. (1996) Three studies on the reliability and validity of a self report measure of posttraumatic stress disorder, *Assessment*, 3: 17–25.

Lauterbach, D. and Vrana, S. (2001) The relationship between personality variables, exposure to traumatic events and severity of posttraumatic stress symptoms, *Journal of Traumatic Stress*, 14(1): 29–46.

Lazarus, R.S. and Folkman, S. (1984) *Stress, Appraisal and Coping*. New York: Springer.

LeDoux J.E. (1992) Emotion as memory: anatomical systems underlying indelible neural traces, in S.-A. Christiansen (ed.) *Handbook of Emotion and Memory*. Hillsdale, NJ: Erlbaum.

Lee, C., Slade, P. and Lygo, V. (1996) The influence of psychological debriefing on emotional adaptations in females following early miscarriage, *British Journal of Medical Psychology*, 69: 47–58.

Leighton, P. (1999) Violence at work: the legal framework, in P. Leather, C. Brady, C. Lawrence, D. Beale and T. Cox (eds) *Work Related Violence – Assessment and Intervention*. London: Routledge.

Leymann, H. (1990) Mobbing and psychological terror at workplaces, *Violence and Victims*, 5: 119–26.

Leymann, H. and Gustafsson, A. (1996) Mobbing at work and the development of post-traumatic stress disorders, *European Journal of Work and Organizational Psychology*, 5(2): 251–75.

Lindy, J.D. (1996) Psychoanalytic psychotherapy of post-traumatic stress disorder: the nature of the therapeutic relationship, in B. van der Kolk, A.C. McFarlane and L. Weisaeth (eds) *Traumatic Stress*. New York: Guilford Press.

Lipsedge, M. (2000) Bullying, post-traumatic stress disorder and violence at work, in P.J. Baxter, P.H.Adams, T-C. Cockcroft and A. Harrington (eds) *J.M. Hunter's Diseases of Occupations*. London: Arnold.

Litz, B.T., Penk, W.F., Gerardi, R.J. and Keane T.M. (1992) Assessment of post-traumatic stress disorder, in P.A. Saigh (ed.) *Posttraumatic Stress Disorder: A Behavioural Approach to Assessment and Treatment*. Boston, MA: Allyn & Bacon.

Lundin, T. (2000) Debriefing after disaster, in B. Raphael and J.P. Wilson (eds) *Psychological Debriefing – Theory, Practice and Evidence*. Cambridge: Cambridge University Press.

Lyons, J. and Keane, T. (1992) Keane PTSD Scale: MMPI and MMPI–2 update, *Journal of Traumatic Stress*, 5: 111–15.

MacDonald, L. (1988) *1914–1918 Voices and Images of the Great War*. London: Michael Joseph.

MacLean, P.D. (1985) Brain evolution relating to family, play and the separation call, *Archives of General Psychiatry*, 42: 405–17.

Maier, S.F. and Seligman, M.E.P. (1976) Learned helplessness: theory and evidence, *Journal of Experimental Psychiatry*, 51: 3–46.

Malt, U., Karlehagen, J. and Leymann, H. (1993) The effect of major railway accidents on the psychosocial health of train drivers: a longitudinal study of the one year outcome after the accident. *Journal of Psychosomatic Research*, 8(37): 807–17.

Mansfield, P. (1998) *Extending EMDR*. New York: Norton.

Marmer, C.R., Weiss, D.S. and Pynoos, R.S. (1995) Dynamic psychotherapy of post-traumatic stress disorder, in M.J. Friedman, D.S. Charney and A.Y. Deutch (ed.) *Neurobiological and Clinical Consequences of Stress from Normal Adaptation to PTSD*. New York: Raven Press.

Marmer, C.R., Weiss, D.S. and Metzler, T.J. (1997) Peritraumatic Dissociative Experiences Questionnaire, in J. P. Wilson and T.M. Keane (eds) *Assessing Psychological Trauma and PTSD*. New York: Guilford Press.

Marshall, S.L.A. (1944) *Island Victory*. Harmondsworth: Penguin.

Maslach, C. and Jackson, S.E. (1981) The measurement and experience of burnout, *Journal of Occupational Behaviour*, 2(2): 99–113.

Mayou, R. (1997) The psychiatry of road traffic accidents, in M. Mitchell (ed.) *The Aftermath of Road Accidents: Psychological, Social and Legal Consequences of Everyday Trauma*. London: Routledge.

Mayou, R., Bryant, B. and Duthie, R. (1993) Psychiatric consequences of road traffic accidents, *British Medical Journal*, 307(6905): 647–51.

McCahill, T.W., Meyer, L.C. and Fishman, A.M. (1979) *The Aftermath of Rape*. Lexington, MA: DC Heath.

McCarroll, J.E., Ursano,R.J. and Fullerton, C.S. (1995) Symptoms of PTSD following recovery of war deal: 13–15-month follow-up, *American Journal of Psychiatry*, 152: 939–41.

McCloy, E. (1992) Management of post incident trauma: a fire service perspective, *Occupational Medicine*, 42, 163–6.

McFarlane v. *EE Caledonia Ltd* (1994) 1 All ER 814.

McFarlane A. and Yehuda, R. (1996) Resilience, vulnerability and the course of post-traumatic reactions, in B. van der Kolk, A.C. McFarlane and L. Weisaeth (eds) *Traumatic Stress*. New York: Guilford Press.

McFarlane, A.C. (1987) Family functioning and overprotection following a natural disaster: the longitudinal effects of post-traumatic morbidity, *Australian and New Zealand Journal of Psychiatry*, 21: 210–18.

McFarlane, A.C. (1988a) The phenomenology of post-traumatic stress disorders following a natural disaster, *Journal of Nervous and Mental Disorders*, 176: 22–9.

McFarlane, A.C. (1988b) The aetiology of post-traumatic stress disorders following a natural disaster, *British Journal of Psychiatry*, 152: 116–21.

McFarlane, A.C. (1992) Avoidance and intrusion in posttraumatic stress disorder, *Psychiatric Clinics of North America*, 17: 393–408.

McFarlane, A.C. (1995) Helping the victims of disasters, in J.R. Freedy and S.E. Hobfoll (eds) *From Theory to Practice*. New York: Plenum Press.

McFarlane, A.C. (1996) Resilience, vulnerability and the course of post-traumatic reactions, in B. van der Kolk, A.C. McFarlane and L. Weisaeth (eds) *Traumatic Stress*. New York: Guilford Press.

McFarlane, A.C. and de Girolamo, G. (1996) The nature of traumatic stressors and the epidemiology of posttraumatic reactions, in B. van der Kolk, A.C. McFarlane and L. Weisaeth (eds) *Traumatic Stress*. New York: Guilford Press.

McLeod, J. (1994) *Doing Counselling Research*. London: Sage.

Merskey, H. (1991) *Shell Shock in 150 Years of British Psychiatry, 1841–1991*. London: Gaskell/The Royal College of Psychiatrists.

Miller, H. (1961) Accident neurosis, *British Medical Journal*, 1: 919.

Miller-Burke, J., Attridge, M. and Fass, P.M. (1999) Impact of traumatic events and organisational response, *Journal of Occupational and Environmental Medicine*, 41(2): 73–83.

Mitchell, J. (1983) *Guidelines for Psychological Debriefing*, emergency management course manual. Emmitsburg, MD: Federal Emergency Management Agency, Emergency Management Institute.

Mitchell, J. and Everly, G.S. (2001) *Critical Incident Stress Debriefing: An Operations Manual for CISD, Defusing and other Group Crisis Intervention Services*, 3rd edn. Ellicott City, MD: Chevron Publishing Corporation.

Mitchell, J.T. (1993) Critical incident stress management in the workplace: a workshop presented at the 3rd European Conference on Traumatic Stress, Bergen, Norway.

Moran, Lord (1945) *Anatomy of Courage*. London: Constable.

Mott, F.W. (1919) *War Neurosis and Shell Shock*. London: Oxford Medical Publications.

Mower, O.A. (1960) *Learning Theory and Behaviour*. New York: Wiley.

Multiple claimants v. *the Ministry of Defence* (2003) EWHC/1134 (QB).

Munck, A. and Guytre, P.M. (1986) Glucocorticoid physiology, pharmacology and stress, in G.P. Chrousos, D.L. Loriaus, M.B. Lipsett (eds) *Steroid Hormone Resistance: Mechanisms and Clinical Aspects*. New York: Plenum.

Murphy, R., Foy, W., Penk, E., Gusman, D., Wetherell, L. and Regan T. (1995) Combat exposure, early combat and alcohol problems, paper presented at the Fourth European Conference on Traumatic Stress.

Muss, D. (1991) *The Trauma Trap*. London: Doubleday.

Myres, C.S. (1915) A contribution to the study of shell shock, *The Lancet*, 13 February, 316–20.

Myres, C.S. (1940) *Shell Shock in France, 1914–1918.* Cambridge: Cambridge University Press.

Napier, M. (1991) The medical and legal trauma of disasters, *Medico-Legal Journal*, 59(3): 157–79.

Napier, M. and Wheat, K. (1995) *Recovering Damages for Psychiatric Injury.* London: Blackstone Press.

Newman, E., Kaloupek, D.G. and Keane, T.M. (1996) Assessment of post-traumatic stress disorder in clinical and research settings, in B. van der Kolk, A.C. McFarlane and L. Weisaeth (eds) *Traumatic Stress.* New York: Guilford Press.

Newman, E., Riggs, D.S. and Roth, S. (1997) Thematic resolution, PTSD and complex PTSD: the relationship between meaning and trauma-related diagnosis, *Journal of Traumatic Stress*, 10(2): 197–213.

Niedl, K. (1996) Mobbing and well-being: economic and personal development implications, *European Journal of Work and Organizational Psychology*, 5(2): 239–49.

Norris, F. (1990) Screening for traumatic stress: a scale for use in the general population, *Journal of Applied Social Psychology*, 20: 1704–18.

Norris, F. and Perilla, J. (1996) Reliability, validity and cross language stability of the Revised Civilian Mississippi Scale for PTSD, *Journal of Traumatic Stress*, 9: 285–98.

Norris, F.H. and Riad, J.K. (1997) Standardised Self Report Measure of Civilian Trauma and Posttraumatic Stress Disorder, in J.P. Wilson and T.M. Keane (eds) *Assessing Psychological Trauma.* New York: Guilford Press.

Norris, F.H., Weisshaar, D.I., Conrad, M.L., Diaz E.M., Murphy, A.D. and Ibanez, G.E. (2001) A qualitative analysis of posttraumatic stress among Mexican victims of disaster, *Journal of Traumatic Stress*, 14(4): 741–56.

Ochberg, F.M. (1993) *Victims of the Media Program.* East Lansing, MI: Instructural Media Center, Michigan State University.

Oppenheim, H. (1889/1996) History of trauma in psychiatry, in B. van der Kolk, A.C. McFarlane and L. Weisaeth (eds) *Traumatic Stress.* New York: Guilford Press.

Orner, R. and Schnyder, U. (2003) *Reconstructing Early Interventions after Trauma – Innovations in the Care of Survivors.* Oxford: Oxford University Press.

Orner, R.J., Avery, A. and Boddy, C. (1997) Status and development of critical incident stress management services in the United Kingdom National Health Service and other emergency services combined, 1993–1996, *Occupational Medicine*, 47(4): 203–9.

Orr, S.P., Lasko, N.B., Shalev, A.Y. and Pitman, R.K. (1995) Physiologic responses to loud tones in Vietnam veterans with posttraumatic stress disorder, *Journal of Abnormal Psychology*, 104: 75–82.

Parkes, C.M. (1975) What becomes of redundant world models? A contribution to the study of adaptation to change, *British Journal of Medical Psychology*, 48: 131–7.

Parkinson, F. (1993) *Post Traumatic Stress*. London: Sheldon Press.

Parry Jones, B. and Parry Jones, W.L.L. (1994) Post-traumatic stress disorder: supportive evidence from an eighteenth-century natural disaster, *Psychological Medicine*, 24: 15–27.

Paton, D. and Smith, L. (1999) Assessment, conceptual and methodological issues in researching traumatic stress in police officers, in J.M. Violanti and D. Paton (eds) *Police Trauma – Psychological Aftermath of Civilian Combat*. Springfield, IL: Charles C. Thomas Books.

Peregrine, A. (1993) After the Perrier bubble burst, *Weekend Telegraph*, 23 January.

Perry, S., Difede, M.A., Musngi, G.F. and Jacobsberg, A.L. (1992) Predictors of post-traumatic stress disorder after burn injury, *American Journal of Psychiatry*, 149: 931–5.

Pitman, R.K., Sparr, L.F., Saunders, L.S. and McFarlane, A.C. (1996) Legal issues in posttraumatic stress disorder, in B. van der Kolk, A.C. McFarlane and L. Weisaeth (eds) *Traumatic Stress*. New York: Guilford Press.

Pocock, S.J. (1983) Publication and interpretation of findings, in S.J. Pocock (ed.) *Clinical Trials: A Practical Approach*. Chichester: Wiley.

Porter, M. and Haslam, N. (2001) Forced displacement in Yugoslavia: a meta-analysis of the psychological consequences and their moderators, *Journal of Traumatic Stress*, 14(4): 817–34.

Quarantelli, E. (1988) Disaster crisis management: a summary of research findings, *Journal of Management Studies*, 25: 373–85.

Raifman, L.J. (1983) Problems of diagnosis and legal causation in courtroom use of post-traumatic stress disorder, *Behavioural Science and the Law*, 1: 115–31.

Rains, S. (2001) Don't suffer in silence: building an effective response to bullying at work, in N. Tehrani (ed.) *Building a Culture of Respect*. London: Taylor & Francis.

Raphael, B. (1986) *When Disaster Strikes: A Handbook for Caring Professions*. London: Hutchinson.

Raphael, B. and Wilson J.P. (2000) *Psychological Debriefing – Theory, Practice and Evidence*. Cambridge: Cambridge University Press.

Rauch, S.L., Shin, L.M. and Pitman, R.K. (1998) Evaluating the effects of psychological trauma using neuro-imaging techniques, in R. Yehuda (ed.) *Psychological Trauma*. Washington, DC: American Psychiatric Press.

Rausch, H.L. (1974) Research, practice and accountability, *American Psychologist*, 29: 678–81.

Ravin, J.M. and Boal, C.K. (1989) Post-traumatic stress disorder in the work setting: psychic injury, medical diagnosis, treatment and litigation, *American Journal of Forensic Psychiatry*, 10(2): 5–23.

Rayner, C. (1997) The incidence of workplace bullying, *Journal of Community & Applied Social Psychology*, 7: 199–208.

Rayner, C. and Cooper, C. (1997) Workplace bullying: myth or reality – can we afford to ignore it? *Leadership and Organisation*, 18(4): 211–4.

Reid, J.I. (2000) *Crisis Management: Planning for the Design and Construction Industry*. Chichester: Wiley.

Resick, P.A. (2001) *Stress and Trauma*. London: Taylor & Francis.

Resick, P.A. and Schnicke, M.K. (1992) Cognitive processing therapy for sexual assault victims, *Journal of Consulting and Clinical Psychology*, 60: 748–56.

Resnick, H., Kilpatrick, D.G. and Dansky B.S (1993) Prevalence of civilian trauma and posttraumatic stress disorder in a representative national sample of women, *Journal of Consulting and Clinical Psychology*, 61: 984–91.

Rick, J., Perryman, S., Young, K., Guppy, A. and Hillage, J. (1998a) *Workplace Trauma and its Measurement*. Sudbury: Health & Safety Executive.

Rick, J., Perryman, S., Young, K., Guppy, A. and Hillage, J. (1998b) *Workplace Trauma and its Management: Review of Literature*. Suffolk: HSE Books.

Rick, J., Young, K. and Guppy, A. (1998c) *From Accidents to Assaults – How Organisational Responses to Traumatic Stress Incidents can Prevent Posttraumatic Stress Disorder (PTSD) in the Workplace*. Suffolk: HSE Books.

Rivers, K. (1993) Traumatic stress: an occupational hazard, *Employee Counselling Today*, 5(1): 4–6.

Roberts, G.L. (2000) Evaluating the prevalence and impact of domestic violence, in A.Y. Shalev, R. Yehuda and A.C. McFarlane (eds) *International Handbook of Human Responses to Trauma*. New York: Kuwer Academic/Plenum Publishers.

Robertson v. Forth Road Bridge Joint Board (1995) IRLR 253.

Robinson, R. (2000) Debriefing with emergency services: critical incident stress management, in B. Raphael and J.P. Wilson (eds) *Psychological Debriefing – Theory, Practice and Evidence*. Cambridge: Cambridge University Press.

Robson C. (2001) *Real World Research*. Oxford: Blackwell.

Rose, S. and Bisson, J. (1998) Brief early psychological intervention following trauma: a systematic review for the literature, *Journal of Traumatic Stress*, 11: 697–710.

Rothbaum, B.O., Meadows, E.A., Resick, P. and Foy D.W. (2000) Cognitive behavioural therapy, in E.B. Foa, T.M. Keane and M.J. Freidman (eds) *Effective Treatments for PTSD*. New York: Guilford Press.

Rothberg J.M. and Wright, K. (1999) Trauma prevention in the line of duty, in J.M Violanti and D. Paton (eds) *Police Trauma – Psychological Aftermath of Civilian Combat*. Springfield, IL: Charles C. Thomas.

Sainsbury's (1997) *Prevention and Management of Violence at Work*. Internal document.

Sayle, A.J. (1987) *Management Audits: The Assessment of Quality Management Systems*. London: McGraw-Hill.

Schein, E.H. (1980) *Organisational Psychology*. Englewood Cliffs, NJ: Prentice Hall.

Scheppele, K.L. and Bart, P.B. (1983) Through women's eyes: defining danger in the wake of sexual assault, *Journal of Social Issues*, 39: 63–81.

Scott, M.J. (2000) Journeying with the traumatised – the Hillsborough disaster, in M.J. Scott and S. Palmer (eds) *Trauma and Post-traumatic Stress Disorder*. London: Cassell.

Scott M.J. and Palmer, S. (2000) *Trauma and Post-traumatic Stress Disorder*. London: Cassell.

Scott, M.J. and Stradling, S.G. (1992a) *Counselling for Post-traumatic Stress Disorder*. London: Sage.

Scott, M.J. and Stradling, S.G. (1992b) Post-traumatic stress disorder without the trauma, *British Journal of Clinical Psychology*, 33: 71–4.

Seguin, E.C. (1890) Traumatic neurosis, in C.E. Dugois (ed.) *Annual of the Universal Medical Scientists: A Yearly Report of the Progress of the General Sanitary Sciences Throughout the World*. Philadelphia, PA: F.A. Davis.

Selye, H. (1956) *The Stress of Life*. New York: McGraw-Hill.

Shalev, A.Y. (1992) Posttraumatic stress disorder among injured survivors of a terrorist attack: predictive value of early intrusion and avoidance symptoms, *Journal of Nervous and Mental Disease*, 180(8): 505–9.

Shalev, A.Y. (1996) Stress versus traumatic stress: from acute homeostatic reactions to chronic psychopathology, in B. van der Kolk, A.C. McFarlane and L. Weisaeth (eds) *Traumatic Stress*. New York: Guilford Press.

Shalev, A.Y. and Yehuda, R (1998) Longitudinal development of traumatic stress disorder, in R. Yehuda (ed.) *Psychological Trauma*. Washington, DC: American Psychiatric Press.

Shalev, A.Y., Peri, T. and Canetti, L. (1996) Predictors of PTSD in injured trauma survivors: a prospective study, *American Journal of Psychiatry*, 153: 219–25.

Shapiro, F. (1989) Efficacy of the eye movement desensitisation procedure in the treatment of traumatic memories, *Journal of Traumatic Stress Studies*, 2: 199–223.

Shepard, M.F. and Campbell, J.A. (1992) The abusive behaviour inventory: a measure of psychological and physical abuse, *Journal of Interpersonal Violence*, 7: 291–305.

Sibicky, M. and Dovidio, J.F. (1986) Stigma of psychological therapy, *Journal of Counselling Psychology*, 33: 148–54.

Silver, S.M. (1986) *An Inpatient Programme for Post-traumatic Stress Disorder in Litigation: Guidelines for Forensic Assessment*. Washington, DC: American Psychiatric Press.

Sim, G. (2001) Aftermath – trauma victim support needs, paper presented at the Association of Traumatic Stress Studies conference, 'Disaster Management : Developing Best Practice', Coventry, UK, 18–19 July.

Smith, E.M., North, C.S., McCool, R.E. and Shea, J.M. (1990) Acute post-traumatic psychiatric disorders: identification of persons at risk, *American Journal of Psychiatry*, 147: 202–6.

Snaith, R.P. and Zigmond, A.S. (1994) *The Hospital Anxiety and Depression Scale Manual*. Windsor: NFER-Nelson.

Solomon, S.D. and Smith, E.M.(1994) Social support and perceived control as moderators of responses to dioxin and flood exposure, in R.J. Ursano, B.G. McCaughy and C.S. Fullerton (eds) *Individual and Community Responses to Trauma and Disaster: The Structure of Human Chaos*. Cambridge: Cambridge University Press.

Southwick, S.M., Morgan, A., Nagy, L.M., Bremner, D., Nicholaou, A.L., Johnson, D.R. and Charney, D.S. (1993) Trauma related symptoms in veterans of Operation Desert Storm: a preliminary report, *American Journal of Psychiatry*, 150: 1524–38.

Spaulding, W.J. (1988) Compensation for mental disability, in R. Michaels (ed.) *Psychiatry*, 3: 1–27.

Spitzer, R.L., Williams, J.B., Gibbon, M. and First, M.B. (1990) *User's Guide for the Structured Clinical Interview for DSM III R*. Washington, DC: American Psychiatric Press.

Stein, M.B., Walker, J.R. and Hazen, A.L. (1997) Full and partial post-traumatic stress disorder: findings from a community survey, *American Journal of Psychiatry*, 154: 1114–19.

Tarsh, M. and Royston, C. (1985) A follow up study of accident neurosis, *British Journal of Psychiatry*, 146: 18–25.

Taylor, P. (1989) *The Hillsborough Stadium Disaster: Interim Report*. London: HMSO.

Tedeschi, R.G. and Calhoun, L.G. (1995) *Trauma and Transformation: Growing in the Aftermath of Suffering*. London: Sage.

Tehrani, N. (1995) An integrated response to trauma in three Post Office businesses, *Work and Stress*, 9(4): 380–93.

Tehrani, N. (1998a) Does debriefing harm victims of trauma? *Counselling Psychology Review*, 13(3): 6–12.

Tehrani, N. (1998b) Trauma debriefing revisited, *Counselling at Work*, 23: 5–6.

Tehrani, N. (1999a) Dealing with disasters – the people issues, *Risk and Continuity*, 2(2): 37–46.

Tehrani, N. (1999b) After the knock on the door – the hidden pain of the road crash victim, paper presented at the 'Counselling Psychology' conference of the British Psychological Society, Brighton.

Tehrani, N. (2000a) Organisational culture affects trauma response, *Counselling at Work*, 33: 6–9.

Tehrani, N. (2000b) Managing traumatic stress in the workplace, *Employee Health Bulletin, IRS Review*, 713: 12–16.

Tehrani, N. (in press) Bullying: a source of chronic post traumatic stress, paper presented at the BACP Research conference 2002.

Tehrani, N. and Westlake, R. (1994) Debriefing individuals affected by violence, *Counselling Psychology Quarterly*, 7(3): 251–9.

Tehrani, N., Walpole, O., Berriman, J. and Reilly, J. (2001) A special courage: dealing with the Paddington rail crash, *Occupational Medicine*, 51(2): 93–9.

Tehrani, N., Cox, T. and Cox, S. (2002) Assessing the impact of traumatic incidents: the development of an extended impact of events scale, *Counselling Psychology Quarterly*, 15(2): 191–200.

Thomas, A. (1996) Clinical audit: setting professional standards for counselling services, *Counselling Psychology Quarterly*, 9: 25–36.

Thompson, J. and Suzuki, I. (1991) Stress in ambulance workers, *Disaster Management*, 2(3): 193–7.

Thompson, J.A., Charlton, P.F.C., Kerry, R., Lee, D. and Turner, S.W. (1995) An open trial of exposure therapy based on de-conditioning for post-traumatic stress disorder, *British Journal of Clinical Psychology*, 34: 407–16.

Toga, A.W. and Mazzoitta, J.C. (1996) *Brain Mapping: The Methods*. Boston, MA: Academic Press.

Tomkinson, A. (1999) Human resources for disaster recovery, *Risk & Continuity*, 2(2): 51–2.

Toscano, G. and Weber, W. (1995) Patterns of fatal workplace assaults differ from those of non-fatal ones, in US Department of Labour Statistics, *Fatal Workplace Injuries in 1993: A Collection of Data and Analysis, Bureau of Labour Statistics Report No. 891*. Washington, DC: US Department of Labour Statistics.

Trimble, M.R. (1981) *Posttraumatic Neurosis*. Chichester: Wiley.

Trimble, M.R. (1985) Posttraumatic stress disorder: history of a concept, in C.R. Figley (ed.) *Trauma and its Wake*. New York: Brunner/Mazel.

Ullman, S.E. and Filipas, H.H. (2001) Predictors of PTSD symptom severity and social reactions in sexual assault victims, *Journal of Traumatic Stress*, 14(2): 369–89.

US National Transportation Safety Board (2000) *Federal Family Assistance Plan for Aviation Disasters*, www.ntsb.gov/publictn/2000/SPC1_tpc.htm.

Van der Kolk, B.A (1996) The body keeps the score: approaches to the psychobiology of post-traumatic stress disorder, in B. van der Kolk, A.C. McFarlane and L. Weisaeth (eds) *Traumatic Stress*. New York: Guilford Press.

Van der Kolk, B.A. and Ducey, C.P. (1989) The psychological processing of traumatic experience: Rorschach patterns in PTSD, *Journal of Traumatic Stress*, 2: 259–74.

Van der Kolk, B.A. and McFarlane, A.C. (1996) The black hole of trauma, in B.A. Van der Kolk, A.C. Mcfarlane and L. Weisaeth (eds) *Traumatic Stress*. New York: Guilford Press.

Van der Kolk, B.A., Greenberg, M.S., Boyd, H. and Krystal, J. (1985) Inescapable shock, neurotransmitters and addiction to trauma: towards a psychobiology of post-traumatic stress, *Biological Psychiatry*, 20: 314–25.

Van der Kolk, B.A., Weisaeth, L. and Van der Hart, O. (1996) History of trauma in psychiatry, in B.A. Van der Kolk, A.C. Mcfarlane and L. Weisaeth (eds) *Traumatic Stress*. New York: Guilford Press.

Vancoppenolle, G. (2001) What are we planning for? in A. Hiles and P. Barnes (eds) *The Definitive Handbook of Business Continuity Management*. Chichester: Wiley.

Violanti, J. and Paton, D. (1999) *Police Trauma – Psychological Aftermath of Civilian Combat*. Springfield, IL: Charles C. Thomas Books.

Vrana, S. and Lauterback, D. (1994) Prevalence of traumatic events and post-traumatic psychological symptoms in a non-clinical sample of college students, *Journal of Traumatic Stress*, 7: 289–302.

Walden, R. (1994) Violence against employees: a legal perspective, *Health and Safety Information Bulletin*, 218.

Walpole, O. (2000) Call to crisis, *Occupational Health*, 52(5): 12–13.

Warshaw, L.J. and Messite, J. (1996) Workplace violence: preventative and interventive strategies, *Journal of Occupational and Environmental Medicine*, 38(10): 993–1006.

Weathers, F.W., Keane, T.M., King, L.A. and King D.W. (1997) Psychometric theory in the development of posttraumatic stress disorder assessment tools, in J.P Wilson and T.M Keane (eds) *Assessing Psychological Trauma and PTSD*. New York: Guilford Press.

Weaver, A. (2000) Can post-traumatic stress disorder be diagnosed in adolescence with catastrophic stressor? A case report, *Clinical Child Psychology and Psychiatry*, 5(1): 2–7.

Weisaeth, L. (1983) The study of a factory fire, doctoral dissertation, University of Oslo.

Weiss, D.S. and Marmer, C.R. (1997) Impact of Events Scale – Revised, in J.P. Wilson and T.M Keane (eds) *Assessing Psychological Trauma and PTSD*. New York: Guilford Press.

Wessely, S., Rose, S. and Bisson, J. (1998) A systematic review of brief psychological interventions (debriefing) for the treatment of immediate trauma related symptoms and the prevention of post-traumatic stress disorder (Cochrane review), *Cochrane Library*, 3.

West, M.A. and Reynolds, S. (1995) Employee attitudes to work-based counselling services, *Work & Stress*, 9(1): 31–44.

White, M. (1995) Re-authoring Lives: Interviews and Essays. *Adelaide: Dulwich Press*.

Wilson, J.P. and Keane, T.M. (1997) *Assessing Psychological Trauma and PTSD*. New York: Guilford Press.

Wilson, J.P., Friedman, M.J. and Lindy, J.D. (2001) *Treating Psychological Trauma and PTSD*. New York: Guilford Press.

Wilson, J.R. (1999) A framework and a context for ergonomics methodology, in J.R. Wilson and E.N. Corlett, *Evaluation of Human Work – A Practical Ergonomics Methodology*, 2nd edn. London: Taylor & Francis.

Wilsons & Clyde Coal Co. Ltd v. *English* (1937) 3AII ER 628.

Woolf, Lord (1996) *Access to Justice Inquiry Report*. London: HMSO.

World Health Organisation (1993) *Mental Disorders: Glossary and Guide to their Classification in Accordance with the Ninth Revision of the International Classification of Diseases (ICD 10)*. Geneva: WHO.

Wynne, R. and Clarkin, N. (1995) Workplace violence in Europe: it is time to act, *Work & Stress*, 9(4): 377–9.

Wynne, R., Clarkin, N., Cox, T. and Griffiths, A. (1995) *Guidance on the Prevention of Violence at Work*, draft report for the European Commission. Luxembourg: European Commission.

Yalom, I.D. (1989) *Love's Executioner and Other Tales of Psychotherapy*. Harmondsworth: Penguin.

Yehuda, R. (1998) Neuroendocrinology of trauma and posttraumatic stress disorder, in R. Yehuda (ed.) *Psychological Trauma*. Washington, DC: American Psychiatric Press.

Yehuda, R., Southwick, S.M. and Perry B.D. (1990) Hypothalmic-pituitary adrenal and noradrenergic interactions, in E.L. Giller (ed.) *PTSD: Progress in Psychiatry*. Washington, DC: American Psychiatric Press.

Yehuda, R., Boisoneau, D. and Lowy, M.T. (1995) Dose response changes in cortisol and lymphocyte glucocorticoid receptors following dexamethasone administration in combat veterans with and without posttraumatic stress disorder, *Archives of General Psychiatry*, 52: 583–93.

Yin R.K. (1994) *Case Study Research: Design and Methods*, 2nd edn. London: Sage.

Yule, W. (1999) *Post-traumatic Stress Disorders: Concepts and Theory*. Chichester: Wiley.

Yule, W., Perrin, S. and Smith, P. (1999) Post-traumatic stress reactions in children and adolescents, in W. Yule (ed.) *Post-traumatic Stress Disorders: Concepts and Theory*. Chichester: Wiley.

Zapf, D., Knoz, C. and Kulla, M. (1996) On the relationship between mobbing factors and job content: social work environment and health outcomes, *European Journal of Work and Organizational Psychology*, 5(2): 215–37.

Zilberg, N.J., Weiss, D.S. and Horowitz, M.J. (1982) Impact of Events Scale: a cross validation study and some empirical evidence supporting a conceptual model of stress response syndromes, *Journal of Consulting and Clinical Psychology*, 50(3): 407–14.

Index

abuse: childhood 15, 37–8, 195;
sexual 37–8, 171
accidents 42, 48, 73–4; *see also*
injury
ACTH *see* adreno-cortico-
trophin hormone
acute stress: barriers to 25, 30–2;
symptoms of 11
adrenaline 17–18, 23
adreno-cortico-trophin
hormone (ACTH) 17
aftermath 76–7, 81, 82
age 170
aggression: fight response 26;
'psychoneurosis' 9
Aitkins, Lord 51–2
alcoholism 38–9, 62, 110
ambulance workers 46
American Psychiatric
Association 3, 9, 158
amygdala 20, 21, 22, 23
anger 10
anxiety: assertiveness training
92; bullying relationship 187;
disaster research 197;
epidemiological studies 15;
exposure therapy 91; eye
movement desensitisation and

reprocessing 93; increased
likelihood of post-traumatic
stress 170, 176–7, 179, 180,
219; long-term effects of
trauma 62; Manchester bomb
case study 211, 214, 215;
Paddington rail crash case
study 202, 203
Armed Forces group action 57
armed robberies: employee
reactions 27, 28, 29, 30, 31–2,
34–5; identification of people
vulnerable to traumatic stress
72–3; level of threat to
personal safety 171; Post
Office trauma care
programme 101, 102, 105,
106–7, 167, 173–85; *see also*
criminal attacks; violence
Armstrong, B. 86, 87, 89
arousal: bullying 192, 193, 194,
195, 196, 219; cognitive
behavioural therapy 91;
diagnostic criteria for post-
traumatic stress 10;
Manchester bomb case study
211, 213–14, 215; Paddington
rail crash case study 202, 203;

exploratory factor analysis
(EFA) 144, 145–8
exposure therapy 91
external providers of post-
trauma support 112, 117–26
externalisation 212
eye movement desensitisation
and reprocessing (EMDR) 93

Falklands War 56
families: crisis management plan
82; links to victims 47, 54; US
Federal Family Assistance
Plan for aviation disasters 77
fatalities *see* death
fear 5, 26; brain functioning 21,
23; conditioned 91; diagnostic
criteria for post-traumatic
stress 10, 134
feelings *see* emotions
fight response 17, 26
Figley, C.R. 46
Findlay v. *MoD* (1994) 56
Finland 45, 50
firefighters 16, 46, 56, 143, 171
first aid 82
First Line Debriefing Model
103, 104, 107, 109–11, 114,
115–16
First World War 5, 6, 7–9
Flannery, R.B. 35
flight response 17, 26
Foa, E.B. 154
Folkman, S. 27
follow-up: Paddington rail crash
case study 202; Post Office
trauma care programme 108,
112–13
Forth Road Bridge 55–6
freezing 26, 29

Freud, Sigmund 7, 8
Friedman, M.J. 85
Frost and others v.
*Chief
Constable of South Yorkshire
Police and others* (1996) 47,
54–5
funeral arrangements 82

general practitioners (GPs) 111,
112, 180, 181, 182, 183
GHQ *see* General Health
Questionnaire
Goldberg Anxiety and
Depression Scale 200, 202,
203, 211, 213
GPs *see* general practitioners
Great Fire of London 6
Green, B.L. 26
'gross stress reaction' 9
group interventions 85–6, 111;
see also debriefing
'group meaning' 201
guilt 33, 73, 210, 212
Gustafsson, A. 187–8
Guytre, P.M. 18

HADS *see* Hospital Anxiety
Depression Scale
Hale v. *London Underground Ltd*
(1993) 56
Hatton v. *Sutherland and others*
(2002) 172
Health and Safety at Work Act
(1974) 52
Health and Safety Executive 46,
53, 58, 70, 101, 105, 127
Heiskanen, M. 45
helplessness 10, 26, 134, 196
Henry, Lord 55
Hillsborough disaster 47, 54–5

social and demographic factors 169–71, 176–7, 179–80, 219, 228; situational factors 171, 177–9, 180, 219, 228; witnesses 48; *see also* stress; trauma; trauma care programmes
post-traumatic stress disorder (PTSD): biological responses 14, 18–19, 23, 139; brain functioning 14, 19–22, 23; bullying 188, 192, 195–6; CAPS-1 Scale 136–7; classification of 5, 9, 11–12, 13, 14; diagnosis 9, 10, 11–12, 61, 131, 134; dissociation 157; emergency workers 46; employee reactions 36–9; epidemiology of 14, 15–16, 22–3; expert opinions 158; Falklands War 56; legal issues 50–1; measurement tools 140; personal, social and demographic factors 169–71, 177; Purdue PTSD Scale-Revised 137; situational factors 171
PPTSD-R *see* Purdue PTSD Scale-Revised
practice 226–7, 229–30
preparation 25, 69–70
prevention 68, 74–5
primary defusing *see* defusing
procedures 74
process evaluation 153, 230
prolonged duress stress disorder (PDSD) 11, 104
prospective studies 157
psychiatric care 108, 112
psychiatric disorder: First World

War 8; nineteenth-century view of 6–7; *see also* mental illness
psychobiology 14–23, 139, 141, 211, 212
psychodynamic therapy 92–3
psychological contract 24–5
psychological debriefing 85–6, 88; external providers 117–26; Post Office trauma care programme 104, 107, 111, 113, 173, 180; randomised controlled trials 159–60; *see also* debriefing
psychometric questionnaires 155, 227, 228
'psychoneurosis' 8–9
psychotherapy *see* therapy
PTSD *see* post-traumatic stress disorder
public houses 43

QEs *see* quasi-experiments
qualitative research methods 131, 154, 158, 160
quantitative research methods 131, 154, 158, 160
quasi-experiments (QEs) 155–6, 158, 164
questionnaires 140, 141, 143, 231; bullying 188–9, 236–9; lifetime trauma exposure 134–5; Manchester bomb case study 210; Paddington rail crash case study 202–3; Post Office trauma care programme 173–85, 232–5; psychometric 155, 227, 228; selection of external providers 122–3;